ROUTLEDGE LIBRARY EDITIONS:
INEQUALITY

Volume 6

HOUSING POLICY
& EQUALITY

HOUSING POLICY & EQUALITY

A Comparative Study of Tenure Conversions and their Effects

LENNART J. LUNDQVIST

Routledge
Taylor & Francis Group

LONDON AND NEW YORK

First published in 1986 by Croom Helm Ltd

This edition first published in 2023
by Routledge
4 Park Square, Milton Park, Abingdon, Oxon OX14 4RN

and by Routledge
605 Third Avenue, New York, NY 10158

Routledge is an imprint of the Taylor & Francis Group, an informa business

British Library Cataloguing in Publication Data
A catalogue record for this book is available from the British Library

ISBN: 978-1-032-43329-5 (Set)
ISBN: 978-1-032-43769-9 (Volume 6) (hbk)
ISBN: 978-1-032-43779-8 (Volume 6) (pbk)
ISBN: 978-1-003-36880-9 (Volume 6) (ebk)

DOI: 10.4324/9781003368809

Publisher's Note
The publisher has gone to great lengths to ensure the quality of this reprint but points out that some imperfections in the original copies may be apparent.

Disclaimer
The publisher has made every effort to trace copyright holders and would welcome correspondence from those they have been unable to trace.

HOUSING POLICY & EQUALITY

A Comparative Study of Tenure
Conversions and their Effects

Lennart J. Lundqvist

CROOM HELM
London • Sydney • Dover, New Hampshire

©1986 Lennart J. Lundqvist
Croom Helm Ltd, Provident House, Burrell Row,
Beckenham, Kent BR3 1AT
Croom Helm Australia Pty Ltd, Suite 4, 6th Floor,
64-76 Kippax Street, Surry Hills, NSW 2010, Australia

British Library Cataloguing in Publication Data

Lundqvist, Lennart J.
    Housing policy and equality: a comparative
    study of tenure conversions and their effects.
    1. Home ownership 2. Rental housing
    I. Title
    333.33'8   HD7287.8
    ISBN 0-7099-1676-0

Croom Helm, 51 Washington Street, Dover,
New Hampshire 03820, USA

Library of Congress Cataloging in Publication Data

Lundqvist, Lennart, 1939-
    Housing policy and equality: a comparative study of tenure
    conversions and their effects.

    Bibliography: p.222
    Includes index.
    1. Condominiums–United States–conversion–case
studies. 2. Condominiums–Great Britain–conversion–
case studies. 3. Condominiums–Germany (West)–
conversion–case studies. I. Title.
HD7287.66.L86   1986   363.5'1   85-30856
ISBN 0-7099-1676-0

Printed and bound in Great Britain by Mackays of Chatham Ltd, Kent

CONTENTS

FIGURES

TABLES

To Solveig for making me change tenures

PREFACE AND ACKNOWLEDGEMENTS

Why does a Swede write a book on tenure conversions in other countries? The question is all the more pertinent since Sweden so far does not allow conversions from rental tenure to owner occupation.

Part of the answer is found in the growing interest in such conversions among Swedish housing policy actors in the late 1970s and early 1980s. The Bourgeois coalition then in power initiated a Governmental Commission to study the legal possibilities of introducing condominium ownership in Sweden. Assurances and allegations about possible consequences of such a step crossed each other in an intense political debate. They did, however, lack empirical backing, and I felt it would be a good thing to find out what has actually happened in countries experiencing a wave of conversions, and under what specific conditions particular consequences seem to occur. In this way, the continued Swedish debate over the costs and benefits of tenure conversions could be more informed and provide a firmer basis for future decisions.

The main answer, however, is found in my own research interest. I came into housing research a few yeras ago with a background in comparative studies of the politics of policy formulation and its effects on policy content, and thought it would be interesting to follow the process one step further by looking at the actual effects of implementing policies. Conversions seemed a good topic to pursue. In terms of their role in housing policy, they range from being the keystone or show case (as in Great Britain), to constituting a more traditional and integrated part (as in West Germany), to having occurred as a spontaneous market phenomenon to which policy-makers have reacted afterwards (as in the United States). With such a shifting background, I felt that if one could isolate the consequences of conversions - especially on the distribution of housing standards and housing costs - it might be possible to draw some conclusions both about generalisable and context-specific distributive effects of tenure conversions. In this way, I hoped to be able to provide some input into the important scientific discourse on the issue of social welfare and its distribution in modern society.

The data base has been a problem. National investigations have been made in the United States and West Germany. The reliability of these investigations does not totally fulfil the criteria spelled in textbooks on social science method. However, they are the main sources of knowledge for these countries. British data concern certain municipalities and local authorities; no nationwide inquiry into conversion effects has been made. On the other hand, British national statistics on conversions are far better than those of the other two countries. I have tried to keep these reservations in mind when drawing my conclusions.

The study was carried out within the framework of the long-term Research Programme of the Housing Market and Housing Policy Division of the National Swedish Institute for Building Research. My colleagues have provided an invaluable background of intellectual and spiritual support by commenting on earlier drafts and providing encouragement and help whenever I needed it. Special thanks are due to Jim Kemeny for giving me valuable insight into British housing problems and for straightening my English whenever I seemed to warp it. Thanks are also due to the Institute Librarians for excellent service in tracking down elusive background material. My earlier colleagues at the Department of Government, Uppsala University, gave valuable comments on the introductory chapter. I would also like to thank Nathan H. Schwartz and Jurgen Veser for their valuable comments on the US and West German chapters respectively.

All of these people contributed something to my study. Needless to say, I have been as stubborn as most researchers. Therefore, I alone am responsible for whatever use I have made of their contributions.

Lennart J. Lundqvist

Chapter One

THE CONVERSION CONTROVERSY: HOUSING POLICY AND TENURE CONVERSIONS

In industrialised Western countries, the 1980s have brought about a heated controversy over the future of the welfare state. Opponents have charged it with unwanted and unnecessary intrusion on individual freedom of choice, and branded it the primary cause of governmental overspending. Proponents of the welfare state have defended it as a necessary mechanism for correcting the inequitable distribution of goods and services brought about by free markets. A central battlefield has been housing. Here perhaps more than in other fields, the balance between private and public solutions to welfare distribution seems to be questioned.

The purpose of this book is to compare and evaluate the effects of converting rental housing into owner occupancy in the United States, Great Britain and West Germany. The evaluation is done with a view to examining the pros and cons of such conversions. But since these arguments originate in two different and conflicting perspectives on the appropriate role of government in housing as well as in the general provision of welfare, they are closely connected to the main conflicting ideologies concerning the future of the welfare state. The conversion controversy is thus something more than a technical discussion of outcomes of different housing strategies. It concerns the whole issue of governmental involvement in housing, and can thus be seen as an example of conflicts over governmental involvement in other spheres of social welfare. By viewing tenure conversions as strategies for limiting direct governmental involvement, this comparative evaluation may be able to indicate something about the effects not only on housing, but on general social welfare, of such strategies.

The Conversion Debate: Opportunity or Outcome?

In countries coming under conservative rule in the
late 1970s and early 1980s, victorious politicians
preached the vices of state interventionism and the
blessings of free markets. Attacking 'over-spending'
on welfare, they also wanted to change housing
policies. With ideological fervour, conservative
politicians blamed public sector involvement in
housing, instead advocating a policy that stressed
increased freedom of choice for the households
including wider possibilities for home ownership,
and concentrating state subsidies to households in
real need. In these countries, preferences for market
solutions and for a residual state role were evident.
Consider Margaret Thatcher's housing policy
philosophy, as outlined in the debate on the Queen's
Speech after the 1979 victory:

> Thousands of people in council houses and new
> towns came out to support us for the first time
> because they wanted a chance to buy their own
> houses. We will give to every council tenant the
> right to purchase his own home at a substantial
> discount on the market price and with 100 per
> cent mortgages for those who need them. This
> will be a giant stride towards making a reality
> of Anthony Eden's dream of a property-owning
> democracy. It will do something else - it will
> give to more of our people that freedom and
> mobility and that prospect of handing something
> on to their children and grandchildren which
> owner-occupation provides. (1)

Or consider the criteria for British housing policy,
presented two days later by the Secretary of State
for the Environment:

> We intend to provide as far as possible the
> housing policies that the British people want.
> We propose to create a climate in which those
> who are able can prosper, choose their own
> priorities and seek the rewards and
> satisfactions that relate to themselves, their
> families and their communities. We shall
> concentrate the resources of the community
> increasingly on the members of the community who
> are not able to help themselves.
>
> In terms of housing policy, our priority of
> putting people first must mean more home
> ownership, greater freedom of choice of home and

tenure, greater personal independence, whether as a home owner or tenant, and a greater priority on public resources for those with obvious and urgent need. (2)

After less than five months in office, President Ronald Reagan in June 1981 appointed a Commission on Housing. Among other things, the Commission was to 'seek to develop housing and mortgage finance options which strengthen the ability of the private sector to maximise opportunities for homeownership and provide adequate shelter for all Americans', and to 'detail program options for basic reform of federally-subsidised housing'. In its October 1981 interim report, the Republican-dominated Commission laid down a set of recommendations that reflects a market-oriented housing policy for the United States:

> Reliance on the private market as the fundamental mechanism for resolving housing problems can be fully effective only in an open, freely functioning market system. Therefore, the government should continue its efforts to eliminate discriminatory practices that create artificial barriers and inhibit freedom of choice in housing. (3)

For the great majority of Americans, this freedom of choice has traditionally meant home ownership. Encouraging this form of tenure indeed seems to have many virtues. Said the Commission:

> For many homeowners, their home is the most important factor in their general economic well-being, and gives them a direct financial stake in the society. As President Reagan has said, 'The American home ... represents our strength and much of what we strive for.' In addition, owners appear to invest more effort and money in the maintenance of their homes and to take a leading role in local civic affairs, thus creating a better living environment for their neighbourhoods as well as themselves. (4)

By guaranteeing unrestricted access to the private capital markets and by reducing restrictions on the industry and terminating excessive regulation of land development and housing production, the government would best support the majority of Americans in realising their housing aspirations. However, many Americans have difficulties finding adequate housing at prices they can afford to pay. To support those households, the government should not subsidise housing production, the reason being that

> In general, the residual inadequacy of housing today is attributable to inadequate incomes rather than to the lack of available, adequate housing stock. Government efforts to improve access to housing for the poor should therefore emphasise measures to improve incomes and, where necessary, grants to pay for housing obtained in the private market. (5)

Criticising earlier West German housing policy for socialist experimentation leading to inefficient and inequitable use of existing housing, the incoming Christian Democratic Minister for Housing in 1982 offered a more market-oriented, and less public-sector-supported approach to rental housing provision. State intervention should not suffocate private initiatives; government's role is only supplementary. Everyone has a responsibility to do everything he can to support himself and his dependants; only when this is not enough to provide decent housing should the state come to help:

> Welfare provision for the lower income brackets should, in principle, come through supplementary and individual subsidies. The income/housing cost ratio must always be taken into account. Self-support must come before state support. Only when the income is too small to pay for housing costs can individual support from the state be justified. (6)

He made it quite clear that his new housing policy 'model' - (Leitbild) - included the view of housing not only as a social, but also a market good. Commenting on housing tenures, he stated that

> Individual homeownership must be at the forefront of the governmental support to housing, with a conscious view to the goals of our family policy. State support to private home ownership functions as a wealth policy corrective to the distribution of home ownership brought about by the effects of market forces. Without state support, this objective of widespread home ownership could not be achieved. (7)

He stated that in the future, homes used by the owners should be taxed as investment goods, thus widening the possibilities to deduct housing costs from taxable income. At the same time, direct governmental subsidies through housing policy measures should be made more 'accurate' and go only to the 'weak'. (8)

Conservatives thus favour increased home ownership and want to reduce the public involvement, especially in the rental sector. But what about the other end of the ideological spectrum? What are their views on the issue of housing? Originally seeing public rental housing as a tenure to be made attractive to broad sectors of the population, the British Labour Party gradually drifted towards a more favourable view of home ownership. In the famous Green Paper of 1977, the Labour Government recognised that an increasing number of people want to own their homes. Stating that 'owning one's own home is a basic and natural desire', Labour welcomed this trend and recommended that it should be made easier for people to obtain the tenure they want. Therefore, Labour would continue to support home ownership through the current arrangements for tax relief and other measures. Labour expected that the continued growth of home ownership and public renting would lead to a more equal socio-economic structure in these tenures. To bring this development even further, Labour intended to improve tenants' rights, support intermediate forms of tenure, allow the public sector to build homes for sales, and to set up a 'sensibly regulated programme for sale of public sector rented houses.' (9)

Faced with what it called 'Tory onslaught' on public rental housing, a Labour Discussion Document of 1981 wanted to find a way out of 'Labour's own uncertainty, and consequent lack of confidence' on the basic issue of 'what exactly is it (public housing) for?' Stating that 'our ability to turn the tide of the Tory onslaught is significantly dependent on our success in staking out a positive role for public housing in an era of mass home ownership' the Document concluded:

> Theoretically, one possible model would be public housing as a near-universal public service on the lines of health and education. But this is not a serious option; we live in a society where majority home ownership has now been established, at least as much by Labour as by Tory efforts. Between this and the 'welfare'

model, the only alternative future for public housing is a sector offering to all who need or prefer to rent as many as possible of the rights and benefits traditionally but, in the main, unnecessarily tied to home ownership. (10)

The British Labour Party thus saw political danger in opposing widespread home ownership. At the same time, however, they seem to prefer a strategy of tenure modification, trying to give renters a more equal status without going all the way to making them home owners. By making rental housing more attractive, the possibly negative effects of conversions would be avoided.

In West Germany, the Social Democrats helped engineer the 1977 tax reform which widened the rights of tax deductions to converted rental apartments in the housing stock. They also adhered to the wealth-creating objectives of supporting home ownership, a central feature in West Germany housing. However, the Social Democrats clamped down on speculative practices in tenure conversion in order to protect renters in social rental housing. And in the recent housing policy debates, they have fought to preserve the function of social rental housing as an instrument for providing affordable and accessible housing, and as a special market serving to correct the social discriminations brought about by the free rental market. (11)

The conversion debate is thus framed within the ideological warfare over state involvement in social welfare. On the one hand, Conservatives opt for limiting such involvement by directing support exclusively to those whose need can really be established, at the same time as they preach the blessings of freedom of choice to the great majority of citizens. Along this line of thinking, it seems logical to support the conversion of rental housing into owner occupancy; allowing more housing to be allocated through market mechanisms will result in the distribution of housing that people want. For those marginal groups not able to acquire adequate housing this way, the state will provide cash transfers. On the other hand, politicians of the Left seem somewhat on the defensive. They still see state involvement as a means of reaching what they consider a fair distribution of social welfare, but they do not link this to a preference for a particular tenure. While they appreciate the attraction of home ownership as a political factor, their ideas about a just distribution points them to possible negative effects of conversions. Allowing more housing to be allocated through market mechanisms may prove detrimental to the objective of distributing housing according to need.

This study evaluates the effects of tenure conversions, and thus also the validity of the arguments in the conversion controversy. Covering the main points of that controversy, I will outline the major alleged effects by presenting the positive and negative arguments concerning the effects on
1. housing availability (How much of the housing stock is converted? Are there losses, and, if so, in what market sectors, and for which groups?);
2. housing quality and its distribution (What parts of the stock are converted? Who buys, and who does not, and what housing quality do they enjoy?);
3. housing costs and their distribution (Who pays what in the short and long run? Are there genuine 'losers' and 'winners' in tenure conversions?);
4. the public sector economy (What happens to the quantity and incidence of housing subsidies, and to the national as well as the local tax base?).
As far as possible, I will also evaluate the effects on the household's influence over housing matters. After all, much of the argument in favour of tenure conversions rests on the assumption that households' freedom of choice will increase.

Unfortunately, some arguments in favour of increasing tenure conversions are of a character hardly suitable to rigorous evaluation. They are, indeed, linked to the 'myth of home ownership'. Along this more ideological line of thinking, conversions are favoured because they give more people a chance to realise the natural desire to own their homes. In turn, home ownership induces support for the free market economy, gives the individual a stake in society, which all leads to a more stable society. This so-called 'embourgeoisement' argument further claims that home ownership fosters individual thrift, which is morally rewarding, and is a sign of the home owner's rightful belonging to the property-owning democracy. (12)

However, much of the debate concerns more measurable effects of tenure conversions. In terms of the consequences for housing availability, the focus has been on what happens to the stock of low- to moderate-cost but decent-standard rental housing, often publicly owned and managed (except for the USA), which is a main source of housing available to low-income households. Conversion proponents are not particularly worried. The larger the volume of conversions, the larger the amount of capital flowing back from sales into new production. If conversions take place in the public rental sector, proceeds from sales are more or less bound to be used in this way. In the private rental market, freed capital and a possibly changed relation between supply and demand may provide incentives for new housing production. New production will thus balance losses from conversions. Protagonists also argue that the availability of rental housing will not be much affected until 20 to 30 years from now. Tenants purchasing their dwellings would perhaps have stayed in their dwellings for the rest of their lives, so these dwellings would not have become available anyway. Thus the effects on the availability of low-cost, decent rental housing will be much more limited than some seem to fear. (13)

Those who are more sceptical about tenure conversions argue that the consequences for housing availability will indeed be considerable, and concentrated on particular segments of the stock. Conversions will primarily hit the low-cost, decent rental housing so much in demand, especially in the already tight rental markets of inner city areas. Furthermore, capital from conversions may not even flow back into housing. Even if private money were reinvested, it would go into other types of housing catering for other segments of the market than those households replaced by or losing rental opportunities through conversions. Furthermore, capital flowing back into housing, whether private or public, would not be enough to replace the volume of rental housing lost to ownership. The production costs of today are so much higher than those prevailing when the dwellings now converted were built. In sum, losses in the rental sector would be quite substantial. (14)

When it comes to distributive effects of conversions, it seems as if the two sides in the controversy operate with different conceptions of equality. Where those opposing conversions argue in terms of equal outcome, those who are in favour are eager to point to equality of opportunity. (15) As the latter see it, conversions will widen the opportunities for households to fulfil their dreams of home ownership. A broader spectrum of the population will be able to take part in the growth of wealth, and to protect themselves against the unfortunate consequences of rent increases and inflation. This preoccupation with opportunity rather than distributive outcome is summed up in the

Thatcher Government's answer to the question of anticipated conversion effects on the distribution of income and wealth: 'It is impossible to say but by enabling council tenants like others to benefit from the capital appreciation made of housing, sales should distribute wealth more equally.' Underlying this view is another; converted housing is indeed going to appreciate in value. Conversions will be a strong agent in urban renewal and improvement of neighbourhoods, thus improving overall housing quality. That this could lead to a socio-economically segregated distribution of housing quality is held to be less possible; increased ownership means greater mobility in the housing market, and will lead to a social mix on housing estates that prevents segregation. (16)

Conversion opponents argue that the result will be a more unequal distribution of housing quality. Conversions will strip the rental market of the low-cost, adequate-standard - (often public) - rental dwellings in attractive areas. Private rentals of this kind will often undergo renovation before conversions. The high demand for such attractive housing increases prices, thus making it difficult for most low-income renters either to buy or continue to rent their dwellings. To a very large extent, the buyers will be those who can afford the price; even with rebates on dwelling prices, the need for household capital inputs will be high enough to exclude low-income households from buying. The final outcome will thus be a more pronounced socio-economic housing segregation than existed before. Households with high incomes will move in, while less resourceful ones will move out, probably to areas with less attractive housing and lower standards. Newcomers into the rental market will increasingly be restricted to such housing because of the 'asset stripping' associated with conversion from rental housing to ownership. (17)

When it comes to effects on housing costs and household economy, conversion proponents again argue in terms of opportunity rather than distributive outcome. Conversions in the private rental sector help rent-control-plagued landlords to sell - at a profit - property which is otherwise increasingly becoming a liability rather than an asset. Conversions of public rental housing mean a transfer of wealth from the public sector to individual households, who can enjoy the value appreciation of their new property. In general, conversions widen these opportunities to larger groups of households, since prices are lower for converted housing than for traditional single-family housing. More households will thus have the opportunity to improve their economy; ownership of converted housing includes the right to tax relief through mortgage interest deductions, provides a hedge against inflation, and gives the household an economic security not available to renters. (18)

A major counterargument among opponents to conversions is that opportunities will not be equally spread among households. Those who can afford to buy a converted dwelling are already better off in terms of income, education, and social status. The mortgage payments, together with increased running and maintenance costs due to modernisation and increased demand, will in the short run increase the outlays on housing to an extent not affordable to those with lower incomes. It is furthermore possible that rents in the remaining rental dwellings in converted buildings and areas will increase for the reasons just mentioned, thus making continuing renters worse off than before in terms of housing costs. The tax benefits so much hailed by conversion proponents will be unevenly distributed, benefiting high-income buyers more than others. With high-income households buying converted dwellings more often than others, the long-term value appreciation and increase in wealth will largely go to the more resourceful households. In sum, conversions will increase inequalities in the distribution of housing costs and individual wealth. (19)

Conversion proponents are optimistic about the effects on the economy of the public sector. Where heavily subsidised housing is converted, like council housing in Great Britain or Sozialwohnungen in West Germany, the immediate effect will be that the state no longer has to pay the subsidy. Housing authorities receive credit, because mortgage payments or purchase sums will presumably exceed future rent incomes. Resources are thus freed for housing production without burdening the taxpayer. Where local taxes are heavily based on property, conversions will have a positive effect on the community's fiscal status. The condominium sales in the United States entail a substantial increase in property values, significantly upgrading the taxpaying capacity of middle and upper-middle income housing, and thus increasing the municipality's revenue. (20)

Opponents are much less optimistic. Under present subsidy and tax relief systems, the long-term cost to government for owner-occupied - and converted - housing will exceed that of publicly supported rental housing. Ownership, and thus also ownership of converted dwellings, is an attractive way to hold savings so that they maintain and even increase their value. But the tax relief on mortgage interest, and the almost non-existent taxation of capital gain, drains the public purse of revenue. Furthermore, argue the opponents, home ownership places a heavy demand on investment money, thus driving up interest rates. The use of more and more funds just to finance the swapping of existing dwellings rather than fresh investments in productive industry will, in the long run, have serious effects on the economy as a whole. (21)

Even if the conversion debate clearly reflects the general ideological conflict over government's role in economic and social affairs, our main interest here is how it relates to housing policy. For it must be noted that most arguments are practical, not just ideological or theoretical. They concern empirical consequences of actively choosing tenure conversions as part of governmental housing policy, or of allowing conversions without making it part of official policy. To place the conversion issue properly within the housing policy context, we therefore turn to a discussion of the main - and relevant - features of that context, based on existing theoretical literature. We ask how tenure conversions fit into existing housing policy theory, and how that theory could guide the analysis of conversions and their effects.

Housing and the Role of Government: Supplementary or Comprehensive?

The decades following the Second World War witnessed an unprecedented expansion of governmental intervention in housing. To no small extent, much of this had its origin in the exceptional lack of shelter many countries experienced after the war. Governments in war-worn countries simply had to step in to help provide their citizens with adequate housing. But state involvement continued after the recovery from the war. Albeit shifting in scope and intention, the housing sector interventions of governments in the industrialised Western - and Eastern - countries can be interpreted as a reflection of the more general trend towards governmental involvement in social welfare.

Housing policy researchers seem to hold the view

that there are two distinct patterns of governmental involvement in housing. One important criterion for making this distinction concerns the <u>scope</u> of governmental involvement. The so-called <u>supplementary</u> mode of involvement is limited in scope. Its operations are geared towards meeting particular needs and solving specific problems. Supplementary policies are seen as exceptional interventions into an otherwise normally functioning market system:

> In short, government does not have a perspective in which <u>all</u> consumers of housing and <u>all</u> sources of housing appear together. Instead, there is much discussion of the needs of special groups ... who are distinguished by the difficulties they have in the labour market and hence in the 'normal' housing market. (22)

In contrast, the <u>comprehensive</u> mode of intervention in housing is not confined to regulating, supplementing, or restraining the operations of an independent and normally well-functioning housing market. Its operations aim towards meeting more than particular needs and solving specific problems. A comprehensive housing policy means

> channeling the flow of national resources in the housing field in a way that will maximize the welfare of the entire population ... the governments ... exercise significant control over the volume, timing and even the location of residential building for all income levels and for almost all types of builders. (23)

This classification is the one most commonly found in the literature. It is, however, best described as rudimentary. The assumption that governments do intervene to correct unwanted conditions or prohibit them from developing is often made without reference to whether this is the actual objective. Furthermore, the classification is not very different from those found in research on other social policies. It suggests that housing policies can be analysed according to whether and to what extent they involve the idea of 'residual' or 'institutional' welfare; in other words, they refer mostly to the <u>scope</u> of governmental intervention without taking into account the particular charateristics of the good to be produced and distributed – <u>housing</u>.

Apart from using such broad and general categories, proponents of the supplementary-comprehensive typology have been criticised for building into their analysis a historical bias. Most states move from supplementary policies in the early days of housing market interventions towards more and more comprehensive policies. This underlying assumption would seem to indicate some sort of inevitable policy trend. According to the critics, recent developments towards dismantling or redirecting much of governmental involvement in the housing sector refute such assumptions.

A further criticism levelled at the supplementary-comprehensive school of analysis is that it is too focused on policy content and policy intentions, thereby failing to take into account the often crucial differences in national contexts of housing policy. The relative strength of political forces, the peculiarity of institutions relevant to the policy, as well as historical differences, all make it necessary to widen the analysis when comparative housing policy studies are attempted. This is especially crucial if one wants to explain differences in policy contents and developments. It is also crucial for one's understanding of the dynamics of developments within the housing sector; policies help shape the institutional structures, and this in turn leads to very country-specific conditions for the outcomes of particular policies and the further development of policy content. (24)

Despite these criticisms, a case can be made for using the supplementary-comprehensive classification as a point of departure for comparative research. First of all, these categories are central in the ongoing argument over the government's role in housing; both supplementarists and comprehensivists argue in terms of welfare distribution effects of changed governmental policies, and their arguments are clearly connected to these broad categories. Second, the criticism is directed towards the lack of explanatory power of the classification; it does not say much about why policy contents and developments differ. This, however, is not a strong argument when it comes to comparative research on policy effects. Policies are more or less taken as 'givens', and the reasons why they look they way they do are not an immediate concern. Third, insofar as the effects of tenure conversions are found to differ without this being explained by differences in conversion policies, such a result would have to be interpreted in light of the particular legal, economic and social contexts prevailing in each country's housing sector. If, on the other hand, we were to find similarities in the effects of conversions despite differences in policy contexts, the supplementary-comprehensive dichotomy - and the arguments connected with these main categories - may be a possibly fruitful framework for interpreting these similarities. Such similarities would throw light on the tenability of propositions championed by actors in each camp. In order to maximise the returns of our comparative effort, two aspects should be added to our main classification. One is a more thorough analysis of the supplementary-comprehensive dichotomy's relation to principles of welfare distribution and to housing tenures. The other is to outline and assess the importance of the policy contexts - the 'social relations of housing provision' held so important by the critics of traditional comparative housing research. (25)

Supplementary housing policy gives governmental intervention a limited role. The market is the main mechanism for distribution of welfare in housing, since housing is a <u>commodity</u> to be bought and sold, or offered for use (<u>rent</u>), as freely as possible. The level of housing welfare enjoyed is determined by the household's <u>ability to pay</u>. This may lead to a distribution of housing where those who are able to pay also get the best available housing, regardless of such criteria as household size or health. Advocates of supplementary policies find this to be the most efficient use of resources, and even provide an ideological justification. The distributive principle that should govern in general, and also in housing, is that of <u>desert</u>. Through their efforts individuals acquire unequal amounts of income and wealth, and they should have the right to enjoy whatever housing benefits they can afford without any intrusions from government on their freedom of choice. (26)

However, supplementary policies do allow for interventions when the housing market is judged not to be functioning properly. Typically, such interventions aim at helping households in 'real need' to reach some politically defined 'decent' standard of housing, and interventions are seen as 'temporary'. Governments either provide a special supply of dwellings - most often public rentals - or give housing allowances to those households who meet some sort of means-tested criteria. Regardless of whether the welfare provisions are in cash or in kind, the thrust is clear; government's role is to supplement those whose ability to pay is too low to allow a decent standard of housing.

Comprehensive housing policy places governmental interventions in a much more central role.
Although not abandoning the market mechanism, it
views housing less as a commodity than as a <u>social</u>
<u>right</u> for all. The level of housing welfare should be
determined by household <u>need</u>, usually defined
according to such criteria as household size, health,
age, and, of course, income. Since the market does
not work according to such criteria, governmental
intervention should concern a wide array of aspects
of housing, from production and finance to
consumption subsidies. Behind the focus on need as
the criterion for the distribution of housing welfare
is an ideological justification. Comprehensive
policy proponents deny that the acquisition of income
and wealth is also an adequate, or acceptable,
measure of need. Need implies a deficiency of some
kind, the lack of which is harmful in relation to
criteria decided upon by the state for all its
citizens. (27) It is exactly because individuals
acquire unequal amounts of income and wealth that
government should intervene to make sure that the
final outcome of housing welfare distribution
satisfies the criterion of need. The basic thrust is
taken to be that supplementary policies question
government intervention as such and keep it limited,
while comprehensive policies explicitly make housing
part of government's responsibility for the social
welfare of all citizens.

From the viewpoint of this typology of housing
policy, the conversion issue can be interpreted as
one aspect of the controversy over what should be the
appropriate strategy for governmental involvement in
housing. On the one hand, conversion proponents seem
to come from the supplementary camp. They view tenure
conversions as an opportunity to widen the market-
determined segment of the housing sector. They see it
as a way of providing a greater freedom of choice for
households, and as way of freeing the government from
the burdensome subsidisation of the housing sector. A
most typical exponent of this connection between
supplementarism and tenure conversions is the
British Tory Government's argument for selling the
public rental stock. On the other hand, conversion
opponents argue that conversions represent a retreat
from the credo of comprehensive housing policy;
conversions imply abandoning the criterion of need as
well as the objective of equality of outcome in the
distribution of housing standards and costs.

It is, however, important to note that alongside
these ideological arguments, there is a more down-to-

earth discussion of the more practical positive or negative consequences of converting rental housing - be it publicly or privately owned and managed - to owner occupation. From the presentation of each side's principal view on government and housing as well as each camp's assessment of whether conversions are mainly a good or bad thing, it seems as if there is a direct connection between principles and practice. In reality, however, the connections are much more complex, and are very closely related to what stands the different sides take on the issue of housing tenures.

Housing Policy and Tenures: Neutrality or Bias?

In most countries in the industrialised West, households looking for a place to live have had to choose between two main housing tenures, owner occupancy and rental tenure. Other forms, such as housing cooperatives and equity sharing schemes, have developed but usually take only a small share of the housing stock. The proportions between the two main tenures vary from over 70 per cent being owner-occupied (Finland) to more than 50 per cent (English-speaking countries) down to less than 40 per cent (West Germany). (28) There seems to be, however, a common trend; home ownership is the tenure preferred by most households.

At first glance, this may be interpreted as a result of peculiar physical, economic and socio-cultural conditions, all slanting household choice in favour of home ownership. However, the popularity or unpopularity of housing tenures are not brought about by these factors alone. Ultimately, the conditions for household choice among tenures are determined by governmental policies; they may be used to differentiate, or to make more even, those legal and economic differences which shape the opportunities and outcomes in housing. 'Social relations of housing provision' may be tenure neutral, or they may be tenure biased. A neutral policy would include legal measures to make tenures alike in terms of freedom of disposal and security of tenure. Systems of housing finance, and terms of repayment, could be structured in such a way as to neutralise the impact of ability to pay on household choice of tenure. Whether they concern income, property, or capital gain, tax regulations could be structured so that the final economic outcome of housing would be the same regardless of tenure. (29)

In practice, however, housing policies do not seem to achieve such neutrality. In most countries, freedom of disposal and security of tenure are much wider and stronger for home owners than for renters. But more important are the economic differences, which stem from a combination of governmental policies and inflation. Legally and economically, rental apartments are accessible without capital inputs from the households. To become home owners, households in most industrialised countries must make a down payment. At the other end of the cycle, households leaving home ownership can sell their homes at market prices, often at a higher price than at the time of purchase. No such economic opportunity is available to the renter under present tenure regulations. Depending on the peculiarities of tax regulations, the economic outcome of home ownership may vary. Most countries allow home owners to deduct mortgage interest from their taxable income. With increasing costs of housing production and rises in the prices of older homes, and with increasingly high levels of interest, the economic support to home ownership via tax deductions is growing. In addition, taxes on property and on capital gains are not increasing at the same rate. The net result is an increase in economic support to home ownership which is growing much faster than other, 'direct' housing subsidies. In some of the market economies, the tax subsidies to home owners are reported as larger than interest subsidies on government loans and housing allowances taken together. (30)

This actual, but perhaps not always intended, bias toward home ownership also works within that tenure. Higher-income home owners have higher marginal tax rates. This, in turn, increases the value of their tax deductions. As a result, high-income households get larger tax deductions than low-income households, even if they live in the same kind of house with the same mortgage interest payments. Some observers even talk about a 'second welfare state', supporting mainly the middle and upper classes through the tax deduction of mortgage interest. (31) This possibility of lowering real housing costs through tax deduction has increased the ability to pay for owner-occupied housing, especially among the middle and higher income households. In turn, this policy-induced ability has bolstered demand and inflated prices of single-family homes, forcing low-income households out of that market, and enriching those already in at the expense of those trying but not able to get in. (32) At the same time, rapidly increasing construction costs have made new rental housing very expensive in

17

relation to the ability to pay among low-income households. Furthermore, governments trying to cut budget deficits have moved in on housing allowances to those households, both by spending less and by making entitlement regulations more exclusive.

Governments in industrialised countries are thus faced with problems in the housing sector, which seem inextricably linked to the allegedly inequitable 'housing rates of return' (33) from home ownership and rental tenure. The situation has led some observers to state that

> the crucial factors distinguishing desirable from undesirable housing and the well-housed from the ill-housed are now connected ... with tenure, price and the financial status of householders (their right to tax reliefs, to rent controls, to a hedge against inflation, to sell or bequeath their homes, and so on.) (34)

Tax relief to home owners is one example of the changing 'social relations of housing provision' mentioned in the earlier discussion on housing policy theory. It is worth noting that it is practised in both supplementary and comprehensive housing policies. However, this support to home ownership seems much more compatible with the supplementary line of thinking than with the comprehensive ideology. Since the supplementarists view the market as the principal mechanism for housing provision and the distribution of housing welfare, it follows that the marketable part of the housing stock should be as large as possible. Since the demand for commodity housing is clearly evidenced by households' willingness to save for housing, the government's role in housing finance can be limited. This strong demand for home ownership is seen as 'natural'; people tend to use their savings to buy their own homes, because they can then retain a very strong influence over the capital they put in. Housing policy should give as many households as possible an opportunity to fulfil their dreams of ownership. This emphasis on markets, demand, and allegedly 'natural' desires makes supplementary housing politicians biased towards home ownership. Not only is this in line with present household preferences, but it also has a long-term political implication. By extending the opportunities of home ownership to more households, support for the market economy will be strengthened, since more people will have a stake in its future. (35) The irony of this is that home owners will at the same time fiercely demand comprehensive interventions in the form of tax relief.

Comprehensivists have more difficulty in handling the tenure issue. Since they view the market as incapable of providing and allocating housing in accordance with the criteria of need, it follows that the marketable part of housing should be limited. Tenures which require no down payment should be favoured. (36) At the same time, however, the comprehensive school is committed to raising the general level of housing quality. From this point of view, it would be illogical to cut support to owner-occupied housing, since such housing generally has a higher level of quality than other housing, especially in terms of space. One might therefore characterise the comprehensivists as caught between the preoccupation with equality of outcome and the obsession with increasing the level of housing quality. Furthermore, allowing the former to motivate measures against home ownership would be politically dangerous: 'as the numbers of home owners increase, so does their political power, and it would be a brave politician who proposed any major assault upon their tax privileges'. (37)

The problem of tenure-related inequality in housing does have other solutions than making opportunities or outcomes more equal. A third possibility would be to opt for equality in governmental expenditures on housing tenures. (38) This could be done by extending the tax-related benefits of home ownership also to other tenures without resorting to conversions, or to increase direct government support to households in other tenures. However, the budgetary deficits currently occurring in many industrialised countries seem to make it politically difficult for any housing politician to opt for such alternatives.

It is very much in this clash between popular demand for home ownership and fiscal and economic realities that the conversion of rental housing to owner occupancy has come to be so widely discussed and practised. Following the logic of their views on housing and governmental intervention, and riding on a wave of popular demand for home ownership, supplementary policy advocates have welcomed this alternative, either by making it official policy or by giving it their blessings in other ways. Caught between their drive for equality in outcome of housing welfare and their penchant for increased housing standards on the one hand, and the political

19

power of widespread home ownership on the other, those favouring comprehensive governmental involvement in housing have had much difficulty in arriving at a clear-cut stand on the issue, although they have been stressing negative effects.

The conversion controversy thus concerns not only the direct consequences of conversions on the availability of housing, and the distribution of standards and costs, as well as on the public purse and households' freedom of choice. It also concerns the consequences of moving towards a more market-oriented and 'residualistic' government role in housing. This makes it all the more important to evaluate the validity of the arguments.

Evaluating Conversion Effects: The Case for Comparison

Evaluating the validity of the arguments in the conversion debate is, in essence, equivalent to testing competing hypotheses about the effects of conversions. Just to take one example; does X (conversions) lead to Y (better social mix) or to Z (more socio-economic segregation in housing)? However, one would immediately want to know exactly under what circumstances such hypotheses are accepted or rejected. Intuitively, one may think of the conversion case as primarily concerned with the explanation of partial changes within complex system contexts. In this case, the partial change is the introduction of tenure conversions, and the context is the housing sector and the policy determining its way of functioning. On second thoughts, it may well be found very problematic to exclude also other conditions and circumstances from the explanatory framework. In the end, the number of intervening variables, and thus the number of potentially competing hypotheses, may quickly become large enough to make it almost impossible to determine the validity of any of the initially presented arguments.

Confronted with this problem, the social scientist may be tempted to increase the number of cases studied. In this way, he may be able to control for many of the potentially influential contextual circumstances. But he may also be able to ascertain that small differences in the context lead to important variations in the outcome of a partial change such as tenure conversions. In a study of effects at the national level, it would seem natural to extend the number of cases by including more nations and make the study comparative. The problem is, however, that it is impossible to find a pair of (and, even more difficult, a number of) countries which differ only in the characteristics relevant to the study. The possibilities of establishing a 'quasi-experimental' research situation simply are not at hand.

Does this mean that it would be impossible to gain any knowledge from comparative research on tenure conversions, and that research design is a matter of no consequence? Should one give up the idea of using comparison as a means of getting knowledge about the conditions and circumstances under which statements about conversion effects are generally valid? No; because the character of cross-national research is to replace proper country names by those aspects of their structure which play a role in the explanation of a particular phenomenon, knowledge can indeed be gained if the relevant contextual aspects are properly identified. This is no easy task, and does not 'solve' the problem of possible intervention from other than these identified variables. However, if the relevant structural and contextual aspects are properly accounted for, and their importance can be assessed, the problem of determining the effects of conversions - as opposed to other features of housing policy and the housing sector - may be somewhat easier to handle. (39)

The three countries studied here - the United States, Great Britain, and West Germany - did not come out of a random sampling of all the countries in which tenure conversions have taken place. Rather, they were selected because they are alike in some, and different in other respects of relevance to this study. They are all large and highly developed capitalist economies, and they are highly urbanised. They are all liberal democracies, where housing policies are subjected to legislative scrutiny and approval. Of particular importance is that they have all experienced substantial increases in tenure conversions in the last decade.

The three countries also show differences of special importance to the analysis of tenure conversion effects. First, the general housing policy context is different. Governmental involvement in US housing is best described as supplementary in scope and residual in intent. The main programmes aim at guaranteeing the function of credit markets for mortgages. Direct governmental support to housing provision is limited to public rentals, explicitly meant for the poor. In Great Britain, housing policy has been very much concerned with the rental sector. Governmental support for a publicly owned and managed rental stock - in principle meant for all types of household - has been prominent. In reality, the access to such housing has come to be subject to means-testing according to socio-economic criteria. West German governmental involvement has concerned so-called social housing, which is being allocated according to socio-economic, mostly income, criteria. There seems to have been a gradual development towards a more supplementary approach in West Germany in the last decade.

Second, the countries differ with respect to the relation between tenure conversions and official governmental housing policy. In the United States, conversion legislation is a matter for the states and municipalities. Besides, legislation in the United States came more as a response to spontaneous market developments than as a governmental policy initiative. In West Germany, ownership of multi-family housing flats has existed since the 1950s, and conversions were propelled by tax reforms in 1977. The British case is perhaps most clear-cut. The Tory government taking over in 1979 made tenure conversions a centerpiece of its housing policy.

Third, the countries differ with regard to the regulation of conversion procedures. In both the United States and West Germany, property owners/landlords or special 'converters' can initiate conversions, and they can sell the converted dwellings to other parties than the present tenants. In Great Britain, it is the tenants in public rental housing that initiate conversions by using the legally guaranteed Right to Buy. No conversion can thus take place if tenants decide not to use their right. In contrast, US and West German tenants may find that their dwellings are being converted and sold to other households. In such situations, West German tenants enjoy a much stronger legal protection of their security of tenure than do their American counterparts.

Fourth, the three countries differ concerning what part of the housing stock is subject to conversions. In the United States, it is flats in the private rented sector that dominate the picture. In Great Britain, the Right to Buy concerns houses and flats in public rental housing, although conversions in the private rented sector have long been commonplace. In West Germany, flats in both the public and private sectors are concerned, regardless of whether they are privately or governmentally financed.

Figure 1.1: Tenure Conversions in the United States, West Germany, and Great Britain. Some Characteristics of the Objects for Comparison

Country	Initiator of the conversion	Earlier landlord or property owner				
		Private		Public		
		Houses	Flats	Houses	Flats	
US A	Property owner/ landlord or "converter"		Condominium conversions			
	Tenant(s)					
West Germany	Property owner/ landlord or "converter"		Umwandlung zu Eigentumswohnung		Umwandlung zu Eigentumswohnung	
	Tenant(s)					
Great Britain	Property owner/ landlord or "converter"					Council house sales
	Tenant(s)					

23

Fifth, the countries differ in terms of the financial context of conversions. In the United States and West Germany, sales prices (and possible rebates) are a function of the interplay between the seller's judgement of the market and actual demand for converted dwellings. In both countries, buyers must obtain usual bank loans to pay for the dwelling if they cannot raise the money by themselves. In Great Britain, sales prices are determined in a legally regulated valuation process, where even the buyer has the right to an independent valuation. Rebates are given on a scale determined only according to the length of tenure of the tenant purchaser. He also has a legal right to a 100 per cent mortgage from the selling public landlord.

Finally, another less policy-linked difference should be mentioned. The three countries differ with respect to the housing market share of different tenures. In the United States, roughly one-third of the housing is in the rental sector. The corresponding shares for Great Britain and West Germany are 40 and 60 per cent, respectively. The two English-speaking countries are thus 'home ownership' countries, while West Germany is still predominantly a 'nation of renters'.

Apart from these differences, there are a couple of highly relevant similarities in the housing contexts of the three countries. One is that in all three countries, tenure choice for households is in practice restricted to two alternatives, owner occupancy or tenancy. Other tenures, such as cooperatives, shared equity systems, and so on, comprise only very marginal shares of the housing market. Another is that all three countries pursue a comprehensive policy of tax subsidies to owner-occupied housing. All home owners can have tax deductions, regardless of their income, and with no limits to the space or equipment standard home owners enjoy from their consumption of housing.

Admittedly, this account of structural aspects of possible importance to the evaluation of conversion effects is far from exhaustive. One need only to think the possible influence from differences in the nature of demand for converted dwellings. If the socio-economic characteristics of potential buyers differ systematically between countries, this may intervene in ways which make it difficult to ascertain the effects of conversion as such. Even with this choice of countries, one might thus not be in a position to state with confidence that if conversions had not taken place, the situation in the

housing sector would in many ways be different from
what it is after such conversions. Nevertheless, the
comparison of conversion effects in the three
countries chosen here will make it possible to state
with greater confidence under what circumstances the
arguments in the conversion debate may be valid, and
when they may not. In this way, the comparative
perspective makes possible a more qualified
discussion than would be the case if only one country
were studied.

Comparing Conversion Consequences: The Research Outline

The preceding discussion provides the background for
an empirical evaluation of the effects of tenure
conversions. Presenting the pros and cons of the
debate has served the purpose of identifying the
relevant hypotheses concerning the direct actual
consequences of conversions from rental tenure to
home ownership. These include effects on (a) the
quantity of housing, especially the availability of
low-cost, decent rental housing; (b) the
distribution of housing quality among different
socio-economic household strata; (c) the level of
housing costs, and their distribution among
different households; and (d) the public purse,
nationally as well as locally. As far as possible,
the effects on residential influence, by which is
meant household influence over housing management,
will also be evaluated. The questions asked include:

(1a) Do conversions generally have a marginal
effect on the overall supply of rental
housing, or

(1b) are their effects more substantial,
especially on the supply and availability
of particular types of rental housing?

(2a) Have conversions been rather equally
frequent among all types of rental housing
in terms of quality and location, or

(2b) do they reveal a particular pattern in
terms of dwelling quality and area
distribution?

(3a) Have conversions brought all kinds of
households into home ownership of good
quality housing, leading to a socio-
economic integration in converted areas,
or

(3b) have they involved only certain household
strata, thus leading to socio-economic

segregation in converted areas?

(4a) Do tenure conversions lead to a wider socio-economic diffusion of wealth and economic opportunity, or

(4b) do they involve a more irregular distribution of the benefits and costs of housing, and if so, what is the socio-economic pattern?

(5a) Do conversions generally have a positive effect on public finance at national and local levels, or

(5b) do they cause losses to the public purse?

(6) What are the effects of conversions on residential influence?

Evidently, these questions primarily concern the direct, and allegedly causal, relationship between conversion and aspects of housing. In the real world, the relations aren't that simple. Therefore, the comparative perspective serves the purpose of bringing into focus also the situation in which conversions take place. The above discussion identified such potentially important structural and contextual factors as: (a) general housing policies; (b) legal and financial regulations covering conversions; (c) quality and tenure distribution of pre-conversion housing stock; and (d) pre-conversion tenure distribution of household strata. Through the comparative perspective, their importance for conversions and conversion effects can be assessed.

To repeat once more; the central purpose of this comparative study is to evaluate the validity of the arguments for and against tenure conversions, and to establish as exactly as possible under what conditions they seem valid or not. Since these arguments reflect broader and more general views on government's proper role in housing – (as seen in the difference between marginal and structural housing policies) – there is, however, also a broader purpose. Viewing tenure conversions as an example of limiting and minimising the role of government in housing, something could be said about the prospects for the future level and distribution of housing standards and costs held out by such strategies.

Notes

1. Quoted in Ray Forrest and Alan Murie, Right to Buy? Issues of Need, Equity and Polarisation in the Sale of Council Houses (University of Bristol, School for Advanced Urban Studies, Working Paper 39,

1984), p.5.
2. Quoted in ibid., p.6.
3. The President's Commission on Housing, Interim Report, October 30, 1981 (US Governmental Printing Office, Washington DC, 1981), p.3.
4. Ibid., p.22.
5. Ibid., p.4.
6. Oskar Schneider, 'Die soziale Erneuerung der Wohnungspolitik - politische Lösungsaltern-ativen', Politische Studien, 33 (1982), p.567.
7. Ibid.
8. Ibid., p.572.
9. Department of the Environment, Housing Policy - A Consultative Document (HMSO, Cmnd. 6851, London, 1977), pp. 8, 50, 100.
10. Labour Party, A Future for Public Housing - A Labour Party Discussion Document (The Labour Party, London, 1981), pp. 8, 66.
11. 'Haack stoppt Späkulation mit Sozialwohn-ungen', Bundesbaublatt, XXVII (November 1978), p. 523; Helmut Wollman, 'Housing Policy in West Germany - Between State Intervention and the Market', in Klaus von Beyme and Manfred G. Schmidt (eds.), Policy-making in the Federal Republic of Germany (Gower, Farnborough 1984) passim.
12. This ideological line of thinking is well developed within the British Conservative Party. For examples, see discussions and quotations in Keith Bassett, 'The Sale of Council Houses as a Political Issue', Policy and Politic, 8, (1980), pp. 291 ff.; Philip C. Challen, The Sale of Council Houses (Leeds Polytechnic, School of Town Planning, Leeds, BA Dissertation, May 1980), pp. 19 ff.; Alan Murie, The Sale of Council Houses - A Study in Social Policy (Centre for Urban and Regional Studies, Occasional Paper No. 35, University of Birmingham, 1975), pp. 16 ff., 25 ff. It is also clearly visible in the US Presidential Commission on Housing's statements - see note 4 above.
13. Department of the Environment, Appraisal of the Financial Effects of Council House Sales (Welsh Office, Cardiff, 1980), paras. 7, 50; ibid., Council House Sales: The Government's reply to the Second Report from the Environment Committee Session 1980-81, HC 366 (HMSO, London, Cmnd. 8377, October 1981), p. 4 f.; Taschenbuch fur den Wohnungswirt (Hammonia Verladg, Hamburg, 1981) pp. 39 ff.; GEWOS, Wohnungseigentum aus dem Mietwohnungsbestand - Überlegungen, Hinweise und Anregungen einer unabhängigen GEWOS e.V. - Fachkommission (Hammonia Verlag, GEWOS Schriftenreihe, Neue Folge 31,

Hamburg, 1980), p. 18; Gregory J. Kamer, 'Conversion of Rental Housing to Unit Ownership - A Noncrisis', Real Estate Law Journal, 10 (1982), p. 208.

14. House of Commons Environment Committee, Council House Sales, Vol. I, Report (HMSO, London, June 1981), ch. 5; ibid., Vol III, Appendices pp. 18 ff. (note by David Webster); Ursula Klingmüller et al., 'Gemeinwirtschaftliches Eigentum - Eine vorstaatliche Strategie gegen die Vernichtung preisgunstigen Wohnraums', Bauwelt, 73 (1982), p. 1482; cf. arguments summarised by Klaus Ernst, 'Die Umwandlungen von Mietwohnungen in Eigentumswohnungen', Der Gemeinderat, 23 (9/1980), p. 17; Daniel Lauber, 'Condominium Conversions - the Numbers Prompt Controls to Protect the Poor and the Elderly', Journal of Housing, 39, (1982), pp. 201 ff.

15. Cf. Julian Le Grand, The Strategy of Equality. Redistribution and the Social Services (George Allen & Unwin, London, 1982), pp. 14 f., 100 ff. for a discussion on equality of outcome in housing.

16. House of Commons Environment Committee, Council House Sales, Vol. II, Minutes of Evidence (HMSO, London, June 1981), pp. 320 ff. (quote p. 321); GEWOS, pp. 12 ff.,; Hans Häring, 'Fragen bei der Umwandling von Mietwohnungen in Eigentumswohnungen', Zeitschrift fur gemeinnütziges Wohnungswesen in Bayern, 72 (1982), p. 352 f.; Anonymous, 'Displacement Foes Try to Stop Condo Conversions', Savings & Loans News, 99, (10/1978), p. 120 f.

17. Ray Forrest, 'The Social Implications of Council House Sales', in John English (ed.), The Future of Council Housing (Croom Helm, London, 1982), pp. 104 ff.; Klingmüller et al., p. 1482; Hartmut Meuter, 'Eigentumsbildung im Wohnungsbestand - Die Betroffenheit von Altbauquartieren durch Umwandlung von Mietwohnungen', in Adalbert Evers, Hans-Georg Lange & Hellmut Wollman (Hrsg.), Kommunale Wohnungspolitik (Birkhäuser, Basel, Boston, Stuttgart, Stadtforschung aktuell, Band 3, 1983), pp. 182 ff.; Lauber, pp. 197, 202, 206.

18. House of Commons Environment Committee, Council House Sales, Vol. II, Minutes of Evidence, p. 321 (answer from the Department of Environment); Department of Environment, Council House Sales. The Government's Reply pp. 9 f.; Taschenbuch für den Wohnungswirt, p. 39 f; Häring, p. 352, GEWOS, p. 13; Kamer, pp. 187, 191 ff.; 208; F. Scott Jackson, 'The ABCs of Commercial Co-ownership', Real Estate Review, 10 (3/1980), p. 45; Harold A. Lubell, 'Regulating Conversions in New York: A Model for the

Nation', Real Estate Review, 11 (4/1981), p. 42.

19. House of Commons Environment Committee, Council House Sales, Vol. I, Report, chs. 11-12; ibid., Vol. III, Appendices, pp. 10 ff. (note by David Webster); Meuter, pp. 184, 196; Knut Gustafsson, 'Strukturfragen der Wohnungseigentumspolitik', Bundesbaublatt, XXIX (July 1980), p. 428; Erwin Tenschert, 'Wohnungsumwandlung im Für und Wider. Eine Tagung mit wenig neuem', Gemeinnütziges Wohnungswesen, 33, (1980), p. 238 f.; Lauber, p. 205.

20. Department of the Environment, Appraisal of the Financial Effects of Council House Sales, passim; Taschenbuch für den Wohnungswirt, p. 42; GEWOS, p. 13; George Sternlieb, James W. Hughes, 'Condominium Conversion Profiles: Governmental Policy', in Sternlieb and Hughes (eds.), America's Housing: Prospects and Problems (Rutgers University, Centre for Urban Policy Research, New Brunswick, NJ, 1980), p. 309.

21. House of Commons Environment Committee, Council House Sales, Vol. II, Minutes of Evidence, p. 133 (memorandum by Bernard Kilroy); John English, 'The Choice for Council Housing', in English (ed.), The Future of Council Housing, p. 183; Gustafsson, p. 428.

22. David Donnison and Clare Ungerson, Housing Policy (Penguin Books, Harmondsworth, 1982), p. 75.

23. Carolyn Teich Adams, 'Housing Policy', in A. Heidenheimer, H. Heclo, and C.T. Adams, Comparative Public Policy. The Politics of Social Choice in Europe and America, 2nd edn. (St Martin's Press, New York, 1983), p. 94.

24. For a recent example of such criticisms, see Michael Harloe and Maartje Martens, 'Comparative Housing Research', Journal of Social Policy, 13 (1984), pp. 258 ff.

25. Ibid., pp. 264, 270 ff.

26. Gill Burke, Housing and Social Justice. The Role of Policy in British Housing (Longman, London, 1981), pp. 152, 161.

27. Burke, p. 152; cf. Peter Malpass and Alan Murie, Housing Policy and Practice (MacMillan, London, 1982), p. 17f.

28. Jim Kemeny, The Myth of Home-ownership. Private Versus Public Choices in Housing Tenure (Routledge & Kegan Paul, London, 1981), ch. 1.

29. A vivid discussion on tenure neutrality is found in Kemeny, ch. 9.

30. E. Jay Howenstine, Attacking Housing Costs: Foreign Policies and Strategies (Rutgers University, Center for Urban Policy Research, New

Brunswick, NJ, 1983), pp. 43 ff.

31. Bruce Headey, Housing Policy in a Developed Economy - The United Kingdom, Sweden, and the United States (Croom Helm, London, 1978), pp. 22 ff.

32. Stuart Lansley, Housing and Public Policy (Croom Helm, London, 1979), p. 136.

33. Headey, p. 25.

34. Donnison and Ungerson, p. 91 f.

35. Kemeny, chs. 4-5; Sidney Jacobs, 'The Sale of Council Houses: Does it Matter?', Critical Social Policy, 1 (1981), p. 41 f.

36. Headey, pp. 75 ff.

37. Donnison and Ungerson, p. 88.

38. Cf. Le Grand, pp. 14, 127 f.

39. The preceding discussion draws heavily on Adam Przeworski, 'Methods of Cross-National Research 1970-1983: An Overview', paper for the Conference on Cross-National Policy Research, organised by Science Center Berlin and Stanford University, at Science Centre Berlin, 18-21 December, 1983, passim.

Chapter Two

THE UNITED STATES: CONDOMINIUM CONVERSIONS AND THEIR EFFECTS

US Housing Policy: Main Characteristics and Tenure Aspects

American housing policy does not seem to have developed within the same tradition as in Europe, where housing is viewed as a social right and governments are held ultimately responsible for the housing welfare of their citizens. Even if the policy grew out of the depression of the 1930s, its prime motive was to invigorate the collapsing building industry and to protect investor confidence by providing guarantees for a well-functioning mortgage market. The public housing to be built by the supported building industry would be occupied by the unfortunate few who were not able to get into decent housing by themselves.

The 1949 Housing Act may seem to have adopted a social service philosophy by setting 'a decent home in a suitable living environment for all Americans' as a national goal (reaffirmed by the 1968 policy). However, this philosophy has never been unequivocally supported by positive governmental action. At best, it has been sporadically pursued, and then only as one of several objectives, the most important being (a) support to the home-building sector of the economy; (b) development of an effective and stable set of mortgage market institutions; (c) slum clearance and urban redevelopment; and (d) welfare assistance to those unable to find adequate housing in the private market. By the mid-1970s, governmental housing policy measures included such things as

> (1) the building and administration of public housing by the local housing authority; (2) (building) code enforcement by the city; (3) quite limited programs of direct mortgage interest rate subsidies for low-income home

purchasers and rental assistance run by the federal government; (4) similarly limited rehabilitation grants and loans provided by the federal government; (5) public assistance payments for the poor, which already provide, in many states, a form of housing allowance; (6) and federal support of various mortgage market institutions designed to assure a ready supply of mortgage funds on reasonable terms. (1)

The emphasis was on private enterprise as the vehicle for providing housing for the nation's households. Governments at all levels acted in a supplementary role. In terms of tenure, a striking characteristic has been the limited role given to public rental housing. By the end of the 1970s, there were about 1.3 million occupied public rental dwellings, constituting less than 2 per cent of the occupied housing stock. Production of public housing was seen as a major way of alleviating the housing problems of the poor all the way up to the 1970s. Construction subsidies were given and also the running costs were subsidised. In response to a growing recognition of the long-term commitment of governmental money made through this supply policy, large-scale experiments with housing allowances - i.e., cash subsidies - to poor households were launched in the mid-1970s. It would then be up to the households to decide how to use this cash allowance in relation to housing consumption, and this demand-side strategy was seen as a more efficient way of using governmental money to improve housing conditions. (2)

There is no doubt, however, that home ownership has been favoured all along, both in terms of ideological commitment and in terms of fiscal support. Tax expenditures - i.e., deductions of mortgage interest payments from taxable income - have increased rapidly. Between 1977 and 1981, the costs of subsidised housing programmes rose from just under three to nearly six billion dollars. At the same time, tax expenditures caused by mortgage interest deductions rose from $5.5 to $20 billion. (3) Some sources hold that the $20 billion-figure for such tax expenditures was reached as early as 1978. (4)

The late 1970s witnessed a rapid increase in housing costs. Interest rates surged, thus making home buying much more expensive than before. Inflation led to increased running and maintenance costs. Production of new housing fell substantially. President Reagan's Commission on Housing, established in 1981, was clear in its view of what should and should not be done by government in the field of housing. Instead of believing in the potency of governmental policies, it approached

> its task with optimism based on an entirely different belief: that the genius of the market economy, freed of the distortions forced by government housing policies and regulations that swung erratically from loving to hostile, can provide for housing far better than Federal programs. The 1970s taught not only the limits of the good that can be done by government action, but also the depths of the harm that can be wrought by ill-thought or ill-coordinated government policy. (5)

In line with this basic philosophy, the Commission proposed housing policy changes involving (1) a redirection of support to low-income housing from construction of public housing to direct cash allowances to poor households; (2) a greater reliance on (a less regulated) private thrift industry to help generate more money for housing; (3) a deregulation of the building and planning sectors in order to stimulate the construction industry. (6)

Of utmost concern to the Commission was the 'continued importance of homeownership in the nation, and (the need) to develop options to strengthen the ability of the private sector to provide this opportunity, especially for first-time homebuyers'. The Commission saw the new types of home ownership - mobile homes, and condominiums - as a very favourable development. It summarised its view as follows:

> Conversion of multifamily units to cooperatives or condominiums enables many people to become homeowners who otherwise would not have this opportunity. The Commission believes that homeownership is beneficial not only for those who occupy the units, but also to the community as well. The substantial numbers of units that have been purchased under this form of ownership provides evidence of the public awareness of its benefits. (7)

Thus, the overall view of the Presidental Commission could be summarised as one of making the already supplementary character of direct governmental involvement even more supplementary. There should be

more room for private initiatives, and for market
solutions to housing problems. Still, the Commission
seems to recommend a growing indirect involvement by
keeping the favourable tax treatment of home
ownership. The Commission also furnished several
arguments in favour of condominium conversions. At
issue then, is to what extent these arguments are
tenable.

Condominium Conversions: The Political, Legal, and Economic Framework

As presently interpreted, the US Constitution
reserves to the states the regulatory power over real
estate and its use. Federal policy mostly concerns
financial arrangements to guarantee the smooth and
dependable functioning of a credit market for
housing. On the issue of conversions, Congress did
pass the Condominium and Cooperative Conversion Act
of 1980. However, the legislation merely expressed
the view of Congress that state and local governments
should give tenants sufficient prior notice of
conversion, and assured a tenant's right of first
purchase. (8)

The states had passed condominium statutes
already in the 1960s. They were, however, directed
towards new construction of such housing. When
conversions began to be more widespread in the latter
half of the 1970s, public officials and affected
tenants were taken by surprise. Especially at the
local jurisdictional level, there was strong demand
for regulation, or even prohibition, of conversions.
By 1980, almost half of the states had passed
statutes affecting conversions. Although there was a
great variation in the content, these regulations
could be separated into four broad categories: (1)
tenant protections; (2) buyer protections; (3)
rental stock protection; and (4) preservation of low
– and moderate – income housing.

Tenant protection statutes deal with notification of the intended proposed conversions and
occupation/eviction requirements; right to quiet
enjoyment; minimum tenant purchase or tenant
approval; right of first purchase; and relocation
plans and assistance. Notification requirements
mostly specify a minimum period of tenancy following
the notice of intent to convert. If the statutory
minimum period is longer than the remaining lease,
the tenant must often notify the converter in writing
if he wants to stay the minimum period beyond the
lease. In international comparison, the post-

notification period is remarkably short. By 1980, the statutorily defined period of notice varied from 60 to 270 days, the most common being 120 days. American tenants affected by conversions thus enjoy much less security of tenure than their West German counterparts (cf. below p. 141-2).

A few states have passed legislation protecting a tenant's right to quiet enjoyment of the premises during the conversion process. Such regulations typically prohibit construction or improvement during the notice period. Some statutes ensure that the dwelling can not be shown to a third party without the tenant's consent during the notice period, or prohibit the landlord from taking measures to harass tenants in order to speed up the conversion process.

A number of states require the converter to give tenants in occupancy an unqualified exclusive option to purchase their units. Often called the 'right of first refusal', this option must be exercised within a specified period of time, most often linked to the notice of intent period. Right-to-purchase periods vary from 30 to 120 days among the states. The state of New York has a rule requiring that conversions in New York City may proceed only if 35 per cent of the affected tenants agree to buy within a specified period of time.

By 1980, only a few states required developers to pay moving expenses or establish a relocation assistance programme. One state mandated that low-income tenants must receive moving and relocation expenses equal to one month's rent. Three states permitted the developer to shorten or even terminate the notice period by paying moving expenses or other consideration agreed upon with the tenant. (9)

Almost half of the states had statutes including protection for condominium buyers by 1980. These statutes fall into several categories, the most important being requirements for publication of a full building or property report; full disclosure; warranties; escrow funds to ensure completion or renovation of common elements; purchaser's right to cancel or rescind contracts of purchase; and escrow of purchaser deposits.

A property report requires a statement by the converter as to the present condition of all structural and major mechanical components of the building. Usually, this building report is included in the Public Offering Statement or prospectus, which has to be filed with the relevant state agency before there are any offerings for sale. A copy of this statement must be given to prospective buyers, usually at or before the time a contract is executed. Beside the building or property report, this full disclosure requirement also concerns budgets and legal documents. Disclosure of the projected annual budget for the first year of operation as a condominium is required. It is generally equal to disclosure of the actual expenditures on all repairs, maintenance, operation or upkeep of the building. Finally, full disclosure is required for such documents as the declaration, bylaws and articles of incorporation of the condominium association, management contracts, as well as any encumbrances, easements, liens, or other matters affecting the prospective buyer's legal title to the condominium.

Warranty requirements generally apply to the roof, structural, and common mechanical parts for one or two years. By the early 1980s, it still seems to have been an open question whether such requirements actually covered conversions and not only new developments. On the other hand, escrow requirements seem specifically directed towards protecting the purchasers of converted condominiums. Some states require that when dwellings are contracted for prior to completion of repair or renovation works, the developer must either post a bond or place in escrow some or all of the purchase price to ensure completion. Several states require that all deposits or payments received from purchasers on a contract or reservation must be held in escrow until the deal is finally closed. Purchasers in some states also have the right to rescind or cancel for a certain number of days after execution of the contract, or after they have received all required disclosure documents. (10)

By 1980, California was the only state to have legislation aiming at preservation of the low and moderate income level rental stock. Local agencies must consider the housing needs of the region when looking at requests for subdivision of rental buildings - i.e. conversions. This is taken even further at the local level, where some municipalities have adopted ordinances which make the status of the jurisdiction's rental stock a condition for conversions. One mechanism used is to prohibit conversions if the rental vacancy rate falls below a certain level, usually ranging from 3 to 6 per cent. Some Californian municipalities have also adopted ordinances which require converters to set aside a certain percentage of the converted units for persons of low or moderate income. The state of California then offers assistance in the form of loans amounting to a maximum of 45 per cent of the purchase price. At the local level, converters may also be required to set aside funds, pay special taxes, or even construct new units for rent, all in order to preserve the local stock of rental housing. (11)

The economic framework of condominium conversions is less fragmented than the legal one, particularly because of the importance of federal tax laws and the operation of federal programmes and institutions on the secondary mortgage market. Federal tax laws seem to reduce the role of landlords, and to increase the importance of middle-men - i.e., converters, in the process. Under these laws, a landlord converting his building and selling individual units as condominiums would be considered a dealer in real estate. Whatever profits are earned from the conversion would be considered ordinary income and relatively highly taxed. However, if the landlord chooses to sell his whole property to a converter, the landlord's profits would be treated as capital gain and taxed at a much lower rate than in the former case.

Federal tax laws also influence the way converters organise their operations. Usually, they form separate limited partnerships for each individual conversion project they undertake. In this way, any liability arising from one conversion project will not extend to his next venture. As the general partner in this limited partnership, the converter has overall responsibility for completing the conversion and is legally liable for the full amount of any financial losses incurred. On the other hand, profits earned are not taxed until they are distributed to individual partners, and then they are usually treated as ordinary income. This is more favourable than using the corporate form, where earnings are first taxed as corporate profits and then again as income when distributed to the individual stockholders. (12)

Financing of condominium conversions is provided by a combination of equity and debt. There are two forms of debt. Interim loans are obtained by converters to finance the purchase and rehabilit-ation of the building to be converted, and to cover the administrative costs of the conversion. Long-term loans are made to individuals buying units in the converted building. The converter is responsible also for securing such loans. Income from sales of converted units are used to repay the interim loans. When this is done, whatever income the converter gets from sales is his profit.

Financial institutions making mortgage loans usually require that the converter has non-binding agreements from prospective purchasers, representing 60 to 80 per cent of all converted units. This they do in order to be able to meet requirements from the federal mortgage institutions. These institutions buy mortgage loans from mortgage banks and savings and loans associations for resale in the secondary mortgage market. Their prime purpose is to provide an adequate and stable supply of funds for housing. The effects of secondary mortgage programmes on condominium conversions are twofold. First, they help to finance the ultimate sales of units from the converter. Second, the underwriting standards of the federal mortgage institutions have tended to become the converters' minimum standards, thus affecting the quality of the conversion projects. The federal institutions require that (a) all legal matters and documents are in order; (b) the building report is adequate and that the lifetime of the physical and mechanical parts is stated; (c) no exploitative management contracts for the condominium are set up by the converter; (d) budgets for the condominium management are appropriate; (e) 70 per cent of the units are under sales agreements; and (f) at least 80 per cent of the units are sold to individuals who will actually use them as their primary year-round residences. The institutions do not purchase mortgages from people who buy the condominium only as an investment. (13)

Under Section 235 of the National Housing Act, the federal government subsidises home ownership for low-income families. The subsidy takes the form of an interest rate reduction which lowers the buyer's monthly payments. There are limits both in terms of allowable family income and purchase price of the dwelling. The Section 235 programme allows for subsidies also to (first-time) occupants of condominiums. (14) It should be noted that the programme is not well funded and that those eligible have no automatic right to funding. By the early 1980s, some programmes were in progress at the state and local levels to provide loans and grants to assist individuals to purchase converted units. There were also programmes subsidising rents for special household categories - elderly and handicapped - or providing financial assistance to such households if they had to move out of a building subject to conversion. (15)

Once the conversion is completed and the

converter has relinquished control of the building to the condominium owner association formed by the individual unit owners, these owners pay management fees in accordance with the bylaws of the association ad the management contract. Owners also pay for utilities and for other running costs of the unit. As owners, they enjoy the same tax treatment as 'traditional' home owners. The two most important tax deductions for home owners are their real estate taxes and the interest on their mortgage.

Condominium owners may also temporarily escape taxation of the profit from the sale of their unit. If the unit is the taxpayer's principal residence, and if he uses the proceeds from the sale to buy another unit as principal residence for an equal or higher price, the tax is deferred. The only thing happening is that the basis, or cost for tax purposes, of the second condominium is lowered by the amount of the gain from the first one. The process of deferring taxation of capital gain can be continued indefinitely, as long as the price of the next unit equals or is higher than the present one. If the taxpayer does not buy another house or condominium, taxes become due on the entire deferred gain. However, home owners aged 55 or older who sell their homes and do not reinvest in another house or condominium are allowed a one-time exclusion from taxation for a gain of up to $125,000. (16)

Processes and Procedures of Condominium Conversions

The initiative in the typical US conversion process seems to lie neither with the landlord nor with the tenants. As mentioned earlier, tax regulations make it less advantageous for a landlord to become a converter. Tenant-initiated conversions have been sparse, to some extent probably because of the arrangements tenants must make to go through with their conversion initiative. They have to incorporate as a non-profit organisation capable of holding real estate. Even if this tenant association hires a condominium developer to actually carry out the conversion, it still has an overall responsibility for the process. (17)

It is usually the converter/developer who initiates conversions. He buys the building, gets the property report prepared together with all other required documents, and registers his intent to subdivide the building into separate condominiums at the appropriate public office. If necessary, he applies for a permit to go ahead with the conversion.

The converter must notify the sitting tenants (that is, tenants with a contract), and allow them the legally required period of stay, quiet enjoyment and, where required by statute, offer the tenants their right of first purchase. In more than one-fifth of all cases, the conversion process also involves substantial renovation of the converted building, while the rest involve only minor repairs. The converter usually determines the extent and standard of the renovation, although deals are sometimes made allowing prospective buyers to decide on such matters.

As mentioned earlier, the converter is responsible for securing both interim loans - to finance the purchase and rehabilitation of the building - and long-term mortgage loans for condominium purchasers. Since the interim loans are repaid with funds from the sale of individual units, the converter has an incentive to sell a sufficient number of units as quickly as possible to repay the interim loan and thereby the overall carrying costs. In order to ensure rapid sales, units are therefore often offered to sitting tenants, but sometimes also to known outside purchasers at discounts ranging from 10 to 20 per cent. As soon as the converter has got enough money from the conversion sales to repay the interim loan, he may increase the unit price; the proceeds from selling the remaining converted units then represents sheer profit from the conversion venture. (18)

To ensure that sales will not face problems, converters use different methods. One is to pay lending institutions from one-half to two points above actual interest rates to ensure that the institution will go forward and make all long-term mortgage loans to condominium purchasers. Since the lending institutions usually require that the converter has non-binding agreements from enough prospective buyers to equal 60 to 80 per cent of all converted dwellings before they give mortgage loans to indiviudal buyers, the converter has every incentive to engage in another method; a highly visible, and sometimes aggressive marketing and sales promotion of the converted units. To this end, sales offices are usually opened on the premises following the announcement of a conversion. Meetings and social gatherings with tenants are also used as an opportunity to market converted dwellings. The general character of the campaigns may differ:

Emphasis is placed on tenant discounts and the

tax advantages of homeownership, while discussion of increased monthly housing costs is minimized. These conversions managers and the sales firms they employ tend to use low-key sales approaches. Tenants note, however, that more forceful tactics (such as repeated telephone calls or false reports on the number of units actually sold) may be used if sales are lagging or if the developer wants a very rapid sellout. (19)

The dominating force in the conversion process is thus the converter and his main incentive is profit. A study of conversions in Brookline, Mass. bears this out clearly. It found that prices of converted dwellings were often raised two or three times during the marketing and sale stage. At first, the converter is willing to accept a lower profit margin to assure quick sales. Once costs are recovered and interim loans are paid off, he will increase prices. This he can do because when the building is close to being sold out, purchasers have more assurance that the conversion will be successful; lower risk leads to a higher asking price. If the sales period is extended, prices for comparable units will probably increase and the converter will try to take advantage of this. The study characterises the converter's role in the process as Dr Jekyll and Mr Hyde:

> Up to a certain point, he will pursue tenants assiduously to get them to purchase; but once it becomes clear that a particular tenant will not buy, the developer usually has strong incentives to try to get that person to move out ... An individual tenant has very little leverage with the developer once the tenant has decided not to buy, and whatever leverage he or she has must be exercised fairly quickly. (20)

In the role of Mr Hyde, converters engage in such activities as cutting off or making irregular the services to tenants; repeated petitions for rent increases; extremely short notice to vacate, and so on. However, it is still a limited percentage of replaced tenants who report having been harassed.

When all units are sold and a large percentage of them have gone to completion, the converter must relinquish control of the building to the condominium owners association. This stage in the process generally causes no problems. Most converters complete at the appropriate time. Only few cases involving procrastination on the part of the developer were reported in the 1980 national study. Dr Jekyll is again at the front; in jurisdictions with strong consumer protection regulations, converters usually set up mechanisms for solving problems with things repaired or replaced during the conversion process. (21)

The Volume of Condominium Conversions

The US condominum conversions have taken place in an housing market characterised by an increasing dominance of home ownership. The decades following the Second World War witnessed a doubling of the nation's housing stock from about 40 million occupied units in 1950 to more than 80 million in 1980. More than three-quarters of this increase came in the owner-occupied sector, where the number of occupied dwellings rose by over 30 million, compared to fewer than 10 million in the rental sector. By the early 1980s, the owner-occupied sector thus comprised two-thirds of the total US housing stock. In the US rental sector, public housing plays a much less important role than its counterpart in Great Britain. Of the 28 million occupied rental units in 1981, public housing accounted for only 2 million, or 7 per cent of all rental housing.

Figure 2.1: Stock of Dwellings by Tenure in the United States, 1920-80

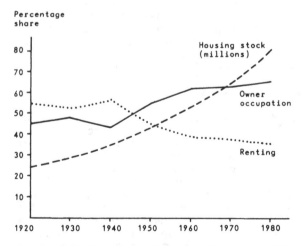

Source: Statistical Abstract of the United States 1984, p. 753

For several reasons, it is difficult to ascertain the importance of condominium conversions in this development towards increased home ownership. First, there are no nationwide figures for conversions after 1979. Second, figures for total stock developments do not reveal the sources of the increase of condominiums - i.e., whether they increase because of new production or conversions. Third, total stock figures seem inadequate at least in comparison to figures for housing starts and available data on conversions. According to <u>Statistical Abstracts 1984</u>, there were just over 1.4 million condominiums in 1981, constituting 1.7 per cent of the housing stock and equalling 5 per cent of the rental stock. (22) Given that the 1977 condominium stock was 665,000, and given the production and conversion figures of Table 2.1. - to which should be added more than 150,000 condominiums produced in single-family units after 1977 - this seems to underestimate the condominium stock by 20 per cent, even if there had been no conversions after 1979.

Limited as they are, the figures in Table 2.1 still reveal some interesting trends. After 1975, the popularity of condominiums shows itself in two ways. One is the increasing share of condominiums in new multi-family housing production. The other is the rapid increase in conversions of rental housing to condominiums. In fact, the volume of conversions seems to have increased seven-fold in the latter part of the 1970s. The contribution of conversions to the growth of the condominium stock became almost equal to that from new production in 1979. It is unfortunate that no data have been available on the development from 1980 onward.

Table 2.2 reveals another trend. Condominium conversions have been concentrated in and around the 37 largest metropolitan areas. These areas stood for 248,000, or 75 per cent, of all conversions during the 1980s. Their proportion of all rental housing, however, was only 46 per cent in 1977. Conversions in these SMSAs split about even between central cities and suburban jurisdictions.

Judging from available data, the proportion of the US rental stock which was converted up to 1980 was quite low. This judgement is, however, dependent on which stock figures are used. If the volume of conversions is viewed as a proportion of the total occupied rental stock of 1977, 1.3. per cent of all rental units had been converted. However, as much as 31 per cent of the rental stock consisted of single-family or attached 'non-convertible' units. About

Table 2.1: Condominiums: Additions from Multi-family Housing Production and from Conversions of Rental Housing in the United States, 1975-82.

Year	Multi-family housing starts				Condominium conversions	
	Total (1)	Rentals (2)	Condo-miniums (3)	(3) as percentage of (1)	Total (4)	(4) as percentage of (3)
1975	259	214	45	17.4	83(a)	-
1976	356	292	64	18.0	20	31.3
1977	510	433	77	15.1	44	57.1
1978	561	448	113	20.1	74	65.5
1979	523	367	156	29.8	135(b)	92.3
1980	426	276	150	35.2	n.a	-
1981	359	214	145	40.4	n.a	-
1982	369	239	130	35.2	n.a	-

Notes: (a)   For the period 1970-5.
            (b)   Estimate based on figures for the first three quarters of 1979.

Sources: <u>Statistical Abstracts of the United States 1984</u>, p. 744; HUD, <u>The Conversion of Rental Housing to Condominiums and Cooperatives A National Study</u>, p. IV-6.

Table 2.2: Condominium Conversions and Percentage of Occupied Rental Units Converted by Location, in the United States, 1970-9 (Thousands).

Area	1970-5	1976	1977	1978	1979 (Jan -Sep)	Total 1970-9	Total 1977-9
All US	83	20	44	74	108	329	226
37 Largest Metro Areas (SMSAs)(a)							
12 High Conversion Activity SMSAs	54	10	30	45	48	187	123
Remaining 25 SMSAs	14	3	9	15	20	61	44
Balance of US	15	7	5	14	40	81	59
Percent Rental Housing Converted							
All US	0.32	0.08	0.17	0.30	0.43	1.31	0.91
12 High Conversion Activity SMSAs	0.75	0.14	0.42	0.68	0.72	2.71	1.83
25 Remaining SMSAs	0.30	0.07	0.18	0.32	0.43	1.30	0.93
Balance of US	0.11	0.04	0.04	0.10	0.28	0.57	0.42

Note: (a) Standard Metropolitan Statistical Areas

Source: HUD, The Conversion of Rental Housing to Condominiums and Cooperatives. A National Study, p. IV-6. (The 12 high activity SMSAs accounted for 28.3 per cent, and the remaining 25 SMSAs for 17.9 per cent of all occupied US rental units in 1977).

41 per cent of all rental units were in buildings with five units or more. If the volume of conversions is seen as a proportion of that stock, 3.56 per cent of the 1977 rental stock had been converted. (23)

As indicated, conversions were much more common in metropolitan areas than in the nation as a whole. Thus, the Chicago SMSA experienced almost 70,000 conversions during the 1970s, which equalled 6.8 per cent of the total Chicago metropolitan rental stock. The central cities of Denver-Boulder had about 11,500 conversions during the same period. However, this represented 10 per cent of the available rental stock and was the highest level of conversion activity in relation to the rental stock of any central city. Among suburban areas, the highest proportions occurred in Chicago with 9 per cent, and in Washington, DC with 8 per cent. (24)

In sum, conversion activities during the 1970s were concentrated to the metropolitan areas of the nation. Twelve of the largest SMSAs, with one-fifth of the total US population, accounted for more than half of the 366,000 condominium conversions occurring in that decade. Conversions split almost even between central city and suburban areas in these SMSAs, the shares being 48 and 52 per cent, respectively. (25) Furthermore, it seems clear that condominiums have become increasingly popular as a means of getting into owner-occupied housing. Of all the home buyers in 1977, only 3.6 per cent purchased a condominium. This share increased to 12.1 per cent in 1980, and further to 16.9 per cent in 1982. (26)

In its 1980 national study, HUD estimated the volume of conversions between 1980 and 1985 at about 1.4 million units. The national supply of 'convertible' rental stock was estimated to 5.2 million units. The study concluded that

> these data suggest that it will be some time before the Nation's supply of convertible rental units is exhausted. In some localities, however, the supply is already low and may be exhausted by 1985 ...
>
> Based on the preceding analysis of supply constraints, conversion activity between 1980 and 1985 cannot proceed at the 1977-79 rate in the 12 high activity areas, taken in the aggregate. In the other 25 SMSAs, and in the balance of the country, conversions could continue at their 1977-79 pace through 1985. (27)

Unfortunately, no national surveys of conversion activities have been carried out after 1979. Annual data on the volume of conversions will be published in governmental reports beginning in 1985. Till then, the actual development during the 1980s is subject to guesswork.

Consequences for the Level and Distribution of Housing Quality

As was shown earlier, neither federal nor state legislation explicitly regulates who has, or who has not, the right to buy a condominium. Conversions occurred mainly as a response to market conditions rather than as a result of conscious housing policy action. Demographic and income developments, and the rapidly increasing prices of single-family homes combined to produce a growing demand for the new form of home ownership offered by condominiums. Tax regulations, and probably rent controls, contributed to an increasing supply of multi-family buildings, which could be converted and sold unit by unit by that new breed called 'converters'.

Thus, any multi-family building can be converted, and any household can become a condominium owner. The analysis of how conversions affect the level and distribution of housing quality must thus be multi-faceted. Not only is it necessary to analyse what kind of housing is converted, and what this means to the quality of the rental supply. One must also look at who is, and who is not, buying among pre-conversion tenants in converted buildings, as well as at the characteristics of households moving into converted units as owners or renters. The fact that outsiders can buy converted units at prevailing market prices furthermore means that many pre-conversion tenants may have to move because they cannot afford to buy their units or rent them at post-conversion rent levels. This of course means that it is of interest to analyse what quality of housing moving tenants enjoy after conversions.

As shown above, the great majority of conversions in the 1970s took place in metropolitan areas. There was, however, a further concentration within these areas. The 1980 HUD report distinguishes three different neighbourhoods; non-revitalising central city, revitalising central city, and non-revitalising suburban. Especially the non-revitalising neighbourhoods are characterised by high-quality buildings in sound or improved condition. Rents are higher than for the rest of the metropolitan areas. Vacancy rates are low, which suggests tight rental markets and attractive areas. Socio-economically, the non-revitalising areas are characterised by upper-middle income, white-collar, professional/managerial, and predominantly white households. Revitalising areas are characterised by a more mixed quality of housing, but have recently experienced an influx of capital for renewal. The socio-economic profile is similar to that of non-revitalising areas; there has been an influx of professional/managerial whites with incomes equal to or above the city's median. Up to 1979-80, conversions in non-revitalising central city areas occurred in 30 SMSAs. Corresponding figures for suburban ares and revitalising central city areas were 27 and 16, respectively. In short, conversions seem concentrated to attractive areas, where buildings in sound or improved conditions are frequently the initial targets for conversions. In revitalising neighbourhoods, converted buildings are more often in substandard condition. On the other hand, the architectural design and size of units often have aesthetic appeal. (28)

Table 2.3 indicates some differences in building characteristics between central city and suburban areas. While only one-third of all units in central cities were less than 20 years old in 1979, over half of suburban units were in that age bracket. However, conversions seem to be concentrated to units built after 1960 in both areas. Current residents predominantly perceived the building age to be less than 20 years in both central cities and suburban areas. However, central city conversions mostly occur in high- and medium-rise buildings, and suburban conversions in low-rise structures. One must, however, draw the conclusion that conversions predominantly occur in modern buildings in sound condition.

This conclusion is supported by the perceptions of continuing residents. A majority of them saw need for only little or minor repairs before conversion. The majority was only slightly larger after conversions, indicating that the buildings may have undergone only limited repairs. This is further corroborated by the continuing residents' perceptions of quality change. A majority perceived the quality to be the same, or just somewhat better. Again, one is led to conclude that condominium conversions occur in modern buildings in good condition. Since they are also located in attractive areas, it may be said that conversions involve asset-

Table 2.3: Selected Characteristics of Buildings in US Metropolitan Areas, 1979. Total Figures, and Perceptions by Current Residents in Converted Buildings.

Building characteristics	Standard Metropolitan Statistical Areas			
	Central Cities		Suburbs	
	Number of units in millions	Percent of all units	Number of units in millions	Percent of all units
Year Structure built				
April 1970-	3.5	14	8.2	26
1960-March 1970	4.4	17	7.9	25
1950-1959	4.0	16	6.2	19
1940-1949	2.7	11	2.8	4
-1939	10.8	42	6.7	21
	25.4	100.0	31.8	100.0
Building age as Perceived by current residents in converted buildings				
-10		24		59
11-20		50		25
21-30		4		3
31-40		2		6
40+		20		7
		100		100
Type of Structure as perceived by current residents in converted buildings				
High-rise (9+ floors)		55		11
Medium-rise (5-8)		19		13
Low-rise (1-4)		26		68
Townhouse, other		-		8
		100		100

Sources: Statistical Abstracts of the United States 1981, p. 764; HUD, The Conversion of Rental Housing to Condominiums and Cooperatives. A National Study, p. VIII-29.

Table 2.4 Quality of Building or Complex, as Perceived by Continuing Residents Before and After Condominium Conversions, United States, 1979, (in percent of respondents)

Quality Aspects	Standard Metropolitan Statistical Areas	
	Central Cities	Suburbs
Perceived need for repair before conversion		
- Little or no repairs	28	34
- Minor repairs	39	44
- Major repairs	33	22
	100	100
Perceived need for repair after conversion		
- Little or no repairs	35	39
- Minor repairs	37	47
- Major repairs	28	14
	100	100
Perceived change in building quality after conversion		
- Much better	9	4
- Somewhat better	26	29
- About the same	56	60
- Somewhat worse	8	7
- Much worse	1	-
	100	100

Source: HUD, The Conversion of Rental Housing to Condominiums and Cooperatives. A National Study, p. VIII-30.

stripping; qualitatively good parts of the rental housing stock are transferred to the owner-occupied sector.

When it comes to the effects of conversions on the distribution of housing quality, several patterns are possible, since the US framework does not restrict conversions to any specific group of households as is the case in Britain. If the buyers of converted units – regardless of whether they are tenant or outside buyers – represent a cross-section of all households, this could result in the distribution of ownership of good-quality housing to a wider spectrum of households. If, on the other hand, buyers represent only specific household strata, conversions could lead to a further concentration of good-quality housing to these strata. Furthermore, the housing quality fate of moving tenants will also have implications for the distribution of housing quality.

Since condominium buyers may come from any tenure and household group, it may be of interest first to have an overview of some of the characteristics of US households at the time of the conversion boom in the late 1970s. As can be seen in Table 2.5, the typical home-owner household in 1977 consisted of two or more persons, was male headed, white, and somewhat older than the average. Among renters, single-person households were much more common than among home owners; one-third of all renter households were singles, compared to one-seventh among home owners. Black and Hispanic households are over-represented among renters, but under-represented among home owners. The median household income was 80 per cent higher for home owners than for renters.

The table also confirms something which could be expected given the kind of neighbourhoods and housing affected by conversions. Renters living in buildings just before conversions differ radically from the average US renter in terms of income. Less than one-quarter of pre-conversion tenants are low income households, compared to three-quarters of all US renter households. The median income for pre-conversion tenants is also far above that of all US home owners. It should, however, be recalled that condominium conversions are an open market phenomenon, and that households outside the conversion buildings can come in and buy – or rent – units, thus affecting the socio-economic profile of the buildings and the neighbourhood. In fact, a rather massive movement of households is caused by

Table 2.5: Tenure Profile of US Households, According to Selected
Characteristics, 1977 and 1979.

Household characteristics	Percentage Share of Households			
	All US Households	Owner occupiers	Renters	Renters in pre-conversion buildings
Household type				
Two or more persons				
Male head	67	78	48	
Female head	12	8	18	
Singles				
Male	8	4	15	
Female	13	10	19	
	100	100	100	
Racial origin				
Black and Hispanic	15	10	25	16
All others	85	90	75	84
	100	100	100	100
Age of head of household				
Under 65	73	69	79	80
65 and Over	27	31	21	20
	100	100	100	100
Household income				
Income under $12,500			74	23
Median income ($000)		18.3	10.0	24.9

Sources: Statistical Abstracts of the United States 1981, pp. 763 ff;
HUD, The Conversion of Rental Housing to Condominiums and
Cooperatives. A National Study, pp. VII-26 ff., VIII-19, 33; ibid.,
Volume of Conversion Activity, pp. 5 ff.; ibid., Impact on Elderly and
Low Income Households, pp. 4 ff.

conversions, as Table 2.6 indicates.

Table 2.6: Pre- and Post-Conversion Status of Residents in Converted Buildings, United States, 1979-80, in per cent.

Tenure status of occupied unit	Residential status		Total
	Continuing residents	New residents	
Owner occupied	22	41	63
Renter occupied	20	17	37
Total	42	58	100

Source: HUD, <u>The Conversion of Rental Housing to Condominiums and Cooperatives. A National Report</u>, p VI-2.

Thus, as many as 58 per cent of pre-conversion tenants move from the converted building, while 42 per cent stay as either condominium owners or renters. It is notable that as many as 37 per cent of the units in converted buildings are rented rather than owned by post-conversion residents.

With nearly six out of ten units being inhabited by new residents after conversion, this is bound to have an impact on the socio-economic and demographic profile. As Table 2.7 shows, incoming households differ from pre-conversion renters in several respects. They are less often low income households; this is true for both outside buyers and new renters. Very few of these new households are elderly, compared to tenant buyers and especially to continuing renters. There is a remarkably high share of single-person households among post-conversion residents. In fact, the share is twice as high as for all households in the twelve high conversion activity areas. (29) Among continuing residents, single females seem to be heavily represented. As a result, the profile of residents has changed. After conversion, the share of low-income households is lower and that of higher-income households higher. The proportion of elderly households is lower and the share of single-person households dramatically higher. There seem to be fewer retired people and a somewhat larger share of people with professional/managerial occupations. The racial mix has not undergone any particular change.

Table 2.7: Selected Characteristics of Households in Conversion Buildings, US High Conversion Activity SMSAs, 1979-80.

Household characteristics	Before conversion	After conversion Owner occupiers		Tenant buyers	Outside renters	Renters		All Residents
	All renters	All owners	All buyers			All renters	Continuing renters	New
Household income								
- under $12,500	23	12	8	14	22	26	17	16
- over $21,500		63	48	35	46	39	51	57
- over $30,000	29	39			23			33
Occupational status								
- professional/managerial	55	65						61
- retired	17	10						13
Racial origin								
- black and hispanic	16	12	14	11	19	19	19	15
Age of head of household								
- under 36	20	48	35	56	51	35	69	49
- 65 and older		9	16	5	17	27	5	15
Household size								
- single male	34(a)	21	8	28	18	13	23	
- single female		36	49	29	29	34	23	53

Note: (a) All renter-occupied housing in the USA (several percentages represent estimates made from information present in these chapters). Percentages do not add up to 100 because of overlapping or missing categories in the original data.

Source: HUD, The Conversion of Rental Housing to Condominiums and Cooperatives. A National Study, ch. VI; ch. VIII; ibid., Volume of Conversion Activity, p.5.

Table 2.8: Pre- and Post-Conversion Characteristics of Households in Buildings Converted to Condominiums, US High-level Conversion Activity SMSAs, 1979-80.

Selected household characteristics	Percentage share of households in area			
	Central cities		Suburban areas	
	Before conversion	After conversion	Before conversion	After conversion
Household income				
- below $12,500 ('low')	18	15	27	16
- above $30,000	31	38	27	27
Occupational status				
- managerial/ professional	59	63	52	59
- retired	16	12	18	13
Racial Origin				
- non-white	21	15	12	17
Age of head of household				
- 65 and older	23	17	18	13
Household type				
- with children under 18	7	7	14	13

Source: HUD, The Conversion of Rental Housing to Condominiums and Cooperatives. A National Study, pp. VIII-19, VIII-33.

These trends are borne out also when one distinguishes between central city and suburban neighbourhoods having experienced conversions. Post-conversion residential profiles suggest a certain pattern. After conversions, residents are more often high-income earners, having professional/managerial jobs, and living as singles. Elderly households are less frequent than before. It is notable that the effects on racial mix differ between central cities and suburbs, the latter having an influx of non-white households into converted buildings.

The households moving out of converted buildings vary considerably with regard to income, occupation, and age. On the other hand, households with heads younger than 36 represent a smaller share among movers than among incoming buyers or renters. Moving households are also larger; while 53 per cent of all post-conversion residents are singles, this group constitutes only 27 per cent of the households moving out of converted buildings. It should also be noted that almost 50 per cent of elderly households whose buildings are converted move rather than stay as buyers or renters, compared to fewer than 10 per cent of all elderly households who move in an average year. Furthermore, this group of elderly movers represent 60 per cent of all low-income households who move out of converted buildings. (30)

What happens to the movers in terms of housing quality? As many as 72 per cent of the households moving out come to live in a new neighbourhood. 26 per cent become owners, 70 per cent renters, and 4 per cent live rent free. The renters have different experiences in terms of housing quality. 31 per cent moved to a higher-quality apartment, while 15 per cent managed to get a unit of equal quality with no cost increase. 18 per cent moved to lower- or equal-quality apartments, but had to pay more for their new dwelling. Another 6 per cent moved to lower-quality cost housing with lower costs. As for household characteristics, the elderly are more likely than others to get less housing value for their dollars; the share is twice as high as that for non-elderly movers from converted buildings. Low-income movers from converted buildings are also much more dissatisfied with their new neighbourhood than any other group affected by conversions. (31)

To sum up, it seems clear that conversions in the 1970s were concentrated in attractive neighbourhoods in metropolitan areas, and in buildings in sound condition needing few or minor repairs. It is also evident that conversions caused a change in the socio-economic and demographic profile of the buildings and neighbourhoods. Post-conversion residents enjoying the good quality of converted units are more often young, single-person households with incomes above average and with professional/managerial positions than was the case among pre-conversion tenants. If anything, outside buyers and and new renters resemble traditional home owners more than they do renters, except for household size. Pre-conversion renters moving out are often larger households. Elderly households represent a large share of moving low-income tenants. About one-fourth of those moving out come to live in housing of lower quality than they enjoyed before.

Although the socio-economic changes are in no way dramatic, they show a specific direction; through conversions, good housing quality is increasingly concentrated to households with resources to enjoy that quality. If buyers look like traditional home owners, then the President's Commission on Housing may not be accurate in its assessment of conversions: 'Conversion of multifamily units to cooperatives or condiminiums enables many people to become homeowners who otherwise would not have this opportunity.' (32) With as many as three-fifths of all pre-conversion tenants moving out from units of allegedly the same standard after as well as before conversion, one might ask whether the costs of converted housing are such as to distribute opportunities far less widely than the Commission seems to believe.

Effects on the Level and Distribution of Housing Costs

As may be recalled from the first chapter, the proponents of conversions argue in terms of equality of opportunity, while the opponents base their objections on arguments concerning equality of outcome. We have just seen that the conversion to condominiums in the United States has tended to result in a more intensive use of the opportunities to buy among households with high incomes. It should, of course, be kept in mind that the pre-conversion residents by no means represented a cross-section of US households. However, if the equality of opportunity argument were valid, there could have been a more even distribution of different socio-economic and demographic household categories after conversion.

What, then, about the argument of equality of

outcome? It could be that the groups affected by conversions experience changes in housing costs which correspond both to their ability to pay and to the quality of housing they enjoy. If so, the opponents' argument would not be tenable.

In assessing the cost effects of conversions, several distinctions must be kept in mind. First of all, it is important to distinguish between short- and long-term effects. In the short run, there may be substantial changes in the outlays of different residential categories. The question here is whether these changes in the level of housing costs show a specific distributive pattern. In the longer run, the different legal and economic conditions surrounding owning and renting will affect the level of housing costs differently for owners and renters. Here, a second distinction becomes important, i.e., between gross and net costs of housing. Tax deductions, and the appreciation of the converted unit, will lead to substantial differences in net expenditures between owners and renters. Insofar as there is a systematic bias in the socio-economic composition of these two groups, the outcome may be correspondingly unequal. Third, there must be a distinction between comparable and uncomparable groups of households. In the US case, the only truly comparable groups in terms of distributive outcome are tenant buyers and continuing renters, since they inhabit units of roughly the same quality before and after conversions, and live in the same buildings.

In short, the assessment focuses on (a) changes in buyer and renter outgoings as a direct result of conversions, and (b) the redistribution of wealth. Although the interest is concentrated on the two groups just mentioned, the consequences for other affected household categories will also be accounted for.

To put the cost effect in perspective, it may be useful to look at the overall development of housing costs in the United States in the 1970s. By 1977, the average renter paid 29 per cent of his income in gross rent. The average home owner's gross expenditures on shelter represented 34 per cent of his income. (33) In 1979, the medium percentage of income paid for housing in the SMSAs was 27 per cent for renters and 22 per cent for owners of conventional units built since 1970 with a mortgage. (34) The mean rent/income ratios – measured in current dollars – increased at different rates for different income quartiles. Between 1960 and 1977, the ratio for the lowest income quartile among renters rose from 0.46 to 0.63, while that of the highest quartile (where most of the renters affected by conversions belong) only rose from 0.13 to 0.14. In real terms, the ratios increased very little between 1973 and 1977. All the change in current dollar ratios seems attributable to inflation, and very little to increases in housing consumption. By 1977, about 45 per cent of all US renters paid more than 25 per cent of their income for gross rent. Twenty-seven per cent paid more than 35 per cent. (35) For home owners, the ratio of gross cash outlay on housing to income differed drastically between income quartiles in 1977. While half of all home owners in the lowest-income quartile had a ratio higher than 0.25, the corresponding shares of the third and fourth quartiles were 10 and 3 per cent, respectively. Of all home owners in 1977, about 20 per cent had gross cash outlays exceeding 25 per cent of their income. (36) During the 1970s an increasing gulf appeared between the initial costs for home buyers and real costs for current home owners. For the latter, net costs after adjusting for taxes and inflation declined; fixed-rate mortgages insulated them from the rise in interest rates, and the resale value of their homes rose faster than other prices, off-setting the rises in fuel costs, taxes, and maintenance. For home buyers, the initial monthly mortgage payment - measured as a percentage of household income - began a rapid increase after 1973 as home prices and interest rates grew much faster than personal incomes. (37)

Given the overall development for renters and home owners and the trends in the market for ownership, it is no surprise to find that condominium buyers seem to have had great economic expectations as a motive for their purchase. As can be seen from Table 2.9, nearly two-thirds of all buyers of condominiums decided to buy for economic reasons such as: (a) to provide a hedge against inflation; (b) to stabilise their rising housing costs; (c) to obtain tax shelters (reliefs) and investments; (d) to get into home ownership 'cheaper' than if buying a single-family home; or (e) to take advantage of a discount on the condominium price offered to them by the converter. As for the last point, about 90 per cent of tenant buyers seem to have been offered discounts varying between 10 and 20 per cent of the purchase price demanded by the converter. (38)

What immediate changes in housing outlays have been felt by conversions? As shown in Table 2.10, the majority of these households incurred increases in

Table 2.9: Factors Most Important in Households' Decisions to Buy or Rent Converted Units, United States, 1979-80.

Most Important factor in decision to buy or rent	Condominium Owners			Condominium Renters
	Tenant buyers	Outside buyers	All buyers	All renters
Economic	47	69	62	13
Location	16	8	11	48
Tenure preference	2	11	16	12
Unit, building	12	8	9	22
Reluctance to move	23	0	7	5

Source: HUD, The Conversion of Rental Housing to Condominiums and Cooperatives. A National Study, pp. VI-8 ff., VI-18.

Table 2.10: Change in Total Monthly Housing Costs Following Condominium Conversion, for Different Categories Affected by Conversions, United States, 1979-80.

Change in total costs	Present condominium residents				Former residents	
	Tenant buyers	Outside buyers	Continuing renters	New renters	Owners	Renters
Lower costs	12	16	3	27	5	30
No change	2	0	48	3	0	5
Higher costs						
25%	19	14	43	22	18	37
26 - 50%	29	13	5	19	12	21
50	38	57	1	29	65	7
	100%	100%	100%	100%	100%	100%

Source: HUD, The Conversion of Rental Housing to Condominiums and Cooperatives. Impacts on Housing Costs, p. 25 f.

housing expenditures following conversions. Renters move into or out of converted dwellings were those most often enjoying lower total costs after conversion, although a majority did get higher costs. Half of the continuing renters in the buildings after conversion had the same costs as before conversion, and most of the other half suffered increases of less than 25 per cent. The most dramatic immediate increases hit buyers from the outside and pre-conversion renters moving into owner-occupied housing elsewhere. The difference between tenant and outside buyers may - to some extent - depend on discounts given to tenant buyers, but also on outside buyers' change in housing quality.

This is further revealed by the figures for average percentage increases in total housing costs. The average outside buyer nearly doubled his outlays after moving to the condominium, while continuing renters had a small average increase, with tenant buyers in between these two extremes. It should be noted that on the average, tenants moving out to rent somewhere else experienced an increase close to one-fifth of their earlier total housing costs. Incoming new renters in converted buildings suffered an average increase of almost two-fifths of their earlier total housing costs. No particular pattern can be elicited from the data on households with increases of 50 per cent or more. The fact that the percentage for 'all' is in some cases higher than for the particular groups presented in the table reflects another phenomenon; high-income earners constitute a large share of buyers, and their immediate cost increases are extremely large in most cases. (39)

It must, of course, be remembered that households moving into or out of converted buildings may change to another standard and quality of housing. Therefore, the changes they experience in total housing costs cannot be directly interpreted as being caused by conversion as such. The problem of interpreting data can be illustrated using the case of former resident renters and new renters. As Table 2.11 shows, these groups experienced increases in total costs amounting to 19 and 38 per cent, respectively. The weighted mean increase for these two groups was 27 per cent. This may be compared to the 9 per cent increase in housing costs experienced by the average renter in the SMSAs between January 1979 and January 1980. Now, we know that three out of seven former resident renters moved to higher quality housing, and thus probably had to pay more for better housing. On the other hand, it seems that only one

Table 2.11: Increases in Total Housing Costs after Conversion, for Different Household Categories, United States, 1979-80.

Increases in total costs of housing	Present condominium residents				Former residents	
	Tenant buyers	Outside buyers	Continuing renters	New renters	Owners	Renters
Average Percentage Increase	44	87	7	38	79	19
Percentage of Households Experiencing 50+ % Increase in Total Costs						
- 65 and older	17	50	2	0	20	2
- income under $12,500	16	38	3	31	75	8
- black	31	35	0	28	100	2
- white	22	44	2	25	63	4
- all	37	57	1	29	65	7

Source: HUD, The Conversion of Rental Housing to Condominiums and Cooperatives. Impacts on Housing Costs, pp. 25 ff., 63 ff.

out of seven former renters incurred higher costs for the same quality of housing. Nothing is known about the earlier housing standards of new renters. Thus, very little can be said about whether or not moving households 'lost' or 'won' in terms of housing standards and costs. (40) Thus, the only truly comparable groups in terms of housing costs are tenant buyers and continuing renters. But before going into a more careful analysis of their fate in terms of housing costs, another trend may be worth noting. According to Table 2.11, there was an average increase in housing costs for all households following conversions. Thus, one may ask whether this consequence is in line with official norms concerning housing affordability. In its 1980 edition of Wise Home Buying, the US Department of Housing and Urban Development recommended that:

(1) The price of the home should not exceed two to two and one half times your annual income. A young couple should stay on the low side of this estimate. If income is substantial and income prospects are good, the upper level can be applied.
(2) A homeowner should not pay more than 35 percent of income for monthly housing expenses (payment of the mortgage loan plus average cost of heat, utilities, repair and maintenance. (41)

As the table shows, a very substantial percentage of condominium buyers exceeded the purchase price/income ratio recommended by national housing authorities. A majority of elderly buyers exceeded this recommended ratio, and so did a majority of female buyers among pre-conversion tenants. With the obvious relationship between high purchase prices and high total monthly housing costs, this would indicate a high percentage of buyers having to pay more than 35 per cent of their income on housing. It should, however, be noted that most buyers, and especially the subgroups just mentioned, were able to bring down the unit mortgage/income ratio by making large down payments. In this way, they may have been able to bring down their monthly total costs enough to get below the recommended 35 per cent housing cost/income ratio (provided, of course, that the interest on the capital used for this down payment is not counted as foregone and thus as a cost to the buyer).

Table 2.12: Ratio of Purchase Price and Unit Mortgage to Household Income for Different Categories of Condominium Buyers, United States, 1979-80.

(Percent of) Household Category with Ratio 2.5	Tenant Buyers		Outside Buyers	
	Purchase price/ income ratio 2.5	Unit mortgage/ income ratio 2.5	Purchase price/ income ratio 2.5	Unit mortgage/ income ratio 2.5
All households	42	25	36	19
Age of head of household				
- under 35	32	21	29	22
- 65 and older	74	56	77	50
Sex of head of household				
- male	33	26	32	25
- female	52	25	40	25

Source: HUD, The Conversion of Rental Housing to Condominiums and Cooperatives. Impacts on Housing Costs, pp. 63 ff.

Table 2.13: Ratios of Total Housing Costs to Income for Households Affected by Condominium Conversions, United States, 1979-80.

Ratio of housing costs to income	Present condominium residents				Former residents	
	Tenant buyers	Outside buyers	Continuing renters	New renters	Owners	Renters
Average % of income spent on housing	31	41	34	35	34	29
Percent of households spending 30+% of income on housing						
- 65 and older	63	60	50	67	70	61
- income under $12,500	85	61	66	70	33	64
- black	51	30	25	8	50	12
- white	39	31	30	20	33	24
- all	40	32	27	22	36	24

Source: HUD, The Conversion of Rental Housing to Condominiums and Cooperatives. Impacts on Housing Costs, pp. 35 ff., 63 ff.

Table 2.13 shows that the average percentage of income spent on housing comes close to the 35 per cent line for most of the household groups affected by conversions. The average percentage is substantially higher for outside buyers. Unfortunately, the HUD national survey used 30 rather than 35 per cent as the dividing line, with the households paying more than 30 per cent of their income on housing being defined as 'burdened'. For almost every group of households affected by conversions, the table reveals that a majority of elderly and low-income households are 'burdened' with high monthly expenditures on housing. As many as 40 per cent of tenant buyers paid more than 30 per cent of their income for housing, compared to about 21 per cent of all US home buyers in 1979. (42)

The data so far seem to support the conclusion that US condominium conversions have a tendency to drive costs of housing upward. Most groups affected have experienced increases - sometimes dramatic ones - in their housing expenditures as a short-term effect of the conversion. The data also seem to indicate that continuing renters have fared better than tenant buyers with respect to short-term gross expenditure changes. Continuing renters have only a small average rent increase, and the proportion paying more than 30 per cent of the income on housing after conversion is lower than for tenant buyers.

On the other hand, these conclusions refer exclusively to gross short-term effects. If we include the effects of tax regulations and value appreciation, the actual housing costs of buyers may well turn out to be quite different from gross expenditures. In the long run, the buyers may be better off than continuing renters in terms of actual costs for the same standard of housing. In the long run, a redistribution of wealth in favour of buyers may occur as a result of conversions.

Table 2.14 sheds some light on this problem. While a small majority of continuing renters experienced no immediate upward change in gross rent, the overwhelming majority of buyers incurred substantial upward increases in total housing costs. The picture changes somewhat, however, if the buyer's possibility of deducting mortgage interest from taxable income is taken into account. The net increase in housing costs is considerably lower than the gross figures indicate. And when the appreciation of the condominium is considered, the picture is totally reversed. Provided the buyer is able to sell at prices indicated by the appreciation rate of 10

Table 2.14: Changes in Housing Costs, With and Without Tax Benefits and Unit Appreciation, for Tenant and Outside Buyers, and Continuing Renters in Converted Buildings in the United States, 1979–80.

Change in total housing costs	Tenant Buyers			Outside Buyers		Continuing Renters	
	Without tax benefits	With tax benefits	With tax benefits, and unit appreciation	Without tax benefits	With tax benefits	With tax benefits, and unit appreciation	Without tax benefits and unit appreciation
Lower costs	12	16	91	17	25	95	3
No change	2	0	0	0	0	0	48
Higher costs							
−25%	19	31	6	15	11	2	43
26–50%	29	23	0	12	16	2	5
50+%	38	30	3	56	48	1	1
	100%	100%	100%	100%	100%	100%	100%
Mean Monthly Values							
Change in percentage	+44	+32	−57	+87	+68	−64	+7
Cost, $	568	521	179	549	492	131	389
Tax savings, $		66	66		72	72	none
Appreciation, $			393			394	none

Source: HUD, The Conversion of Rental Housing to Condominiums and Cooperatives. Impact on Housing Costs, p. 32.

per cent, he will enjoy a remarkable decrease in actual housing costs. The appreciation of the value of his condominium brings the owner into the circle of people that reaps the benefits from the redistribution of wealth occurring in all housing markets subject to inflation.

By using available data on purchase prices, mortgage debts, rent increases, interest rates, tax deductions in different income brackets, as well as income figures, it is possible to compute the present value of the 'economic outcome of housing' over the next five years for tenant buyers and remaining tenants. For the pre-conversion tenant choosing to stay as a renter in a converted building, the present value of his outgoings for rent over the five years after 1979 would have been $20,900. For the pre-conversion tenant who bought his dwelling, the net outgoings over there five years would have had a present value in 1979 of $25,700. If the owner chooses to sell his unit after five years and buys another unit for the same or a higher price, he escapes the capital gains tax and thus enjoys the full value appreciation of his 1979 unit. The 1979 present value of the market price of the unit in 1984 was $50,100, assuming the same value appreciation as the increase in rent for tenants. At the end of the fifth year the present value of the remaining mortgage debt would have been $22,900. The present value of the owner's possible earnings after five years would thus have exceeded that of his outgoings and remaining debt by $1,500. The tenant buyer would thus have been up on the continuing renter by as much as $22,400 after five years in terms of the present value of their 'economic outcome of housing.' (43)

These figures bring us into a position where we can judge the effects of conversions in terms of outcome for comparable groups. Pre-conversion residents staying in a converted building are either renters or owners, depending on whether or not they have taken the opportunity to buy their dwellings at a discount price. As shown especially in Table 2.7, these two groups differ in some ways which indicate that they may have had different possibilities in this respect. More continuing renters are low-income earners, and fewer have high incomes than is the case among tenant buyers. There are also more elderly households among continuing renters than among tenant buyers.

Not only may the tenant buyers have had greater opportunities to buy in the first place, but they are also clearly much better off in terms of economic outcome of living in converted housing. In fact, tenant buyers would be able to leave their unit with a gain after five years, something quite impossible for continuing renters.

To sum up, the immediate cash-flow implications of conversions together with the more long-term wealth accumulation effects, both seem to have identifiable redistributive effects. A study of conversions in a Boston suburb summarises the effects in the following way:

> While current renters in Brookline generally appear to reside in housing units whose costs are reasonably matched to their incomes, the condominium conversion process threatens a change in this relationship of serious proportions ... the proportion of Brookline's current renter population which may be faced with actual buy-or move choices cannot be estimated with any assurance. What is indisputable, however, based on the comparative cost analysis presented above, is that for the less transient, less affluent, and generally older groups in Brookline, conversion of their apartments will generally have the effect of putting the apartments in a price range they cannot afford.
>
> Continued conversion, in other words, will inevitably lead to a significant upward movement in the average income level of Brookline's residents as current renters are displaced by condominium owners. (44)

In terms of our framework, inequalities of opportunity lead to inequality of outcome.

Conversions, Housing Markets, and the Availability of Rental Housing

One central argument in the condominium controversy concerns the effects of conversions on the rental market. Obviously, conversions mean that housing units once occupied by renters change to owner-occupied status, while some converted units continue to be rented rather than occupied by their owners. Some households which once rented become owners, while others move from their owner-occupied homes to become renters in converted buildings. The net effect of conversion in the housing market thus depends upon changes in both the tenure status of households and the occupancy status of the housing units.

The national conversion study by HUD contains a model for estimating the net changes in the rental markets of SMSAs. It is based on the supply and demand changes taking place between 1977 and 1979 in the twelve SMSAs with high conversion activity. Since these metropolitan areas had nearly 60 per cent of all conversions in that period, it seems reasonable to consider the effects estimated from these SMSAs as representative for the nation as a whole.

Based on a careful analysis of the pre- and post-conversion status of the households affected by conversions, the resulting model for net changes in the rental market (see Figure 2.2) shows the following effects. For every 100 rental units converted, 63 units are lost to the rental supply because they are now owner-occupied by purchasers. Thirty-seven continue to be occupied by renting households. Of the 63 households who bought and now occupy their units, 49 were previous renters. Of the 58 households who moved out of the converted building, 11 bought other housing units and thus became owner occupiers. As a result, renter demand is decreased by 60 households, that is, the 49 previous renters who bought converted units and the 11 moving tenants who bought owner-occupied units elsewhere. Since two previous home owners moved into the converted building as renters, they add to renter demand. The actual decrease in that demand as a result of the conversion of 100 units is thus 58 households. The supply of rental units decreases more than rental demand, leading to a net loss to the rental market of 5 units per 100 units converted to owner occupancy. Using these results as a basis for estimating the absolute amount of loss to the rental housing stock attributable to condominium conversions, the HUD report concluded:

> If it is assumed that the conversion effect observed in the 12 SMSAs with high activity between 1977 and 1979 is similar to what occurred nationally during the 1970s, the following took place: between 1970 and 1979, 366,000 units were converted; the Nation's rental housing supply was reduced by 231,000 units; renter demand fell by 212,000 households; and a net total of 18,000 previously vacant rental units were occupied by former tenants of converted buildings. (45)

This figure represents only a tiny fraction of the total rental supply in the United States, and just

Figure 2.2: Estimated Net Loss to the Rental Sector Attributable to Conversions as per Each 100 Units Converted, United States

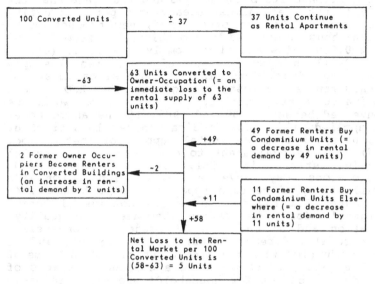

Source: HUD, <u>The Conversion of Rental Housing to Condominiums and Cooperatives. A National Report</u>, pp. VII-5 ff.; esp. p. VII-9.

over 1 per cent of vacant rental housing in 1979. It should be noted that the total rental stock grew by 2.8 million units between 1973 and 1980, and that the vacancy rate held almost steady at 5 per cent during that period. On the other hand, new production of rental housing dropped by two thirds, or from 672,000 to 220,000 units annually from 1973 to 1981. (46)

Still, however, the net effect on rental supply resulting from condominium conversions must be considered as almost negligible. The HUD report estimated that about 1.5 million units would be converted between 1980 and 1985. If the above model is applied, this would indicate a net loss of about 75,000 units from the rental supply for that period. (47) This is equivalent to one third of the rental housing starts in 1981. On the other hand, conversions may have a larger impact on the availability of certain types of rental housing. An estimated 5.1 million units are considered 'prime targets' for conversions because of quality, location and so on. (48) If projected conversions were totally directed towards this segment, and if new production is not a direct substitute in terms of quality etc., there would be a considerable loss of freedom of choice for households who - for economic or other reasons - rent rather than own their dwellings.

Condominium Conversions and Residential Influence

In a way, what was just said about the poorer resident strata indicates that the conversion process will lead to a decrease in these groups' influence over their housing situation. As noted earlier, residential influence is not explicitly mentioned as a primary motive for ownership rather than renting. To converters as well as buyers, the motivating force is money; economic benefits are uppermost in these actors' minds in the conversion process. It is not possible to determine whether or not the motive 'life style' includes a high valuation of residential influence and/or a higher willingness to engage in matters common to all residents.

We noted earlier that when a converter has sold most of the units in a converted building, he relinquishes control of the common parts of the property to a condominium owners' association. This association has a Board of Directors, which negotiates service contracts, determines maintenance fees, and decides on whether or not the renters in the building should be allowed to join the association, as well as what their voting powers should be. Nothing much is known about the work of these associations and their Boards. However, an overwhelming majority of condominium owners receive services through membership or through payment of a service contract or maintenance fee. This would seem to indicate that membership in associations is not 100 per cent among owners. Most owners and renters are, however, satisfied with the services provided.

An issue very much related to residential influence, and seemingly of concern to many condominium residents, is the relationship between owners and renters in a condominium building. Ten per cent of both owners and renters surveyed said they had experience 'confrontations' with members of the opposite tenure group. Owners mostly complained about noise, unruly pets, and children. Renters, on the other hand, complained mostly about conflicts engendered by the process of conversion. On the whole, about 50 per cent of the condominium owners would rather live in buildings without renters. (49)

Available reports give no information about the association's role in solving such conflicts. Nor do they indicate how condominium owners have acted – through the Board of Directors - one the issue of participatory rights to renters. Given the owner views shown in the survey just mentioned, renters in converted buildings may find it difficult to exert much influence over matters common to all households in a converted building.

Conversions and the Public Purse

Property taxes constitute the major source of income for US local governments. Condominium conversions affect a community's fiscal affairs in two principal ways. The primary impact comes from the revaluation of converted property. The tax base becomes broader if all units in a building are assessed separately as condominiums than if the building as a whole is assessed as a rental property. A secondary effect comes through changes in demands for municipal services. As we have seen above, the socio-economic profile of post-conversion residents differs from that of the pre-conversion renters, something that may affect the demand for municipal services. To some, the broadening of the tax base means increased possibilities for local governments to provide better services:

from a strictly fiscal point of view, one can

view the condominium conversion process as
significantly upgrading the taxpaying capacity
of middle and upper middle income housing, thus
providing the wherewithal for financing the
needs of less fortunate residents. (50)

The impact on tax revenues is, however, difficult to
assess. The rules and practices of property value
assessment vary substantially among states and local
governments. On the other hand, property tax relief
programmes covering home ownership seem to be at work
in a large number of jurisdictions. Owner-occupied
property is assessed at a lower percentage of the
market value than other property, or is taxed at a
lower rate of the assessed value than other property.
The result of such rules and practices is of course
to mediate the impact of conversions on tax revenues.
(51)
    The HUD national study contains some rudimental
data on changes in assessment values. The total
assessed value of converted buildings increased
substantially after conversion, as did nominal taxes
owed. On the other hand, the increase is small
compared to the total assessments existing in the
SMSAs with high conversion activity. Among these
areas, only San Francisco experienced a net increase
in assessed values larger than 0.0002 per cent of
total real property assessments as a result of
condominium conversions in 1978. Still, they
represent additional tax revenues to be collected
over the years to come and could thus amount to a
significant sum in the future. (52)
    A local study of conversions in Brookline,
Mass., indicates that post-conversion assessment
values exceeded pre-conversion values by 34 per cent.
At existing property tax rates in Brookline, this
higher valuation would yield an additional $450 in
tax revenues per unit converted. Assuming that there
were no property tax exclusions or abatements, and
that the $450 increase represents the average for all
converted units, the city of Brookline would have
enjoyed an increase in tax revenues of more than
$750,000 in 1979. (53) Unfortunately, no data are
given for the total tax revenues, and thus no
indication can be given as to the relative importance
of the extra revenue caused by post-conversion value
reassessments.
    The effects of conversions on the demand for
municipal services are even more difficult to assess.
They depend totally on the particular demographic
profile that results from conversions. If the post-

conversion neighbourhoods have become more dominated by smaller and older households with few children, this would indicate a lower demand for school services. If the opposite demographic profile occurs, this demand will of course increase. The Brookline study found the latter profile, but concluded that average net tax benefit would be substantial; increased revenues from conversion reassessment would still exceed increases in school expenditures. (54)

Conversions do, however, have effects on the revenues also at the state and federal levels of government. Condominium owners can deduct mortgage interest and local property taxes from their taxable income. Assuming that the average increase in property taxes resulting from conversions is the same as that for Brookline - $450 - and using the assumptions made above about mortgage debts and interest rates, as well as tax rates, the estimate in Table 2.15 admittedly hypothetical - of the overall fiscal effects of conversions can be made. (55)

Table 2.15: Estimated Overall Fiscal Effects of Condominium Conversions in the United States, 1970-9, for Fiscal Year 1979.

Total revenue increase for local governments due to increased property values (average tax increase $450, number of conversions 366,000)	+$165,000,000
Total revenue decrease for federal and state governments due to deduction of increased property taxes (federal tax rate 28 per cent, state tax rate 6 per cent)	-$ 55,000,000
Total revenue decrease for federal and state governments due to deduction of mortgage interest (tax rate 34 per cent, mortgage debt $44,000, interest rate 12.5 per cent)	-$685,000,000
Net revenue result for all governmental levels	-$575,000,000

This estimate indicates an overall loss to the public purse as a result of conversions. From a strictly fiscal point of view it would thus seem as if the optimism of the statement quoted earlier is based on a too one-sided view. Admittedly, local governments increase their revenues as a result of conversions. But at the same time, the loss to the federal and state public purses is much larger. Since so much of local services depends on grants from higher governmental levels, the implications of conversions for the local governments' ability to extend services to 'less fortunate residents' may be somewhat less clear-cut than the optimists would have us believe.

Conclusion

A notable feature of US condominium conversions is that they occurred as a spontaneous market phenomenon, with no specific backing by any governmental policy. Rapid price increases for traditional owner-occupied homes, unfavourable relations between profits from investment in rental housing and from other investments, as well as tax regulations favouring wholesale purchase and subsequent subdivision of rental buildings for sale unit by unit all combined to open up a whole new type of housing market. Only when this development had established itself did governments at different levels react by issuing regulations governing the rights and duties of actors in the conversion market. In 1982, a Presidental Commission on Housing came out strongly in favour of conversions as a means of spreading home ownership, and suggested measures to make the conversion market work more smoothly and effectively.

Several aspects contribute to making the context of US condominium conversions quite special. Conversions are initiated by a special type of developer called converters, who can convert buildings in a more profitable way than landlords because of tax regulations. The initiative lies with the converter, who can sell the converted units in the open market, and not just to sitting tenants. Thus, issues of security of tenure for sitting tenants become important, as do issues of consumer protection for buyers. However, many of these issues are a matter for state and local governments, which means that the legal framework differs considerably among states and municipalities. The motivating force behind the converter's actions is money, meaning that he will use whatever economic measures are available and legal to secure the highest possible profit from conversions. With such a varying legal, and profit-oriented economic context, the effects of conversions will be highly dependent on what buildings and estates are selected by converters as possibly profitable conversion objects. In all likelihood, converters are drawn to the most attractive and best-quality segment of the rental housing stock. This makes for high purchase prices and subsequent high outlays on housing. In turn, this implies that the opportunities for home ownership provided through conversions may not be equally possible for all households affected by conversions, or aspiring to become owner occupiers.

The account given here seems to corroborate this argument. So far, US condominium conversions have concerned a very small part of the rental housing stock. However, they tend to be concentrated in the large metropolitan areas, and within these areas, in attractive neighbourhoods with good-quality housing. The pre-conversion demographic and socio-economic household profiles of high conversion activity areas by no means resemble a cross-section of American households. The median income of pre-conversion renters was much higher than that of all home owners, and two and a half times higher than that of all US renters.

If all pre-conversion tenants took advantage of the discounts offered by converters, thus buying their attractive high-quality units at a favourable price, this could hardly be described as a widening of opportunities for home ownership to new strata. If, on the other hand, many pre-conversion tenants move and are replaced by households showing a broader socio-economic and demographic profile, this would be at least some step in this direction.

The evidence provided here points to a rather high degree of movement following conversions. Nearly six out of ten pre-conversion residents have moved from the building within two years of the conversion. There is a tendency that households moving out are more often elderly, have lower incomes and are larger than those remaining in the converted building. Furthermore, those who buy and stay, and those who buy and move in, are more often young, have higher incomes and form smaller households than those moving out. Thus the US conversions could be described as leading to an even higher concentration of households with good ability to pay in the best-quality segment of US multi-family housing.

Indeed, an ability to pay seems to be a prerequisite for households who want to use the opportunity for home ownership provided by conversions. The immediate effect of condominium conversions is to drive the gross outlays on housing dramatically upward. This is true for all households moving in or out of converted buildings, as well as for tenant buyers. Continuing renters seem to fare better in this respect. On the other hand, households buying their units thereby enjoy the benefits provided by tax regulations and by the appreciation of their unit's value. Thus, a redistribution of wealth occurs, favouring households who purchase rather than rent their units. The economic outcome of housing for pre-conversion tenants who can afford to buy their units is really different from that of tenants moving out to rent a lower-quality unit at the same or higher price as their earlier dwelling.

Thus, the market-oriented economic context leads to a concentration of conversion activity to high-quality buildings holding the prospect of a good profit to the converter. In turn, this is paralleled by a concentration of opportunities to those segments of households who already have a high ability to pay for housing. The final result seems to be a greater inequality of outcome. Thus, the President's Commission on Housing seems only half right in its assessment of conversion effects. Condominium conversions <u>do</u> provide benefits to those who occupy the units as owners; it is only that conversions <u>do not</u> seem to enable many people to become home owners who would not otherwise have this opportunity. The volume of conversions does provide evidence of public awareness of the benefits; it is only that the evidence provided here indicates that it takes a solid ability to pay to act on this awareness and enjoy the benefits.

The Commission believed that conversions are beneficial to the community as well. The estimates made here - and based on the empirical data available - indicate that there will be an overall fiscal loss to the public purse as a result of conversions. This seems to have some strange implications for <u>supplementary</u> housing policy, which offers direct economic subsidies only to those households who would otherwise never be able to live in decent housing. By allowing those with good ability to pay to enjoy the benefits of home ownership, governments forego tax revenues which could be used to subsidise less resourceful households. The more home ownership is favoured and spread, especially among high-income groups, the fewer resources will be available to governments for redistribution in accordance with the principles of supplementary policy. By being <u>comprehensive</u> towards home owners, the government has even less to offer as a supplement to the poorer tenants.

Notes

1. Harold L. Wolman, <u>Housing and Housing Policy in the U.S. and the U.K.</u> (Lexington Books, Lexington, Mass., 1975), chs. 1 and 2 <u>passim</u>; quote from p.20.

2. See, e.g. Joseph Friedman and Daniel H. Weinberg, <u>The Economics of Housing Vouchers</u> (Academic Press, New York, 1982), and Joseph Friedman and Daniel H. Weinberg (eds.), <u>The Great Housing Experiment</u> (Sage, Beverly Hills, Urban Affairs Annual Reviews, vol. 24, 1983).

3. Nathan H. Schwartz, 'Reagan's Housing Policies', in Anthony Champagne and Edward J. Harpham (eds.), <u>The Attack on the Welfare State</u> (Waveland Press, Prospect Heights, Ill., 1984), p. 162.

4. Barry G. Jacobs <u>et al.</u>, <u>Guide to Federal Housing Programs</u> (The Bureau of National Affairs, Inc., Washington, DC, 1982), p. 229.

5. <u>The Report of the President's Commission on Housing</u> (Washington, DC, 1982), p. xvii.

6. Ibid., p. xvii.

7. Ibid., p. 81.

8. C.F. Horowitz, 'Condominium Conversion Controls', <u>Society,</u> <u>21</u> (March/April 1984), pp. 58 ff.

9. HUD, <u>The Conversion of Rental Housing to Condominiums and Cooperatives. A National Study of Scope, Causes and Impacts</u> (US Department of Housing and Urban Development, Washington, DC, 1980), p. X-4 ff.

10. Ibid., pp. XI-100 ff.

11. Ibid., pp. XI-19 f., XII-26 f.

12. Ibid., p. III-5; Jack Beren, 'The Condominium Corner', <u>Journal of Real Estate Taxation,</u> <u>3</u> (Winter 1985), pp. 221 ff.; Asa Baber, 'The Condominum Conspiracy', <u>Playboy</u> (November 1979), p. 204.

13. HUD, <u>The Conversion of Rental Housing to Condominiums and Cooperatives. A National Study,</u> pp. X-7 ff.

14. Jacobs <u>et al.</u>, pp. 89 ff.

15. HUD, <u>The Conversion of Rental Housing to Condominiums and Cooperatives. A National Study,</u> p. X-13 f.

16. Jacobs <u>et al.</u>, pp. 229 ff.

17. HUD, <u>The Conversion of Rental Housing to Condominiums and Cooperatives. A National Study,</u> p. III-7.

18. Ibid., p. III-10.
19. Ibid., p. III-21.
20. John R. Dinkenspiel, Joel Uchenick, and Herbert L. Selesnick, Condominiums. The Effects of Conversion on a Community (Auburn House, Boston, Mass., 1981), pp. 31, 59 (quote).
21. HUD, The Conversion of Rental Housing to Condominiums and Cooperatives. A National Study, p. III-22.
22. Statistical Abstracts of the United States 1984 (US Department of Commerce/Bureau of Census, Washington, DC, 1984), p. 748.
23. HUD, The Conversion of Rental Housing to Condominiums and Cooperatives. Volume of Conversion Activity in Selected Metropolitan Areas (US Department of Housing and Urban Development, Washington, DC, 1981), p. 3.
24. Ibid., p. 13; HUD, The Conversion of Rental Housing to Condominiums and Cooperatives. A National Study, p. IV-9.
25. HUD, The Conversion of Rental Housing to Condominiums and Cooperatives. Volume of Conversion Activity, p. 5.
26. Statistical Abstracts of the United States 1984, p. 758.
27. HUD, The Conversion of Rental Housing to Condominiums and Cooperatives. A National Study, p. VII-22 f.
28. Ibid., p. VII-12 f.
29. NDS, 1980 U.S. Census - The Population & Housing Characteristics (National Decision Systems, San Diego, 1982), pp. 29 ff.
30. HUD, The Conversion of Rental Housing to Condominiums and Cooperatives. A National Study, p. VI-17 f.,; ibid., Impact on Elderly and Low-Income Households, p. 20.
31. Ibid., A National Study, pp. IX-18, IX-26 ff.
32. The Report of the President's Commission on Housing, p. 81.
33. Judith D. Feins and Terry Saunders Lane, How Much for Housing? New Perspectives on Affordability and Risk (Abt Books, Cambridge, Mass., 1981), pp. 28, 92.
34. HUD, The Conversion on Rental Housing to Condominiums and Cooperatives. Impacts on Housing Costs, p. 33.
35. Feins and Saunders Lane, pp. 36 ff.; 49.
36. Ibid., pp. 84, 89. Gross cash outlay is defined as mortgage payment + utilities + property tax + insurance + maintenance and repairs.

37. <u>The Report of the President's Commission on Housing</u>, p. xxv.

38. HUD, <u>The Conversion of Rental Housing to Condominiums and Cooperatives. A National Study</u>, pp. VI-8; IX-2; IX-7.

39. Ibid., <u>Impact of Housing Costs</u>, pp. 63 ff.

40. HUD, <u>The Conversion of Rental Housing to Condominiums and Cooperatives. A National Study</u>, p. IX-23; ibid., <u>Impacts on Housing Costs</u>, pp. 40 ff.

41. HUD, <u>Wise Home Buying</u> (US Department of Housing and Urban Development, Washington, DC, 1980), p. 3.

42. Feins and Saunders Lane, p. 133. It may be noted that 27 per cent of the US renters paid more than 35 per cent of their income for rent purposes in 1977; ibid., p. 48.

43. The assumptions underlying these figures are based on the material found in the HUD reports on conversions. However, assumptions concerning rates of increase for rents and appreciation are much lower here, given the fact that developments in the condominium market have been much slower in the early 1980s than during the period studied by HUD. It is assumed that the rates of increase are uniform over the five years following conversion in 1979. The interest rate for alternative investment of the rent is 12.5 per cent. This holds also for the cash outlays of tenant buyers. The figures used are as follows:

Average valuation (V)	$55,000
Average discount	$ 8,000
Average down payment (D)	£ 3,000
Average initial mortgage debt (M)	$44,000
Average repayment period	25 years
Standard annual repayment (A)	$ 1,760
Mortgage interest rate (r)	12.5 per cent
Average tax rate for deductions (T)	28 per cent
Average annual upkeep and insurance (no annual increase is assumed) (U)	$ 400
Average annual increase (v) on sales value (V)	7 per cent
Average annual increase in rents (R)	7 per cent

Present value of renter outgoings is computed as

$$P_R = R_0 \sum_{t=0}^{4} \left(\frac{1 + \frac{\Delta R}{R}}{1 + r(1 - T)} \right)^t = \$20,926$$

Present value of V - also at the end of year 5 - is computed as

$$P_V = \frac{V(1+v)^5}{\left[1+r(1-T)\right]^5} = \$50,135$$

Present value of owner occupier outgoings at the end of year 5 is computed as

$$P_{OO} = D + \sum_{t=1}^{5} \frac{A+U+r(1-T)(M - \sum_{\tau=2}^{t} A_\tau)}{\left[1+r(1-T)\right]^t} = \$25,678$$

Present value of remaining mortgage debt at the end of year 5 is computed as

$$P_M = \frac{M-5A}{\left[1+r(1-T)\right]^5}$$

The empirical basis of the assumptions are found in HUD, The Conversion of Rental Housing to Condominiums and Cooperatives. A National Study, pp. IX-27 ff., and in ibid., Impacts on Housing Costs, pp. 28 ff. For helping me through the maze of assumptions and formulas, I thank my colleague, Dr Rune Wigren.

44. Dinkelspiel, Uchenick and Selsneick, p. 113 f.

45. HUD, The Conversion of Rental Housing to Condominums and Cooperatives. A National Study, p. VII-10.

46. HUD, 1982 National Housing Production Report (US Department of Housing and Urban Development, Washington, DC, 1983), pp. 34, 36.

47. HUD, The Conversion of Rental Housing to Condominiums and Cooperatives. A National Study, p. VII-16.

48. Ibid., p. VII-20 f.

49. Ibid., pp. III-22, IX-30 f.

50. George Sternlieb and James W. Hughes, 'Condominium Conversion Profiles: Governmental Policy', in Sternlieb and Hughes (eds.), America's Housing. Prospects and Problems (Rutgers University /Centre for Urban Policy Research, New Brunswick, NJ, 1980), p. 307.

51. HUD, The Conversion of Rental Housing to Condominiums and Cooperatives. A National Study, pp. VIII-2 ff.

52. Ibid., p. VIII-9; see also Horowitz, p. 63.

53. Dinkelspiel, Uchenick and Selesnick, p. 120 f.

54. Ibid., pp. 134 ff.

55. Cf. above, p. 000 and footnote 43. See also Jacobs et al., pp. 229 ff.

Chapter Three

GREAT BRITAIN: COUNCIL HOUSE SALES AND THEIR EFFECTS

British Housing Policy: Main Characteristics and Tenure Aspects

Post-war British housing policy is characterised by oscillations between <u>supplementary</u> and <u>comprehensive</u> principles. These shifts seem to be ideological in origin, with Tories going in the former and Labour in the latter direction. Over time, however, Labour seems to have become less determined in pursuing more comprehensive alternatives. Common to both parties seems to have been that their housing policies have been among the first to be adjusted to the realities of the British economy.

The 1945-51 Labour government launched a comprehensive housing policy. Wartime experiences seemed to prove the capability of government to plan the development of whole sectors. Public rental housing - <u>council housing</u> - was to be the core. Through municipal land acquisition, special subsidies, and favourable interest rates, such housing increased by 150,000 dwellings annually from 1948. Private housebuilding was seen as 'speculative', and even diminished in volume. In Labour's view, the public rental sector should provide good housing for all at reasonable costs.

The Tory government coming to power in 1951 had promised to increase housing completions to 300,000 dwellings annually. Ironically, the immediate means for this policy was council housing. Production was increased up to 1954. However, the standard of such new housing was lowered. After 1954, the Tories allowed the public sector's share of new production to decrease, instead favouring private sector construction to make it the larger from 1958 to 1964. Other measures to favour home ownership included freeing home owners from income tax on imputed rent. Council house rents were allowed to increase, and the public sector's role was defined as <u>residual</u>; it should take care of slum clearance and provide households in such areas with new housing. The effects of this policy in combination with pent-up demand caused by long-term demographic trends are said to have contributed to the Labour victory in 1964. Labour's housing programme called for an annual housing production of 500,000 dwellings by 1970, half of which should be in the public rental sector. However, expansion of council housing was to meet 'exceptional needs: it is borne partly of short term necessity ... Expansion of owner-occupation on the other hand is normal; it effects a long term social advance ...' For a while, Labour's policy was relatively successful. However, the economic crisis and the 1967 devaluation caused a drastic reduction of support to public housing construction. Furthermore, subsidies were to be increasingly channelled into the improvement of already existing housing.

The Tory government of 1970-4 took several measures to favour home owership over council housing. The possibilities to get option mortgages - with partial governmental subsidy of mortgage interest - were improved. Building societies were given support to keep mortgage interest rates down. Local authorities were encouraged to sell council housing to tenants. Rents in council housing were allowed to increase. At the same time, the poorest tenants were given rent rebates. In this way, Tories counted on better-off tenants to opt for home ownership. Central government also took over the power to set rents from the local authorities. New public sector construction dropped to a post-war low, as did private completions after the 1973 oil crisis.

Returning to power in 1974, Labour gave back the rent-setting power to local authorities. Rent rebates were increased and new council housing production favoured. However, Labour now had to adjust its housing policy to the politically crucial fact that home ownership made up well over 50 per cent of all housing. Labour thus refrained from changing the tax deduction rules. In the 1977 Green Paper on housing policy, Labour even stated that 'owning one's home is a basic and natural desire'. It is notable that while the crisis policy from 1975-6 onwards allowed tax benefits to remain untouched, support to the public sector was reduced and the completion figures for that sector decreased.

The Conservative Thatcher government in power since 1979 is characterised by an ardent belief in the benefits of free economic markets and private initiative and ownership. Tories have made housing a showcase. Fulfilling their campaign promises, they instituted a policy of converting council housing into owner occupancy by giving council housing tenants a legal Right to Buy their dwellings. Local authorities must provide 100 per cent mortgages, and sell at discount rates spelled out in the 1980 Housing Act. Tax deduction possibilities for home owners have been increased, while subsidies to council housing have been cut dramatically and new public sector completions are down to an all-time low. Central government has effectively taken over the powers of rent-setting to implement its policy of increasing rents in the public sector. The explicit aim of Thatcher's housing policy is to increase the importance of the private sector and of home ownership, and to reduce government's role to one of providing housing support only to those in real need. (1)

The shifting emphasis of British housing policy can be seen in the distribution of new production. From a modest 20 per cent of all completions in the 1945-50 period, new private sector completion - almost all of which is for home ownership - reached an average of 54 per cent of all completions during the 1960s and 1970s. The corresponding figure for 1980-3 is 70 per cent. (2) Since private sector production is not governmentally subsidised - with the exception of option mortgages - the production side of the housing sector clearly bears witness to an increasingly limited role for government.

But what about housing consumption? Support to home ownership is indirect, through tax relief on mortgage interest. As mentioned earlier, there is no income tax on imputed rent. Option mortgages provide interest support to households who might otherwise not be able to pay all mortgage costs. In the fiscal year 1970/71, total support to the home ownership sector amounted to £300 million. Ten years later, it had increased to £2,200 million. Direct subsidies to the public rental sector come through central government, local rate funds, and rent rebates. In 1974/75 they amounted to about £900 million, and increased to £2,300 million in 1979/80. (3)

The Thatcher government's policy of reducing support to the housing sector has not cut the tax relief (but indeed improved it). The expenditure cuts for the whole governmental budget would go from £5,300 million in 1979/80 to £2,800 million in 1983/84. Throughout the period, cuts in direct housing subsidies would represent one third of all budget cuts. Between 1980/81 and 1983/84, direct subsidies (except housing benefits) dropped from £1,853 to £660 million. (4)

As part of the conscious drive for a more market-oriented state of affairs in housing, conversions of council housing to home ownership play a key role. The major housing policy objectives have recently been described as

> to maximise the public sector contribution, in partnership with the private sector, towards satisfying the demand for home ownership, while continuing to encourage and provide for a total approach to housing, embracing all sections of the community, on a cost effective basis. (5)

It is to the effects of this tenure-centred conversion policy that we now turn.

Council House Sales: The Political, Legal, and Economic Framework

The introduction of the Right to Buy in the 1980 Housing Act was not the starting point for tenure conversions in Britain. For decades, houses have been transferred from the private rental sector to owner occupancy. As for the public rental sector, the 1936 Housing Act empowered local authorities to sell council houses provided they got Ministerial permission. The Labour government of 1945-51 consistently refused to grant such permissions. When the Tories took over, they reversed this policy and gave a general consent to local authorities to sell council houses, only notifying the Minister afterwards. During the Labour reign between 1964 and 1970, this general consent remained in principle. It was, however, subjected to more and more restrictions. In 1967-8, rules restricting sales in major conurbations were promulgated and a quota system for sales introduced. The Tory government taking over in 1970 replace these restrictions with a general consent allowing local authorities to proceed with council house sales as they saw fit. With Labour returning to power in 1974, the policy was again changed. In areas with shortages of rental housing, the Minister considered it generally wrong to sell council houses. (6)

What was really new in the 1980 Housing Act was the shifting of the initiative from the local authority to the tenant. Regardless of the sales policy of a local authority, the tenant has a legal Right to Buy his house or flat, and the authority must go ahead with the sale whenever the tenant decides to exercise his right.

Entitled to buy are all tenants who for a total of three years have been 'secure tenants' of a local council, a New Town development, and some other types of public landlords. For a tenancy to be secure, the house or flat must be a separate dwelling and the tenant must occupy it as his only or principal home. Some dwellings especially designed or adapted for elderly or disabled persons are excluded from the Right to Buy. A secure tenant can require that as many as three other members of his family should be allowed to buy jointly with him. Buying one's house means buying the freehold, while buying one's flat means buying a lease, usually for 125 years.

Following the tenant's application to buy, his house or flat is valued at its open market value with vacant possession, less the improvements paid for by the tenant. With the exceptions of applications made in the first few months after the law took effect, valuations will be as of the day of application. Tenants have the right to a discount on this assessed value, the size of which depends on the length of tenancy. Having been a secure tenant for three complete years means getting 33 per cent off the valuation. The discount then goes up by 1 per cent for each complete year up to a maximum of 50 per cent after 20 complete years as a secure tenant.

Buying tenants have a legal right to a mortgage from the landlord. They are entitled to an amount which is 2½ times the available annual income of one purchaser, plus once the income of each other purchaser. If the tenant finds that he and his co-purchasers do not qualify for a mortgage big enough to buy immediately, he has the option of paying a deposit of £100, which will enable him to buy his home any time within two years of his first application to buy at the price his home was originally valued at.

Prior to 1980, local authorities could prohibit resales during the first five years, either through special contract clauses or through their right to first purchase. Since then, however, the buying tenant has the right to sell his home whenever he wants and - with some minor restrictions - to whomever he wants. But if he resells his home within the first five years he must repay some of his discount, according to the following pattern: resale in year one, a 100 per cent repayment; in year two,

80 per cent; in year three, 60 per cent; in year four, 40 per cent, and in year five, 20 per cent of the amount of the discount. After five years, buying tenants are free to resell without any repayment at all and to put the capital gain in their own pockets. (7)

This they can do because there is no tax on capital gains from selling one's home in Great Britain. Furthermore, the homeowner does not have to pay tax on imputed rent, that is, the income the owner would receive from letting his property. The owner can also deduct mortgage interest from his taxable income, provided the loan is less than £30,000. Home owners pay local rates on their property. (8) In this, however, they do not differ much from tenants. Rates on property are the main source of income for British local governments, and landlords simply pass the rates on to the renters.

The home owner does of course have to pay the running costs the same way he did as a renter. But he also becomes responsible for maintenance and repair of his property. When a tenant buys the flat he lives in, the landlord normally continues to be responsible for external repair and maintenance as well as for providing agreed services, and the lease may require the buying tenant to make a reasonable contribution towards the costs involved. Structural defects must be put right at the landlord's expense insofar as they have not been notified to the tenant at the time of the purchase, or if they come to light 10 years or more after the sale. This holds for flats, not for houses. (9)

As a rule, then, it is the secure tenant who enjoys the Right to Buy. However, the Ministerial consent of September 1980 also gives local authorities the right to sell empty or unlet rental dwellings to people who want to buy such dwellings as their permanent home, provided such persons are first-time buyers (or have not owned a home during the last two years), have a firm offer of regular employment in the area, or have been forced to move in the last six months due to slum clearance. If they qualify under these or a few other conditions, they can buy a home with a 30 per cent discount on the assessed value of the dwelling. They enjoy the same right as secure tenants to get a mortgage from the seller, that is, from the housing authority. (10)

Several aspects of the new legislative framework are evidently favourable to the prospective tenant buyer. Discounts would now be maximised to 50 per cent, compared to the maximum of

30 per cent prior to the Right to Buy. The rules governing valuation of property give the purchasing tenant the right to carry out a valuation to check the one made by the local authority. It also gives the buyer the right to appeal against the local authority's valuation. Of course, the legal right to a mortgage from the selling public landlord is also favourable to the buyer.

Other aspects of the 1980 Housing Act provide central government with considerable powers to limit local variation in the implementation of the Right to Buy. Examples of this are (a) the powers of the Secretary of State to determine procedures for mortgages from landlord to buyer, and (b) the power of central government to take over policy implementation from procrastinating local author- ities. There has already been at least one example of such action, when a central government commissioner in February 1982 took over the Right to Buy implementation in Norwich. It seems fair to say that the Conservative government - through the 1980 Housing Act - allocated powers in such a way as to make sure its ideologically motivated drive to promote home ownership would not be hindered by local authorities who do not share the Tory view on sales.

Processes and Procedures of Council House Sales

The Right to Buy introduced in 1980 thus radically changed the relations between sellers and buyers in the public rental sector. The local authorities could no longer control sales, since they no longer had the initiative. Earlier, they could decide if and when to sell housing from their stock. They decided what sort of housing should be sold, and they also controlled in what areas sales should take place. Furthermore, they had a certain influence over the pricing by their power to introduce some form of rebates. Local authorities could also influence later transactions by widening their right to first purchase - or in this case, right to repurchase - and to set the prices of such later sales. Several studies have shown the existence and extent of such local sales policies for the public rental sector. (11)

Since 1980 it is the buyer who starts the sales process by sending an application to buy his home to the landlord. The council sends the applicant a response notice, telling the tenant whether or not in the landlord's opinion he has the right to buy, that is, if he is considered a 'secure' tenant as defined in the Act. As soon as is practically possible, the landlord then has to send the prospective purchaser an offer notice indicating the valuation of his home, the discount, the sales price, the basic conditions of sale, and informing the tenant about his right to get a mortgage from the landlord - the council. Should the tenant decide he wants a mortgage from his landlord, he sends the mortgage notice to the landlord. In turn, the landlord sends the tenant a mortgage response notice saying how large a mortgage the tenant is entitled to. When all mortgage and sales matters have been agreed between tenant and landlord, the latter can ask the tenant to complete the purchase within 28 days, except where the tenant has claimed the option to complete the sale within two years of the original valuation.

During this procedure, the landlord has the right to control the information given by the tenant purchaser. For example, the landlord may want to control with other public landlords whether the tenant actually has lived in council housing for as long as he claims to have done so. However, the public landlord also has duties. If the sale concerns a flat, the landlord must provide information about the services the buyer can count on from the landlord and what the charges will be. The landlord cannot deny a mortgage to a tenant if the tenant wants to exercise his right in this respect. In the end, it is the tenant who decides whether or not the sale will be completed. The 28 days mentioned above are not mandatory, and the buyer can consider the option for a longer period of time without forfeiting his Right to Buy. In some instances, this seems to have caused some problems for local authorities and their processing of the sales. (13)

The Right to Buy was introduced on 3 October, 1980. Reports from the Greater London Council's Housing Committee provide some information on the process started by the new policy. Up to December 1981, just over 5,000 applications to buy had been received by the GLC. The Right to Buy was denied in about 12 per cent of cases, mostly because tenants did not meet the three-year condition. For the slightly fewer than 2,000 houses, valuations had been carried out for more than 90 per cent and offers made in about 75 per cent of the cases. Only 3 to 4 per cent of the sales were completed, while about 12 per cent had been cancelled by the applicants. As for the sale of flats, the Council was facing difficulties. With its cost setting system based on pooled costs, it was very problematic to calculate the service charges as required in the Housing Act. The Housing

Committee was still investigating 'the lawfulness of charging an individual purchaser a service charge calculated by reference to overall costs rather than to those directly attributable to his dwelling'. In fact, none of the nearly 2,900 cases where the Right to Buy had been admitted had come to a completion by the end of 1981. (14)

Table 3.1: The Scope of the Sales Process in England and Wales, 1980-3: Right to Buy (RTB) Claims Received, Acceptances Issued, Sales Completed.

Year	RTB claims received	RTB acceptances issued	RTB sales completed
1980	149,600	106,500	1,120
1981	279,500	286,100	72,560
1982	175,500	163,200	188,625
1983	140,100	136,500	132,780

Source: DoE, <u>Housing and Construction Statistics</u>, December 1983, Part 2.

Table 3.1 indicates that more than 90 per cent of all Right to Buy claims are actually admitted by local authorities. It also indicates that the sales process is lengthy. Finally completed sales were trailing behind by 100,000 at the end of 1980, by more than 300,000 one year later, and by just under 300,000 at the end of 1982. Since applications, acceptances and completions seem to have held the same pace during 1983, there were still around 300,000 uncompleted sales at the end of 1983. The table also seems to convey that the volume of the sales reached a peak in the first years after the introduction of the Right to Buy, but then gradually decreased. Whether or not this decrease will continue or level out remains to be seen.

The Volume of Council House Sales
To put the extent of sales in proper perspective, one has to look at developments of the total British housing stock. The two decades preceding the 1980 introduction of the Right to Buy were characterised by several interesting features. First of all, the total stock increased by nearly 5 million dwellings. A second and very important aspect is that this growth can be attributed totally to the owner occupied sector. In absolute terms, the whole rental

sector did not grow at all in the 1960s and 1970s. This is due to the fact that the growth in the public rental sector was just equal to the losses from the private rental sector during the period. In relative terms, owner occupation's share rose to 55 per cent of the total stock. At the same time as the public rental sector's share increased the private rental sector dropped from one third to a mere 13 per cent of all housing in Great Britain.

Table 3.2: Stock of Dwellings by Tenure, Great Britain 1960-80.
(N = total number in millions, % = percentage of stock)

Year		Tenure Owner- occupied	Rented from local authority or new town	Other tenures	Total
1960	N	6.97	4.40	5.24	16.61
	%	42	26	32	100
1970	N	9.57	5.85	3.77	19.18
	%	50	30	20	100
1980	N	11.91	6.82	2.80	21.54
	%	55	32	13	100

Sources: Donnison and Ungerson, Housing Policy, p. 166; Central Statistical Office, Social Trends 13, (1983), p.111.

The losses from the private rental sector were due not only to slum clearance and demolition but also to conversions to owner occupancy. Between 1960 and 1975, an estimated 70,000 to 75,000 privately rented dwellings were sold annually. (15) However, it was not until 1980 - the same year the Right to Buy was introduced - that the growth of the public rental sector no longer balanced private sector losses. Then the public rental stock diminished by 20,000 dwellings.

As can be seen from Table 3.3, 1980 was also the first year when sales from the council housing stock outnumbered additions from new production. During the 1960s and 1970s, sales totalled about 290,000 in England and Wales (figures for Scotland are hard to come by, but indications are that sales there were negligible). (16) The pattern seems to have followed quite closely the shifts in government between Tories and Labour, and the resulting shifts in sales

Table 3.3: Public Sector Completions Compared to Sales from Local Authorities and New Towns in England and Wales, 1961-83.

Year	Public sector completions	Sales from local authorities and new towns	Public sector sales as a percentage of public sector completions
1961	98,500	4,148	4.2
1962	111,700	5,061	4.5
1963	102,400	4,158	4.1
1964	126,100	4,282	3.4
1965	140,900	4,369	3.1
1966	142,400	5,825	4.1
1967	159,347	5,497	3.4
1968	148,049	10,434	7.0
1969	139,850	9,094	6.5
1970	134,874	7,367	5.5
1971	117,215	20,652	17.6
1972	93,635	61,957	66.1
1973	79,289	41,831	52.8
1974	99,423	5,372	5.4
1975	122,857	2,950	2.4
1976	124,152	5,895	4.7
1977	121,246	13,387	11.0
1978	96,752	30,619	31.6
1979	74,952	42,473	56.7
1980	78,405	85,700	109.3
1981	58,933	106,485	180.7
1982	33,089	207,050	625.7
1983	31,501	150,420	477.5

Sources: Murie, Council House Sales, p. 57; Social Trends 13, p.113; DoE, Housing and Construction Statistics, December 1980, Part 1; December 1982, Part 1; December 1983, Part 1 and Part 2; DoE, Housing Policy - A Consultative Document, (HMSO, London, Cmnd. 6851, 1977), p. 143.

policies. With the Right to Buy sales increased considerably. Already at the end of 1983 almost 550,000 dwellings had been sold from council housing under the Right to Buy. Since about 200,000 dwellings were completed between 1980 and 1983, the first four years of the new sales policy meant a loss to the public rental sector in England and Wales of 350,000 dwellings. Compared to the British public stock of 1980 this means a loss of 3.4 per cent. Since new production is falling so dramatically, the impact of sales on the public rental stock is of course even more pronounced. It is, however, not possible to predict whether or not the sales volume of the first years will continue.

Table 3.4: Private Sector Completions Compared to Sales from Local Authorities and New Towns in England and Wales, 1971-83.

Year	Public sector completions	Sales from local authorities and new towns	Public sector sales as a percentage of private sector completions
1971	179,998	20,652	11.5
1972	184,622	61,597	33.4
1973	174,413	41,831	24.0
1974	129,626	5,372	4.1
1975	140,381	2,950	2.1
1976	138,477	5,895	4.3
1977	127,540	13,387	10.5
1978	134,216	30,619	22.8
1979	120,192	42,473	35.3
1980	113,677	85,700	75.4
1981	102,695	106,485	103.7
1982	110,484	207,050	187.4
1983	152,633	150,420	98.6

Sources: DoE, Housing Policy – A Consultative Document, p. 143; Murie, Council House Sales, p. 57; DoE, Housing and Construction Statistics, December 1980, Part 1; December 1982, Part 1; December 1983, Parts 1 and 2.

The volume of sales can also be seen as a contribution to the private owner occupied sector. During the 1970s, about 225,000 dwellings were sold from the public sector. This amounted to about one sixth of the volume added to owner occupation through new production. The Right to Buy changed this pattern too. As can be seen from Table 3.4, additions to the owner occupied sector from sales exceeded additions from new production by almost 75,000 dwellings already during the first three years of the new sales policy. In fact, the addition from sales exceeded additions from new construction in 1981 and 1982, and equalled new construction in 1983.

The effects of the increased volume of council house sales following the Right to Buy thus have been quite pronounced. During the 1960s and 1970s, council house sales totalled 0.29 million dwellings. In the same period, new production added 2.23 million to the public housing stock. In other words, sales detracted no more than 12 per cent from the total possible growth during the period. In these two decades, the owner occupied stock increased by 4.8 million; council house sales thus contributed only 6 per cent to that growth. Between 1980 and 1983, however, the public rental stock had only 0.2 million new dwellings added to the stock, while about 0.55 million were sold to owner occupation. In turn, new production in the private owner occupied sector was 0.48 million. It seems fair to conclude that council house sales have been instrumental in bringing about this change in the public sector, from one of slow but steady absolute growth to one of quite pronounced absolute decline. During the first four years of the Right to Buy the public rental stock decreased by 5 per cent. In turn, this loss constituted more than half of the growth of the owner occupied stock during those years. The post-1980 pattern suggests that home ownership is rapidly approaching the same dominant tenure position in Britain as in the United States; some projections indicate a home ownership rate of 64 per cent already in 1986. (17)

In view of the actual volume of sales after 1980, it may be of interest to note the predictions made before the Right to Buy was introduced. Some of the witnesses giving information to the House of Commons Environment Committee during its 1980 investigation on council house sales supported the forecast of about 100,000 sales annually. Governmental spokesmen gave figures ranging from 62,500 in 1980/81 to 120,000 in 1981/82. Noting the views of its Advisers that 'the highest level of sales in England which could be safely assumed in the period 1981/82 to 1983/84 was 100,000 a year', the Committee continued:

> Sales on the scale envisaged by the Committee's Advisers would be bound to have a major social impact. For example, a decade of sales of 100,000 houses annually would mean the disposal of nearly one-third of the present stock of council houses (excluding flats, and dwellings

built for the elderly). This could imply a major change in the nature of the local housing service, depending on the rate of replacement ... The possibility that even higher rates of sales may occur increases the need seriously and systematically to evaluate their effects. (18)

Indeed, evidence so far indicates that the Committee was right in assuming that local authorities were underestimating the potential rate of sales. With the rates exceeding the most commonly presented projections, it may also be that the social impacts are even more pronounced than was foreseen before the Right to Buy was introduced.

Consequences for the Level and Distribution of Housing Quality

The British legal framework explicitly defines both the buyer and the commodity in relation to tenure conversions. The 1980 Housing Act gives the Right to Buy to 'secure' tenants in rental housing owned and managed by local authorities and new towns. Consequently, it becomes important to know the quality characteristics of that stock and the socio-economic characteristics of the tenants at the time when the Right to Buy was introduced. From that one can proceed to an analysis of who buys what, which in turn provides the basis for conclusions concerning the effects of sales on the level and distribution of housing quality.

Selling to sitting tenants could lead to a very special match of tenant and dwelling character-istics, provided that the allocation of housing has some specific characteristics in terms of who is allocated to what kind of housing. In Britain, there seems to be a general pattern in the allocation of public housing. This 'housing career' means that the public tenant at first rents a flat. Gradually, he is allocated to other types of housing - terraced, semi-detached or, if he is very lucky, a detached house. Those lucky enough to be allocated to a house early on in their housing career, e.g. larger families, now have an economic situation which makes it possible for them to buy their house, which also happens to be the most sought-after form of council housing. There are, however, findings which indicate that the housing career does not run similarly for all households. Although the allocation procedures are built on seemingly objective principles of need, allocation officers seem to run a parallel and highly subjective system which advances the housing career of 'decent' and retards that of 'troublesome' households. In fact, there seems to be a tendency for the latter group to be almost equivalent to the socially and economically less resourceful households. Housing quality may thus be unevenly distributed among public tenants already before the Right to Buy is applicable. (19)

Using the experiences of earlier sales as a basis for predictions, the House of Commons Environment Committee summed up the expected consequences of the Right to Buy in the following way:

> The sum of the available evidence and opinion on this issue is not entirely conclusive, but it does suggest that sales will be disproportionately of houses rather than of flats, and that sales of houses will tend towards the better quality properties in more attractive areas, or areas in which there is already a high proportion of owner-occupation. This will, of course, make the position of many who remain in the rented public sector worse as their chances of being able to move, say, from a flat in a tower block to a house, and particularly in more popular areas, will be reduced. (20)

Since these arguments were related to sales before the Right to Buy, it could be dismissed as irrelevant. Before 1980, sales were governed by the policies of the individual councils which often excluded flats from the sales. Unfortunately for the evaluation, there are no national surveys of the Right to Buy sales. Instead, one must rely on gross national statistics and on surveys from specific municipalities.

Evidently, sales after 1980 have been 'disproportionately of houses rather than flats'. Although flats constitute nearly one third of the council housing stock, they have so far been a tiny fraction of sales. It could be argued, however, that, this is at least partly due to the problems inherent in assessing the services charges for individual flats converted into owner occupation. The tendency towards an increase in the share of flats could be seen as a sign that local authorities are coming to grips with these problems after the initial difficulties. However, the pattern so far seems to confirm the predictions of the Environment Committee.

Table 3.5: The Share of Houses and Flats in the 1977 Council House Stock, and in the Sales after 1980, in England and Wales.

Housing type	Share of council house stock in 1977, in %	Share of council house sales in %			
		1980	1981	1982	1983
Houses					
- terraced	35				
- semi-detached or detached	35	70	98.0	98.1	97.1	95.5
Flats	30	30	2.0	1.9	2.9	4.5
Total		100	100	100	100	100

Sources: Maggie Jones, 'Choice in Housing Tenure in Britain', in Hans Kroes and Fritz Ijmkers (eds.), Buitenlandse vormen van woningbeheer (Delft, RIW-instituut voor volkshuisvestingsonderzoek, 1982), p. 184 f.; DoE, Housing and Construction Statistics, December 1980, Part 2; September 1983, Part 2.

Table 3.6: Council House Stock Characteristics in England and Wales, 1980 and 1982: Age of Stock, and Share of Different Dwelling Types and Sizes.

Stock characteristics	Share of council house stock, in %		
	April 1980	April 1982	Difference
Period of completion			
- before 1945	26	25	-1
- 1945 to 1964	43	41	-2
- after 1964	32	34	+2
Type and size of dwellings			
- two and three + bedroom houses	56	54	-2
- two and three bedroom flats	17	18	+1
- one bedroom dwellings	17	18	+1

Source: Forrest and Murie, Right to Buy?, p. 27.

Already after one and a half years, the Right to Buy seems to have led to a discernible shift in the composition of the council house stock. It seems as

if two and three+ bedroom houses in areas approaching
mature age are the ones that go first. Flats in newer
housing remain untouched by sales, and consequently
increase their share of the total council house
stock. In some areas, for instance, West Midlands,
the share of houses decreased by as much as 4 per
cent. Sales in Birmingham in 1979/80 were
concentrated to three+ bedroom houses (86 per cent)
constructed after 1945 (56 per cent). Corresponding
figures for the whole 1980 Birmingham stock of
council housing were 54 and 67 per cent,
respectively. British observers conclude that

> the evidence available continues to show that
> sales do not represent a cross section of
> council properties. Previous research on sales
> further demonstrates that sales alter not just
> the quantity of council housing but its
> characteristics and location. New evidence on
> the quality of property sold is not available
> unless dwelling type and size is regarded as
> indicative. However, there is nothing in the
> evidence available to justify modifying the
> view that it is better quality family dwellings
> that are sold. (21)

The previous research referred to indeed seems to
point towards a picture of asset stripping of British
council housing. Invariably, sales seem to concern
estates with very low movement and transfer
frequences – that is, very popular estates. Such
areas are often 'cottage housing' areas in the
suburbs, where the council house share is already low
and that of owner occupancy high. Also invariably,
flats have remained almost untouched by sales even in
local authorities where their share of the council
housing stock is high and sales policies have
permitted the sale of flats. (22)

As long as this pattern of sales continues, the
quality level of council housing will go down. If
quality is interpreted as space and amenities, the
dwellings sold must be considered good-quality
housing. The share of less attractive and less
spacious dwellings is increasing in the public
sector. In terms of the distribution of housing
quality, several developments are conceivable. If
buying tenants do represent a cross-section of
council house tenants, this would lead to the socio-
economic widening of home ownership expected by the
promotors of sales. If, however, tenant buyers come
only from very special socio-economic and

Table 3.7: Tenure Profile of British Households, According to Different Household Characteristics, 1978

Household characteristics	Percentage share of households in different tenures, 1978			
	All households	Owner occupancy	Private renting	Public renting
Socio-economic group of head of household				
Economically active heads:				
Professional managerial	15	24	9	3
Intermediate and junior non-manual	13	16	15	9
Skilled manual and own account non-professional	25	24	20	27
Semi-skilled manual, personal service and unskilled manual	13	9	11	20
Economically inactive heads	33	27	45	40
	100	100	100	100
Household type				
1 adult 16-59	7	5	20	6
2 adults 16-59	14	16	16	10
Small family	22	25	10	18
Large family	10	9	4	13
2 adults, 1 or both aged 60 or over	16	17	19	16
1 adult aged 60 or over	15	11	23	20
	100	100	100	100
Age of head of household				
Under 25	4	2	14	3
25-29	8	7	11	6
30-44	26	32	16	21
45-64	35	36	23	39
65 and over	27	23	36	30
	100	100	100	100

Sources: Forrest and Murie, Right to Buy? Appendices C and F; Alan Murie, Housing Inequality and Deprivation (London, Heineman, 1983), pp. 102 ff.

demographic strata, this could represent a cream-skimming of such groups from the public rental sector. Given the asset-stripping pattern just found, both alternatives lead to a bias in the distribution of housing quality among tenures, with the owner-occupied sector rapidly becoming identified with good quality, while the public rental sector gets the opposite reputation. If buyers come only from high-income strata, housing quality becomes distributed according to economic rather than social or demographic criteria. Poorer households are left with lower-standard housing. A pattern of residualisation occurs.

Before looking at buyer characteristics, it may be of interest to compare the composition of households in council housing with those of other tenures. As can be seen from Table 3.7, tenure and socio-economic characteristics show a very clear pattern. Upper strata tend to be over-represented in the owner-occupied, but under-represented in the public rental sector. The opposite is true for working-class households. Among household types, small families and households with two adults under 60 are more often found among home owners than their shares among all households would indicate. Again, the opposite is true for the public rental sector. Households in the owner-occupied sector seem to be somewhat younger than those in the public rental sector. The private rental sector seems to have a concentration of economically inactive, single member, elderly households, although there is also a large share of young small households.

Another way of comparing council housing tenants with other groups is to look at incomes and income distribution. As can be seen from Table 3.8, incomes for households in public renting are considerably lower than those of owner occupied households and also lower than the national averages. The same is true for incomes of heads of households. There is also a very clear relationship between income and tenure. The higher the mean annual income, the more probable that the household is in the owner-occupied sector. For the public rental sector, the relationship is reversed. The lower the income, the more probable that the household lives in council housing (cf. Table 3.9).

What is, then, the socio-economic and demographic profile of public tenants who buy their dwellings? Unfortunately, data on Right to Buy sales are scant in this respect. There has been no national survey like in the United States and West Germany.

Table 3.8: Tenure and Gross Annual Income, Great Britain, 1978

Income strata	Form of tenure			
	Owner occupancy	Public renting	Private renting or other	Total
Households				
Mean income	5,400	3,610	3,540	4,500
Lower quartile	3,340	1,570	2,100	2,040
Median	4,680	3,180	2,840	4,110
Upper quartile	6,700	5,040	4,830	6,070
Heads of household				
Mean income	4,040	2,600	3,330	3,370
Lower quartile	2,580	1,350	1,790	1,590
Median	3,560	2,420	2,770	3,160
Upper quartile	4,900	3,650	4,460	4,460

Source: Murie, Housing Inequality and Deprivation, pp. 98 ff.

Table 3.9: Income Distribution (1979/80), and Tenure Distribution of British Households by Income Deciles (1978)

Income decile	Mean annual income £	Percentage share of income earners	Percentage of households in		
			Owner occupancy	Public renting	Private renting & other
1	1,550	2.9	20.0	56.1	23.9
2	2,140	4.0	33.9	46.3	19.8
3	2,640	5.3	41.0	37.9	21.1
4	3,530	6.6	40.4	38.7	20.9
5	4,170	7.8	48.7	37.7	13.6
6	4,920	9.2	54.1	30.4	15.5
7	5,880	11.0	63.1	26.6	10.3
8	6,850	12.8	67.8	23.0	9.2
9	8,340	15.6	70.0	22.0	8.0
10	13,300	24.8	79.5	15.3	5.2
All incomes	7,400	100.0	51.8	33.4	14.8

Source: Social Trends 13, p. 77; Ray Robinson and Tony O'Sullivan, 'Housing Tenure Polarisation - Some Empirical Evidence', Housing Review, 32, (July-August 1983), p. 116.

Table 3.10: Socio-economic and Demographic Characteristics of Tenants and Tenant Buyers in Selected Municipalities.

Percentage share of public renters and council house buyers in selected municipalities

Household characteristics	Birmingham Public renters 1977	Birmingham Buyers 1979/80	Carrick Public Renters 1978	Carrick Buyers TRB	Slough Public Renters 1978	Slough Buyers 1980/81	Solihull Public Renters 1978	Solihull Buyers RTB	Sutton Public Renters 1977	Sutton Buyers 1980
Socio-economic group of head of household										
Economically active heads:										
Professional managerial	3	7	5	13	6	12	4	10	7	2
Intermediate and junior non-manual	20	6	19	8	15	33	21	10	28	5
Skilled manual and own account non-professional	33	50	38	57	44	46	33	71	31	31
Semi-skilled manual, personal service and unskilled manual	43	18	38	18	36	10	40	8	34	12
Economically inactive heads	2	19(a)	–	5	–	–	2	–	1	38
Household type										
1 adult 16–59	5	–	4	–	5	2	5	–	4	
2 adults 16–59	9	16	7	26	7	35	10	18	9	
Small family	14	13	21	30	20	23	25	30	21	
Large family	14	13	9	12	12	25	16	33	9	
Large adult household	18	45	13	24	19	15	15	16	19	
2 adults, 1 or both aged 60 or over	19	14	20	7	23	–	14	4	20	12
1 adult aged 60 or over	20	–	21	–	13	–	15	–	18	–
Age of Head of Household										
Under 25		–		4	2					–
25–34		12		11	13					24
35–44		20		17	13					19
45–54		39		43	17					27
55–64		18		14	23					19
65 and over		12		1	32					11

Source: Forrest and Murie, Right to Buy?, Appendices C and F. (a) Higher figure depends on different categorisation of households.

The only available data come from a limited number of local authorities researched by Forrest and Murie. Their data does, however, suggest a clear pattern. Buyers do not represent a cross-section of public tenants; rather, they are very much like the households already in the owner-occupied sector.

As can be seen from Table 3.10, upper classes are more often found among buyers than their share of all public tenancies would have us believe. Professional/managerial groups show this pattern quite regularly, while intermediate and junior non-manual groups are less predictable in this respect. Skilled manual and own account non-professional strata are the ones most commonly found among council house buyers, far out of proportion to their share of all public tenancies. The lower classes show an opposite pattern. Semi-skilled and unskilled workers, and service personnel are clearly under-represented among buyers.

Two types of household seem to be most common among buyers - small families and large adult households. Especially the latter are very over-represented among buyers in the local authorities for which there are data. As could be expected, the youngest and oldest households are not found among buyers to the extent that could be expected if buyers were a cross-section of all tenants. The most commonly found age groups among buyers are those between 35 and 54 and, more especially, those between 45 and 54.

The age pattern also comes out quite clearly in Table 3.11, which shows that heads of households among buyers are usually around the age of 45 at the time of purchase. The table furthermore shows that buying households have been public tenants for quite some time before the purchase. It also reveals a very important feature of those using the Right to Buy; they are evidently to be found among the upper income brackets among public tenants. A comparison with the income figures given in Table 3.8 bears this out very clearly even in view of income developments after 1978.

A pattern seems to emerge. Tenant purchasers are not representative of all public tenants. Instead, they tend to come from very distinct groups. The most typical buyer is in the skilled manual and own account non-professional stratum, about 45 of age, and has lived for at last 15 years in council housing. His income is far above the average for public renters. And it is exactly these groups of households who happen to live in the type of council

Table 3.11: Characteristics of Council House Tenant Purchasers in Six Local Authorities, 1980/81.

| Buyer characteristics | Local Authorities | | | | | |
	Solihull	Plymouth	Hounslow	Slough	Carrick	New Forest
Average income of principal earner (£)	6,467	6,269	8,034	7,204	7,204	5,679
Average age of principle earner	46	44	43	41	46	44
Average length of tenancy	18	18	18		12	16

Sources: Forrest and Murie, *Right to Buy?* p. 35. Cf. their 'The Great Divide', ROOF, 7 (December 1982), p. 20.

housing that is most attractive and most often sold. Thus, the best-quality public housing is sold to the households who can best afford to buy. In terms of the distribution of housing quality, the effect of council house sales is to make it more dependent on tenure. Good-quality housing is taken away from the public rental sector and transferred into the owner occupied sector. Since so many of the higher-income public tenants happen to live in such housing, their use of the Right to Buy leads to <u>residualisation</u>; the public rental sector will increasingly have only lower-quality housing to offer to the remaining, lower-income households who are not in a position to buy.

The last point is important. The pattern just found may be explained by life-cycle patterns and allocation procedures. Through these procedures, local authorities to a large extent determine which households will live in what kind of public housing at each stage in their life-cycle. Tenant purchasers' 'housing careers' have brought them into the dwellings they have now bought. But not all tenants at this position in the life-cycle have done so. It is predominantly the 'upper' socio-economic strata in their forties who have used their Right to Buy. The Environment Committee's earlier discussion on this point was inconclusive:

> What is not entirely clear to us is how far the higher incomes of tenant purchasers can be explained as being a result of the stage which they have reached in their life-cycle: incomes tend to be highest for people in their forties, and this has been the typical age for council house purchase. There appears to be insufficient evidence available to settle this issue.
>
> However, evidence on socio-economic group membership, because it is largely free of life-cycle distortions, is also valuable in establishing whether tenant purchasers are 'better off' than other tenants. Although some of this evidence is unsatisfactory, it suggests that there is a higher proportion of professional and managerial workers among purchasers than among tenants as a whole. On the proportion of unskilled manual workers, the worst paid group, the evidence is unclear ... (23)

Although allocation procedures and life-cycle

patterns are important, evidence now available suggests that socio-economic factors are decisive in determining who does and who does not make use of their Right to Buy. In the end, poorer households may never get into the housing quality enjoyed by those strata who bought during the first years of Right to Buy sales.

Effects on the Level and Distribution of Housing Costs

In assessing the possible gains and losses for tenant purchasers and remaining tenants, the House of Commons Environment Committee concluded that there are 'various financial advantages of council house sales for tenant purchasers'. Purchasers would acquire an asset which could be expected to appreciate in real value. Mortgage payments would decline in real terms. Discounts would be generous and give the purchaser a possibility of enhanced ability to borrow. Purchasers would enjoy tax relief on mortgage payments. However, the Committee also foresaw some disadvantages for purchasers: immediately higher housing costs because mortgage payments would be considerably higher than the rent purchasers would otherwise pay; extra maintenance costs; insurance expenditures; in the case of flats, service charges additional to mortgage payments; and some restriction on mobility during the five years when part of the discount is repayable on sale. As for remaining tenants, the Committee concluded that 'in the long run, the financial effects of sales may be disadvantageous for those tenants who remain'. Pointing out that the dwellings most likely to be sold are also the ones with the lowest maintenance costs to local authorities, the Committee concluded that increased management and maintenance costs 'could lead eventually to rent increases for tenants who do not buy'. (24)

The Committee thus identified two possible effects: (a) the redistribution of wealth, and (b) the changes in purchaser and tenant outgoings as a direct result of sales. There are, however, also other effects to be taken into account which especially concern remaining tenants. They have to do with how the whole rent-setting system of local authorities is related to the volume and character of sales, and how that system is furthermore affected by government policy towards subsidies to the public rental sector. With the cost-pooling and rent-averaging system used by British local authorities,

the sale of older housing with low capital,
management and maintenance costs will drive rents in
the remaining public stock upward. This may be even
more pronounced if government policy is changed
towards less subsidies to that stock. In fact, such
changes were introduced in the 1980 Housing Act
alongside the Right to Buy provision. The rules are
such that they practially force local authorities to
increase rents. (25)

Before looking at these effects, it may be of
interest to look at the overall development of
housing costs in Great Britain. By 1980, the average
household paid 13 per cent of its expenditures on
housing. So did high-income households, while those
with lower incomes paid 16 per cent. In 1981, the
percentage of total consumers' expenditure going to
housing was about 16 per cent. There are several
signs of an increase in the weight and importance of
housing expenditures in household budgets. The
weights used to combine the various components of the
price index reflect the relative importance of
various categories in the typical basket of goods an
services. Between 1961 and 1981, the weight of
housing went from 87 to 135, an increase second only
to transport and vehicles. At the same time, the
weight of food decreased from 350 to 207. In fact,
housing was the only item showing a significant
increase in 1981. And while the average annual
increase in the Retail Price Index showed a downward
trend after 1979, the opposite was true for housing.
Between 1971 and 1979, the average increase for
housing was just under 13 per cent, slightly above
the rate of increase for the general index. After
1979, however, the annual increase jumped to more
than 22 per cent for the period up to early 1982.
(26)

As can be seen from Figure 3.1, average annual
housing costs for owner occupiers increased rapidly
after 1977-8, almost totally due to increases in
mortgage interest because of rising interest rates
and rapidly rising dwelling prices. By 1980-1,
average total costs for home owners amounted to £849,
having increased by 40 per cent in 1980-1 prices
since 1977-8. Home owner outgoings (after allowing
for tax relief) increased by 46 per cent over that
period, amounting to £650 on the average in 1980-1.
During the same period, the average annual housing
cost per household in the public sector increased by
only 11 per cent in real terms, or to £843. The cost
to the tenant rose by only 4.5 per cent, the average
being £369 in 1980-1.

109

Figure 3.1: Average Annual Housing Costs per Household, Great Britain, 1970-1 to 1980-1

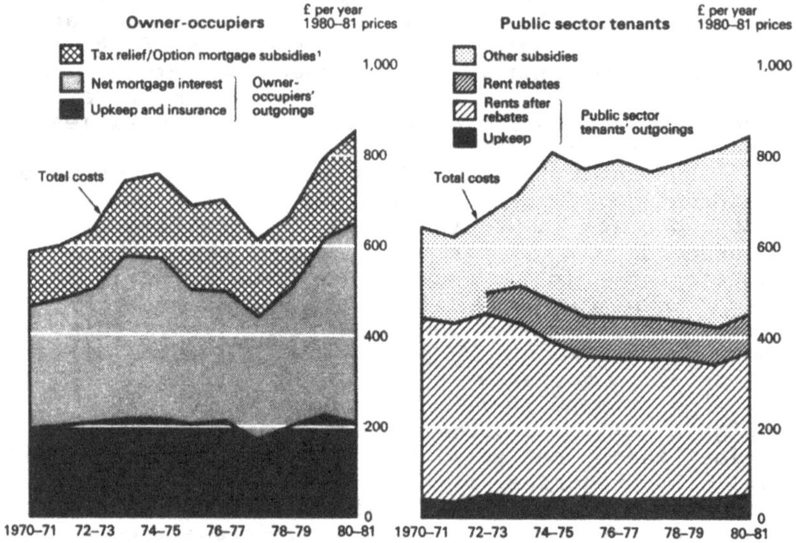

Source: <u>Social Trends 13</u>, p. 120

Are there any signs that tenant purchasers have experienced cost increases placing them in the same range as other home owners, and way above the outgoings they experienced as tenants? Unfortunately, the data available are notoriously scarce concerning earlier rent expenditures by tenant purchasers. Estimates made in the hearings before the Environment Committee were vague, showing widely differing changes, but <u>not</u> taking into account the effects of tax relief. (27) The effects are also dependent on what discount the purchasers get on the sales price. In the Birmingham study, Forrest and Murie found that buyers got an average discount of 45 per cent. Thanks to this, the purchasers could get their annual total housing costs down to £830. With an average tax relief of £200 (cf. Figure 3.1) the net outgoings per week would come down to about £12. This should be compared to the rent for a three-bedroom house. The typical rent level for such dwellings in Birmingham in May 1981 ranged from £11 to £14. The authors conclude: 'Taking into account subsequent rent increases and changes in interest rates, the majority of council house purchasers are likely to be paying less in mortgage repayments than

Table 3.12: Economic Aspects of Council House Sales, 1980/81. Averages for Six Authorities.

Economic aspect	Authority					
	Solihull	Plymouth	Hounslow	Slough	Carrick	New Forest
Valuation (£)	15,534	16,403	26,804	23,862	16,375	21,921
Price (£)	8,565	9,251	14,754	13,462	9,164	12,206
Discount (%)	45	44	45	43	44	44
Cash value of discount (£)	6,969	7,152	12,050	10,400	7,211	9,715
Income of principal earner (£)	6,467	6,269	8,034	7,204	5,679	7,358
Price/income ratio	1.3	1.5	1.2	1.9	1.6	1.6
Monthly repayment (£)	93	87	165	156	92	143

Source: Forrest and Murie, Right to Buy?, p. 35; Forrest and Murie, 'The Great Divide', p. 20.

in rents (net of rates) within 2 or 3 years of purchase.' (28)

There are also other considerations to be taken into account. Tenant purchasers take over the responsibility for insurance and the maintenance burden may become heavier. As Figure 3.1 shows, there are great differences between owner occupiers and tenants in this respect. On the other hand, the dwellings sold are of good quality and should not need more outlays than the average for the owner occupied sector - £200 for 1980-1. If this sum is added to net mortgage repayments for Birmingham tenant purchasers we arrive at a weekly outlay of £16, which is only slightly above the average rent for equivalent dwellings.

Still, there is a considerable local variation to take into account. As can be seen from Table 3.12, sales prices vary quite a lot between different local authorities. This makes it very difficult to draw any generally valid conclusions concerning whether, and to what extent, the tenants purchasing their homes have experienced higher net outgoings after the purchase. We may therefore not be in a position to say much about the distributive effects of sales on housing costs. It may be noted though that in Hounslow where the share of unskilled manual workers among public tenants was 34 per cent, only 1 per cent of the purchasers came from this category. (29)

This is important in terms of the redistribution of wealth that takes place in the process of council house sales. What Table 3.12 shows here is a pattern of consistency. Regardless of valuation figures, the discounts are everywhere just under 45 per cent. This means a massive redistribution of wealth to the buyers. However, if the sales prices are too high for certain categories of tenant, these categories cannot share in the redistribution.

The figures are impressive. As Table 3.13 shows, sales from local authorities provided an average discount of 41 per cent of the valuation in the years 1980-3, corresponding to an average amount of £6,910. During the first four years with the Right to Buy, just over half a million tenant purchasers were thus given an amount of wealth in the order of £3,700 million. The purchasers represented 8 per cent of public tenants in 1981, and the amount of wealth acquired through the discount corresponded to about 1.6 per cent of the marketable wealth of dwellings (net of mortgage debt) in 1980. (30)

Given the fact that tenant purchasers are better off than the majority of public tenants, it is hard

Table 3.13: Council House Sales and the Redistribution of Wealth: Sales, Valuations, and Discounts, 1980-3.

Year	All local authority sales	Capital value of sales (net of discount) £ million	Average discount in percent	Capital value of discount £ million	Average capital value of discount per sale £
1980	81,485	769.0	38	471.3	5,780
1981	102,825	991.7	41	689.1	6,700
1982	201,880	1,941.7	43	1,464.8	7,250
1983	145,585	1,513.1	41	1,051.4	7,220
Total	531,775	5,215.5	41	3,676.6	6,910

Source: DoE, Housing and Construction Statistics, September and December 1983, Part 2.

to agree that council house sales contribute to a more equal distribution of wealth. The picture seems much clearer than the House of Commons Environment Committee was prepared to accept:

> (If) equalisation is defined as a reduction in the extent to which the distribution of personal wealth deviates from perfect equality, then it is not clear whether council house sales produce a more equal distribution. Certainly, many families with low incomes have succeeded in buying, but many have not, and many are likely to be permanently excluded from the opportunity to buy. The complex question of who pays for the capital gains, and the discounts, received by buyers, also needs to be considered. (31)

What has been, then, the fate of remaining tenants? As already shown, council house sales imply a creaming-off of higher-income households from council housing. The lower the skill and income levels, the lower the proportion of tenant purchasers. This means that the earlier characteristic of council housing - the lower the income and skill levels, the higher the proportion of households who are council tenants - will become even more pronounced. It should also be kept in mind that somewhere between 40 and 50 per cent of council tenants were in receipt of either rent rebates of a contribution towards rent from welfare benefits in the early 1980s. (32) Their housing costs are affected by sales through the rent-setting system, but also by governmental policies for subsidising the public rental sector.

Rents in local authority housing are pooled. There is no relationship between the cost of providing each dwelling and its rent. In this way, the rent for new dwellings can be kept at levels tenants can afford. The system means that a local authority with a large share of older dwellings, and low new production, can keep both rents low and take in a large amount of its income through rents. In the opposite case, a local authority with little stock and much new production must rely more heavily on government subsidies and locally raised rates to cover the costs of its operations. Around 1980, the average local authority's rent income (before rebates) covered about 50 per cent of that authority's costs. (33)

Dwellings produced before 1960 are considered to provide resources that enable authorities to lower rents in new production. Since a large part of the houses sold come from that stock, the possibilities of lowering the rents in new housing becomes more and more limited. A smaller share of the stock provides a surplus, which will press rents in the remaining stock upward, especially if compensating governmental subsidies are not forthcoming. Of course, capital from the sales could be used to keep rents down, but that would only provide a temporary solution. Thus the remaining tenants who for economic and other reasons have not been able to use their Right to Buy, and who often happen to live in the less attractive public stock, will have to pay higher rents as a result of the sales.

Unfortunately, there are no empirical studies of these effects of the sales. On the other hand, it is quite easy to show the effects of the new subsidy policy for the remaining public tenants. Introduced for the fiscal year 1981-2, the system has three components:

(a) <u>Base amount</u>; the starting base for subsidy, consisting of a local authority's entitlement to subsidy in the previous year.
(b) <u>Housing costs differential</u>; for any given year, this is the amount by which reckonable Housing Revenue Account (HRA) expenditure exceeds that for previous years. In essence, this means new housing capital expenditure carried out by the local authority and eligible for subsidy, <u>and</u> the annual determination made by the Secretary of State for uprating reckonable expenditure on management and maintenance.
(c) <u>Local contribution differential</u>; the amount by which an authority's 'reckonable income' in any one year exceeds that of the previous year. This is decided on an annual basis by the Secretary of State and is basically his assumption on how much local authorities should raise in rents that year. (34)

Annual subsidy entitlement for a local authority is then (a) + (b) - (c). Of course, if c is larger than b, the subsidy decreases. In terms of (b), low new production and the government's tendency to determine lower rates of increase for reckonable expenditures than the rate of inflation have contributed to holding it down. At the same time, government has kept increasing (c). The end result has been a rapid decrease in government subsidies and an equally rapid increase in rents. Furthermore, local authorities have entered a profit position, while they were earlier only allowed to keep a working balance in the Housing Revenue Account. In fact, as many as 300 local authorities showed a surplus in 1984.

Table 3.14: Governmental Subsidies and Local Rate Fund Contributions to Council Housing in England and Wales, 1980-4.

Year	Central government subsidy to council housing, £ million	Local rate fund contributions to council housing, £ million
1980/81	1,423	430
1981/82	903	402
1982/83	552	443
1983/84	370	290

Source: Nick Fielding, 'Who is Subsidising Whom'?, ROOF, 9 (March/April 1984), p. 11.

In four years, central governmental subsidies to council housing have thus decreased by almost 75 per cent. The rent increase has been on less dramatic. From 1979/80 to 1983/84, the average unrebated weekly rent in council housing rose from £6.48 to £13.77 - that is, by more than 50 per cent. (35) There is thus a process of redistribution going on within the British housing sector which makes tenant purchasers double winners. First, they purchase the best-quality housing in the public stock and get tax relief on their mortgage interest payments. Second, the repayments decrease over time in real terms, while the rents now increase faster than the general inflation rate:

> In other words, council tenants are financing through rents the accumulated and future costs of local authority housing provision. No such reforms have been introduced or proposed in the owner occupier sector. Tax relief on mortgage interest on all outstanding mortgage debt in the UK in 1981-82 is estimated at approximately £2,030m. This sum is unlikely to fall in the foreseeable future. (36)

To assess the magnitude of this redistributive process it would be necessary to have nationwide, representative data. It is, however, also possible to give an idea of the outcome by using available data on the averages for sales prices, discounts, mortgage debts, repayment periods, and so on, for council house sales, and what is known about the developments of average rents for comparable council house dwellings.

By using such data in combination with what is known about the tax regulations, it is possible to compute the present value of the 'economic outcome of housing' for the next five years for tenant purchasers and remaining tenants, taking 1980 as the starting point. For the tenant who chose, or was forced by circumstances, to remain as a tenant in his three-bedroom house instead of using his Right to Buy in 1980, the present value of his outgoings for the following five years would have been £3,420 (no rent rebates assumed). For the tenant able to use his Right to Buy, the net outgoings for the following five years would have had a present value of £5,560. However, after five full years the tenant purchaser would have been able to sell his house at the then prevailing market value without having to pay any tax on his original discount or any capital gains tax on possible value increase above the original valuation. Assuming an annual value increase of 5 per cent, the present value of the average purchaser's house would have been about £12,350 in 1980. The present value of his remaining mortgage would have been £4,580. The present value of the market price after five years would thus be up to exceed those of the net outgoings and remaining mortgage by £2,210. The buying tenant would thus have on the continuing renter by as much as £5,630 in terms of the present value of their 'economic outcome of housing'. (37)

The tenant purchaser can look forward not only to enjoy living in his good quality house, but to do so with a 'profit' (provided he is willing to trade his home at some point). The remaining tenant can only look forward to an increasing present value of his outgoings. Given the socio-economic profiles of purchasers and remaining tenants, it seems somewhat difficult to conclude that sales provide a more equal distribution of housing costs.

Sales, Housing Markets and the Availability of Rental Housing

The council house sales have been surrounded by a lively discussion concerning the possible effects on the housing market. What would happen to those

looking for housing in the public sector? Would it
become more difficult to find housing? And what would
be the consequences for present public tenants?
Would it become more difficult to move or to get a
transfer to a dwelling corresponding to the
household's special needs? In a wider perspective,
what are the consequences for the public rental
sector as a whole? Will it be able to provide housing
for all types of households, or will council housing
become special housing for special people?

In the long run, all council houses sold are
lost from the rental market. As we have seen almost
100 per cent of all dwellings sold are houses, not
flats. Assuming an annual sales volume for the 1980s
of 150,000 dwellings – mostly houses – this would
mean that between 40 to 50 per cent of the public
rental stock of houses would be transferred to the
owner-occupied sector. (38) Assuming further that
the annual volume of new production will be around
30,000 dwellings, half of which are houses, it is
easily seen that the supply of public rental housing
will have changed its character quite dramatically.
This in turn means that the functions of council
housing in the housing market will also change.

In the short run, the question is whether sales
lead to a loss of relets. Here, opinion is divided.
The Tory government claimed that effects would be
minimal. Most of the tenant purchasers could be
expected to be in their forties. They would probably
have stayed as public tenants in their dwellings for
another 30 to 40 years, if the Right to Buy had not
been enacted. Before then, the loss of relets from
sales would thus not be a substantial problem. (39)
Founding their argument on data on moving rates,
death rates, and the age distribution of tenant
purchasers, witnesses before the House of Commons
Environment Committee held that the loss would be
considerable. Estimates of the annual immediate loss
varied from 2.5 to 4.1 per cent of the sales volume,
to be compared to the overall relet rate in the
public sector of 3.8 per cent of the stock. The
Committee settled on 2.6 per cent as a 'reasonable'
estimate. With an annual sales volume of 100,000
dwellings, the loss of relets in the first year would
be 2,600 dwellings. Over a decade following the
sales, there would be a cumulated loss of relets due
to the sales in the first year amounting to 26,000
dwellings. Assuming a decade with an annual sales
volume of 100,000 dwellings, the cumulated loss at
the end of the decade would be 140,000 relets. (40)

Unfortunately, the lively controversy over the

loss of relets (41) is not paralleled by empirical research on developments after 1980. However, one could use available data on sales volumes (cf. Table 3.3) and on the age distribution of tenant purchasers (cf. Table 3.10) to estimate the losses caused by the first four years of Right to Buy sales. Combining this informtion with the moving and other rates presented to the Environment Committee, (42) it seems reasonable to assume a loss rate of 3 per cent rather than the 2.6 figure used by the Committee. Given the 1980-3 sales volumes, this would imply a cumulated loss of 37,000 relets for the first four years of Right to Buy sales. If one assumes that the annual sales volume goes down by 10,000 dwellings every year compared to the 1983 volume, the cumulated loss of relets caused by sales would be more than 210,000 by the end of the 1980s. The annual loss of relets would reach 30,000 in 1986/87. With new council house production staying at that level, it means that in the second half of the 1980s, annual losses of relets due to sales will equal lets provided through new production. It was shown above that sales have an impact not only on the number of council house dwellings, but also on the types of dwelling. British researchers conclude that the latter impact will have serious consequences for remaining tenants when it comes to the possibility of making the kind of housing career which brought tenant purchasers into the attractive houses they bought. They argue that those households with the least bargaining power will be allocated the less popular public rental dwellings. When their family circumstances change, the inevitable decline in transfer possibilities caused by the character of the sales means that they may get stuck in their dwellings:

> Given the selective nature of sales, it is unlikely that tenants moving into the public sector today will have the same opportunities. In future, many tenants may be in a financial position to purchase but will be occupying highrise flats with little chance of a transfer. The Right to Buy is an opportunity on offer to one generation of council tenants at the expense of the next. (43)

Chances are, however, that the majority of remaining tenants will not be in a financial position to buy. As we have seen, tenant purchasers are better off than tenants in general. As these better-off households leave the public rental sector, sales

119

compound the trend towards residualisation - or perhaps more correct, categorisation - of council housing. During the 1970s, the proportion of supplementary benefit recipients who were also council tenants rose form 51 to 61 per cent. Also during the 1970s the share of semi-skilled workers living in public housing rose from 44 to 51 per cent, and that of unskilled workers from 56 to 66 per cent. The share of those not in paid employment who were public tenants rose from 39 to 44 per cent between 1974 and 1980. Between 1968 and 1978, the share of income earners in the highest decile who were public tenants went down from 20 to 15 per cent while that for the lowest decile increased from 32 to 56 per cent. (44) Public renting is becoming a sector providing only special types of housing to special categories of household.

Council House Sales and Residential Influence

British public sector tenants have never had much influence over their housing situation. It was not until the 1980 Housing Act that they got a legally guaranteed security of tenure. Under the 1980 Tenants Charter, such tenants can be evicted only on special grounds - rent arrears, breach of tenancy obligations, nuisance to neighbours, or damage to dwelling or furniture, or false statements on a tenancy application. Secure tenants also have a number of rights; the right to sublet and take in lodgers, to do improvements, to be notified of changes in tenancy conditions, and - this is the 1980s! - the right to a written tenancy agreement. (45)

The conditions for tenant influence in council housing are described as follows in two recent books on British housing:

> Council housing is a parternalistic housing type in which households are visited, selected and allocated dwellings by the housing managers, who set their rents, decide the colour of their doors and determine the rules and regulations which cover tenancy agreements. (46)

> It is fashionable to argue that housing management is suffering from an excess of paternalism. But 'paternalism' is not a true description: 'oppressive' and 'regulatory' would be more accurate. Management policies are

divisive and individualistic and, whilst purporting to be for the good of the majority, do in fact assist the 'respectables' and discredit and stigmatise the less fortunate. Problems are defined bureaucratically and the response is management-oriented. Whilst it is possible to discover individual authorities that have adopted good practices, underlying assumptions and the basic values of housing management are common to most local authority landlords. The dominant ideology favours owner occupation whilst housing management is left to pick up those who cannot compete in the market and, in so doing, confirms the image of council housing as a residual 'welfare' sector. (47)

According to Short, the 1980 Tenants Charter eliminated or lifted some of the 'petty limitations' placed on public tenants. However, the ideological context of housing management – managers rule and tenants are ruled – still determines everyday management practice. This ideology has two elements. One is the notion of council housing as a welfare provision. It is a benefit, something the 'unfortunate' and 'deserving' should see as a privilege rather than a right. The other is paternalism. Since they view council housing as a privilege to be granted the needy, housing managers adopt an authoritarian style towards applicants and tenants. (48)

Under such conditions, tenants may view purchase of their own dwelling as a means of increasing their freedom of disposal and security of tenure. But when asked what importance such motives have, prospective buyers ranked 'security' only fifth in one survey. In another, prospective tenant purchasers ranked freedom of disposal and security of tenure as the third and fourth motives for buying. By far the most important – or at least popular – reason was economic. The financial advantages of home ownership seem to be the first or second motive for buying. (49)

If most buyers connect such advantages of ownership with the possibility to influence their housing situation, at least some of them may come to have second thoughts about the tenability of such a connection. A May 1983 survey of metropolitan districts showed that one out of six buyers with a local authority mortgage was already in repayment arrears. In fact, the survey showed that already

there have been 3.5 repossessions per 10,000
right to buy local authority mortgages, and
repossession action has started on 93 more per
10,000 mortgages. In contrast, the building
societies in the first half of 1982 repossessed
nine out of every 10,000 mortgages. For every
10,000 right to buy local authority mortgages,
there have been 57 voluntary sales. (50)

Council house sales have undoubtedly increased the
influence over their housing for the majority of
tenant purchasers; for some, however, the financial
difficulties brought by the purchase may actually
make things worse. And since sales limit the options
of transfer, they limit the residential influence of
remaining tenants.

Sales and the Public Purse

The economic consequences for local authorities of
selling council housing have been subject to lively
discussion. At issue has been whether sales are
economically advantageous compared to continued
letting. It has also been discussed whether sales
would lead to a 'subsidising effect' in the form of
tax relief to tenant purchasers, which in the long
run would cost the Exchequer more than the subsidies
hitherto linked to the local authority dwellings
concerned by sales.

In the very short run, local authorities 'lose'
considerable sums because of the rebates given to
tenant purchasers. As shown earlier, the average
discount has been over 40 per cent of the valuation.
For the 550,000 dwellings sold under the Right to Buy
betweeen 1980 and 1983, the average rebate has been
£6,910. This means that local authorities have
foregone about £3,700 million, provided they would
have been able to sell the dwellings on the market at
valuation prices (cf. Table 3.13 above).

But what happens in the long run? The discussion
shows that the answer is very much dependent on the
assumptions made about the present value of net rent
incomes in relation to the net income from sales.
When the Tory government presented its projections of
these long-term financial effects, it assumed that
the rents would fall in real terms. It would
therefore be advantageous for local authorities to
sell rather than continue to let. Those attacking the
government's appraisals point to the new rent-
setting policy introduced with the 1980 Housing Act,
saying that this policy will indeed lead to real rent

increases or at least to rents keeping their real value. Shelter has argued that with rents increasing by 8 per cent annually, local authorities would experience losses from sales already after six years. (51) Arguing that rents historically have followed interest rates, another critic has concluded that sales under the conditions prevailing in the early 1980s would all lead to losses provided that (a) rents keep their value in real terms, and (b) dwellings sold have an expected lifespan of more than the average 25-year mortgage period. (52) Others have argued that with a projected rent increase of more than 2 per cent above the Retail Price Index, and with a real interest rate of less than 1 per cent, the long-term loss would be £15,000 per sale. (53) Of course, all appraisals are extremely sensitive to the time periods used. Using a modified variant of the government's appraisal, an expert to the House of Commons Environment Committee came up with results that differed widely depending on whether 20 or 50 years was used as the appropriate period for analysis. (54)

No effort will be made here to settle the issue once and for all. But by using some of the sales data presented earlier, it may be possible to shed more light on at least some of the problems. In 1981, the typical unrebated rent for a three-bedroom council house was £14.40 a week. Assuming an annual rent increase of 11 per cent (the average for 1979/80 to 1983/84 - and further assuming that inflation is 11 per cent (i.e., rents keep their real value) the present value of cumulated rent incomes over the next 25 years would be £18,750. Also in 1981, the average mortgage on council house sales was £9,400, repayable in 25 years. The interest rate was 13.5 per cent, and the initial deposit £400. The present value of cumulated incomes from sales for the next 25 years would then be £12,400.

As presented in Figure 3.2, these figures show the present values of annual and cumulated gross local authority receipts from the two alternatives, selling and continued renting. As such, they indicate that the cumulated present value of future rent receipts becomes larger than that of sales receipts 15 to 16 years after the sale. Present value of annual rent receipts is larger than that of sales already after 7 years.

To be at all realistic, appraisals should take into account present values of management and maintenance costs, as well as renovation costs. But even if such items could be projected with some

Figure 3.2: Present Value of Gross Local Authority
Income from Selling or Continued Letting of Typical
Three-Bedroom House, 1981-2006

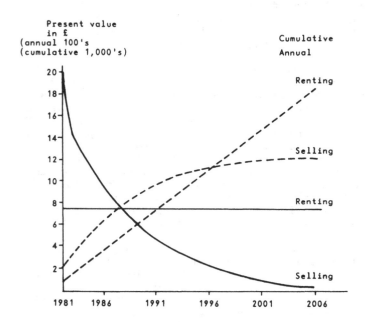

degree of plausibility, the most crucial thing
remains - what should be the appropriate time period
for the appraisal? For if the point at issue is
'whether the gains from sales in the years before the
cross-over exceed the losses in the years after the
cross-over', then everything depends on what
assumptions are made concerning the lifespan of the
house after the present value of one alternative
crosses the other. (55)

Another effect on the public purse of council
house sales has to do with tax regulations for home
owners. The tenant purchaser will enjoy tax
deductions on his mortgage interest payments.
Whenever he sells his house to another person, the
latter will also enjoy such a tax deduction. In this
way, council house sales will give rise to a
continuous subsidy effect. The tax effect will
probably be more pronounced than the subsidy linked
to historic capital costs in the public rental stock.

The latter diminishes over time in real terms, while subsequent mortgages keep tax deductions at a high level.

How pronounced the effect will be is difficult to state with any confidence. It is interesting, however, to compare the direct effect on tax incomes with the development of governmental subsidies to the public sector (cf. Table 3.14 above). For each year of council house sales between 1980 and 1983, the average sales price can be deducted from Table 3.13. Given the total sales figures presented in Table 3.3 and given further an average mortgage of 95 per cent of the sales price, a 25-year mortgage with an interest of 13.5 per cent, and a tax effect of 30 per cent, the total sum of taxes foregone by council house sales increased from £32 million in 1980/81, £70 million in 1981/82, and £144 million in 1982/83 to about £200 million in 1983/84. For the public purse, this loss of tax income was more than compensated for by the simultaneous cut in direct subsidies to public rental housing by more than £1,000 million (almost £1,200 if the cuts in local rate fund contributions are included). Assuming that local rates have not changed dramatically for tenant purchasers - after all, they live in the same house as before - they did not contribute to this fiscal gain as much as remaining tenants. While the latter saw their average governmental subsidy go down from £270 to £100, housing benefits not included, the average tenant purchaser's tax relief amounted to £360 in 1983/84.

Conclusion

The most notable characteristic of British tenure conversions is that they are part and parcel of a conscious governmental housing policy, aimed at spreading home ownership and reducing direct government subsidies to the housing sector, especially the public rental part of it. The British policy is thus representative of the marginalist type of housing policy that was discussed in the introductory chapter, and the policy of selling the public rental stock to the tenants is at the core of it. The evaluation of conversion effects is thus at the same time an evaluation of the consequences of supplementary housing policy strategies.

Several features contribute to making the context of British tenure conversions very specific. Conversions concern only sitting tenants. When they exercise their Right to Buy it is only their

125

particular dwelling that is concerned, not a whole building or a block of flats. Thus, security of tenure for non-buying tenants is not an issue. This is further accentuated by the peculiar composition of the public rental stock with its large share of houses in relation to flats. The legal context gives the buyer an upper hand in relation to the seller. The buyer has a legally defined right to a rebate on the sales price and to a 100 per cent mortgage from the seller. It is the buyer who has the initiative in the process, not the seller.

With such a rigidly defined legal and economic context for conversions, the effects will be highly dependent on the existing social composition of households in the public rental sector, and the prevailing 'match' of socio-economic and demographic household characteristics on the one hand, and dwelling characteristics on the other. This is so because all in the target group may not have the resources needed to exercise their Right to Buy, and all dwellings may not be attractive enough to seem worth buying.

What is presented as a way of spreading home ownership to all households – and whatever the benefits implied from such a strategy – may thus have quite different effects, especially if the better-off households already occupy the most attractive parts of the public rental stock. Thus, even if the volume of sales may be such that one can talk about a substantial increase in home ownership, the distribution in terms of buyer and dwelling characteristics may convey another picture.

The account given here clearly corroborates this proposition. The part of the stock concerned by sales is not a cross-section of public sector dwellings. Very few flats have been sold, while houses in attractive areas have tended to sell very quickly. Thanks to the allocation system of British council housing, the attractive houses have been occupied by households who are in such stages of their family cycle that they have the resources necessary to exercise their Right to Buy. The typical tenant purchaser is in his mid-forties, with adult children, and with an income much higher than the average council tenant. In fact, the characteristics of tenant purchasers are more similar to home owners in the private sector than to tenants.

Given this pattern, it seems difficult to conclude that council house sales so far have led to a wider distribution of home ownership in socio-economic or demographic terms. With the prevailing discount rates, the sales do not seem to spread wealth more equally either; over time, the discounts shift economic wealth from the public rental sector to the tenant buyers, who were already better off economically than the rest of tenants. Given the cost-pooling and rent-averaging system in British council housing, the sales of older 'surplus' housing leads to increased rents for remaining tenants, who happen to live in housing that was earlier made cheaper thanks to these surpluses. This effects on rents for remaining tenants is further accentuated by the rent increase policy adopted by the central government.

Unfortunately, there are no data available to allow a comparison of housing expenditures for tenant purchasers before and after the sale. Indications are, however, that net outgoings for purchasers are not considerably higher than for tenants. Based on average economic data on sales, the present 'net' value to the purchaser of owning for five full years - after that, he can sell without having to repay any of his discount - shows a surplus of more than £2,000. For the tenant remaining in a three-bedroom house, the present value of his outgoings show a deficit of more than £3,000.

Remaining tenants seem to become double losers in the sales game. Not only do they lose out to purchasers in terms of housing costs, but they also lose in terms of freedom of choice and prospects of buying in the future. With so many attractive houses in the public stock being sold, remaining tenants will find less opportunity for transfer to such housing in the future, and thus have fewer possibilities to buy the kind of housing most people seem to want. Some studies of sales content that sales compound and make more pronounced the tendency towards residualisation already at work in council housing. The public rental sector is increasingly providing less attractive housing to less resourceful households. It may become a residual - or supplementary - tenure catering for people at the margin of the regular housing market - that is, for those in 'real need'.

There are no indications that sales have a positive effect on the public purse. Given the discounts, this is certainly true in the short run. In a longer perspective, conclusions are heavily dependent on assumptions concerning the future life-span of dwellings sold, repair and maintenance costs, and so on. In terms of present value of receipts from sales and rents, a comparison shows that receipts from rents are higher than from sales, given the present rent increase policy.

In one sense, the sales policy can be termed a resounding success. The volume of sales exceeds even the most daring projections. If the present trend continues, sales will have taken 10 per cent of the council housing stock already after five full years of sales. And to the great majority of purchasers, the shift from tenancy to home ownership will increase their influence over housing matters, so remarkably underdeveloped for tenants in the British public housing sector.

However, the main effect is distributive. Council house sales do extend home ownership – and the benefits flowing from it – to a wider circle of households. But these households are already very much like other home owners, and may well have bought a house in the private sector, had it not been for the sales policy. Thus, the effects of sales – and housing policy – on the distribution of housing standard and housing costs do not lead to greater equality in housing. They rather make differences between tenures, and households in different tenures, more pronounced. In terms of the ideology behind the sales policy this may, however, be interpreted as a positive thing. Sales do indeed seem to 'create a climate in which those who are able can prosper, chose their own priorities and seek the rewards and satisfactions that relate to themselves', while the resources of the community can be concentrated 'increasingly on the members of the community who are not able to help themselves.' (56)

Notes

1. The preceding paragraphs are based on David Donnison and Clare Ungerson, <u>Housing Policy</u> (Penguin, Harmondsworth, 1982), chs. 9–10; and John R. Short, <u>Housing in Britain – The Post-War Experience</u> (Methuen, London and New York, 1982), ch. 3. Quotes of Labour statements are from Short, pp. 55 and 62.

2. Donnison and Ungerson, <u>Housing Policy</u>, p. 148. Cf. below, Tables 3.3 and 3.4.

3. Building Societies Association, <u>BSA Bulletin</u>, No. 27 (July 1981), p.22; Donnison and Ungerson, <u>Housing Policy</u>, p.214.

4. Nick Fielding, 'Who is Subsidising Whom?' <u>ROOF</u>, <u>9</u> (March/April 1984), p. 11; Donnison and Ungerson, <u>Housing Policy</u>, pp. 162, 215, 225.

5. The quote is found in 'DoE's first Annual

Report', Housing Review, 33 (January/February, 1984), p.3.

6. Alan Murie, The Sale of Council Houses - A Study in Social Policy (CURS Occasional Paper No. 35, University of Birmingham, 1975), ch. 3.

7. Department of the Environment/Welsh Office, The Right to Buy. A Guide for Council, New Town and Housing Association Tenants (DoE Welsh Office, Housing Booklet No. 2, Cardiff, March 1980), passim.

8. P.J. Welham, 'The Tax Treatment of Owner-occupier Housing in the U.K.' Scottish Journal of Political Economy, 29 (1982), p. 139 f.

9. DoE/Welsh Office, The Right to Buy, p.8.

10. Department of the Environment, 'Sales of Council Houses and Flats and Disposal of Land' (DoE, London, 2 September 1980, mimeo), p. 2.

11. Murie, The Sale of Council Houses, pp. 79 ff.; Andrew Friend, A Giant Step Backwards. Council House Sales and Housing Policy (Catholic Housing Aid Society, CHAS Occasional Paper/5, London, 1980), pp. 8, 14, 19; Philip Challen, The Sale of Council Houses (Leeds Polytechnic, School of Town Planning, Leeds, BA Dissertation, 1980), p. 74 f.

12. DoE/Welsh Office, The Right to Buy, p. 11.

13. Greater London Council Housing Policy Committee, 'Right-to-Buy: Progress' (GLC, London, Housing Policy Committee, HG 187, Report (11.12.81) by the Controller of Housing and Technical Services).

14. Ibid., App. A.

15. Murie, Council House Sales, p. 52 f. Cf. Stephen Merrett (with Fred Gray), Owner-Occupation in Britain (Routledge & Kegan Paul, London, 1982), where a figure of just under 70,000 per year is given for the same period.

16. Murie, The Sale of Council Houses, p. 51 f.

17. Ray Forrest and Alan Murie, Right to Buy? Issues of Need, Equity and Polarisation in the Sale of Council Houses (University of Bristol, School for Advanced Urban Studies, Working Paper 39, 1984), p. 22.

18. House of Commons Environment Committee, Session 1980-81, Council House Sales Vol. I Report (HMSO, London, 1981), p. xviii.

19. John R. Short, Housing in Britain - The Post-war Experience, pp. 163 ff.; Peter Malpass and Alan Murie, Housing Policy and Practice (MacMillan, London, 1982), pp. 142 ff.; Valerie Karn, 'Class, Race and Gender Stratification in the Allocation of Council Housing', in Lennart J. Lundqvist & Marianne Wiktorin (eds.), Current Trends in British Housing -

Proceedings from a British-Swedish Workshop on Current Housing Policy Research (The National Swedish Institute for Building Research, Gavle, Bulletin M 83:17, 1983), pp. 79-90.

20. House of Commons Environment Committee, Council House Sales, Vol. 1, Report, p. xxvii.

21. Forrest and Murie, Right to Buy?, pp. 29 ff.

22. See, e.g., Murie, The Sale of Council Houses, p. 111 f.; Challen, The Sale of Council Houses, p. 53; M. Beazley et al., The Sale of Council Houses in a Rural Area - A Case Study of South Oxfordshire (Oxford Polytechic, Department of Town Planning, Oxford, Working Paper No. 44, (1980), passim; Keith Bassett, 'Council House Sales in Bristol, 1960-1979', Policy and Politics, 8 (1980), pp.324-33.

23. House of Commons Environment Committee, Council House Sales, Vol. 1, Report, p. liii. These conclusions are also confirmed by the findings about sales in Aberdeen; see J. Sewel, F. Twine and N. Williams, 'The Sale of Council Houses. Some Empirical Evidence', Urban Studies, 21 (1984), pp. 422 ff.

24. House of Commons Environment Committee, Council House Sales.

25. Peter Malpass and Alan Murie, Housing Policy and Practice, p. 65.

26. Central Statistical Office, Social Trends 13 (HMSO, London, 1983), pp. 80 ff., 120 ff.

27. House of Commons Environment Committee, Council House Sales, Vol. II Minutes of Evidence, pp. 245, 266, 282.

28. Ray Forrest and Alan Murie, Council House Sales and Council Housing in Birmingham. Summary of Research Findings (School of Advanced Urban Studies, Bristol University, 1982, mimeo), p. 29.

29. Ray Forrest and Alan Murie, 'The Great Divide', ROOF, 7 (November/December 1982), p. 20.

30. Cf. Social Trends, 13, p. 78.

31. House of Commons Environment Committee, Council House Sales Vol. I, Report, p. liv.

32. Maggie Jones, 'Choice in Housing Tenure in Britain', in Hans Kroes and Fritz Ijmkers (eds.), Buitenlandse vormen van woningbeheer (RIW-instituut voor volkshuisvestingsonderzoek, Delft, 1982), p. 193.

33. Ibid., p. 192.

34. D. McCulloch, 'The New Housing Finance System', Local Government Studies, 8 (May/June 1982), p. 98.

35. Fielding, 'Who is Subsidising Whom?',

p. 11.
    36. McCulloch, 'The New Housing Finance System', p. 100.
    37. The assumptions underlying the discussion are as follows. The average unrebated rent for council housing in England and Wales rose by about 52 per cent between 1979/80 and 1983/84 (Fielding, p. 11), with the average rent (R) for a 3 bedroomed house (in Birmingham) being about £13 a week in 1979/80 (Forrest and Murie, p. 29). It is further assumed that the rate of increase was uniform over those years, or slightly above 11 per cent. The interest rate for alternative investment of the rent is 13.5 per cent; this holds also for the case of tenant purchasers. For sales, the following assumptions are further made for 1980:

Average valuation (V)	£15,200
Average discount	£ 5,800
Average sales price	£ 9,400
Average deposit (D)	£ 400
Average initial mortgage debt (M)	£ 9,000
Average repayment period	25 years
Standard annual repayment (A)	£ 360
Mortgage interest rate (r)	13.5 per cent
Average tax rate for deductions (T)	30 per cent
Average annual upkeep and insurance costs (no annual increase is assumed) (U)	£ 200
Average annual increase (v) on sales value (V)	5 per cent

The discount is fully realisable after 5 years. (Data from Housing and Construction Statistics – see Table 3.12 – and Social Trends 13, p. 120 f).

Present value of owner occupier outgoings is computed as

$$P_{OO} = D + \sum_{t=1}^{5} \frac{A+U+r(1-T)(M - \sum_{\tau=2}^{t}A_\tau)}{\left[1+r(1-T)\right]^t} = £5,564$$

Present value of V at the end of year 5 is computed as

$$P_V = \frac{V(1+v)^5}{\left[1+r(1-T)\right]^5} = £12,351$$

131

$$P_M = \frac{M-5A}{\left[1+r(1-T)\right]^5} = £4,584$$

This gives

$$P_V - P_{00} - P_M = £2,203$$

which means that after 5 years, the tenant purchaser has a gain from his purchase, the present value of which is £2,203.

For the remaining tenant, the present value of rent outgoings is computed as

$$P_R = R_0 \sum_{t=0}^{4} \left(\frac{1 + \frac{\Delta R}{R}}{1 + r(1-T)} \right)^t = £3,418$$

This means that after five years, the remaining tenant will have spent a sum on living the present value of which is of that magnitude. In the end, the tenant purchaser is up on the remaining tenant by £5,625 in terms of the present value of their outgoings on housing. (Thanks are due to Dr Rune Wigren for helping me through the maze of assumptions and formulas).

38. Cf. House of Commons Environment Committee, <u>Council House Sales Vol. I, Report</u>, p. xviii.

39. Ibid., <u>Vol. III, Appendices</u>, p. 18.

40. Ibid., <u>Vol. I, Report</u>, p. xx. Cf. <u>Vol. III, Appendices</u>, pp. 19 ff.

41. Labour Party, <u>The Sale of Council Houses</u> (Labour Party Research Department, London, Information Paper No. 16, 1979), p. 11; Shelter, <u>Facts on Council House Sales</u> (Shelter, National Campaign for the Homeless, London, 1979), p. 5; Stuart Lansley, <u>Housing and Public Policy</u> (Croom Helm, London, 1979), p. 180; DoE, <u>Council House Sales: The Government's Reply to the Second Report from the Environment Committee, Session 1980-81, HC 366</u> (HMSO, London, Cmnd. 8377, October 1981), p. 4.

42. House of Commons Environment Committee, <u>Council House Sales, Vol. III, Appendices</u>, pp. 19 ff.

43. Forrest and Murie, 'The Great Divide', p. 20.

44. Ray Forrest and Alan Murie, 'Residualization and Council Housing: Aspects of the Changing Social Relations of Housing Tenure', Journal of Social Policy, 12 (October 1983), p. 455 f.; Ray Robinson and Tony O'Sullivan, 'Housing Tenure Polarisation: Some Empirical Evidence', Housing Review, 32 (July/August 1983), p. 116.

45. Steve Schifferes, 'Housing Bill 1980 - The Beginning of the End for Council Housing', ROOF, 5 (January 1980), p.13.

46. Short, Housing in Britain - The Post-war Experience, p. 171.

47. Pam Gallagher, 'Ideology and Housing Management', in John English (ed.), The Future of Council Housing (Croom Helm, London, 1982), p. 132.

48. Short, Housing in Britain - The Post-war Experience, p. 162.

49. Cf. Colin Jones, 'The Demand for Home Ownership', in English (ed.), The Future of Council Housing, pp. 122 ff.; S.T. Charles, 'Council House Sales', Social Policy & Administration, 16 (Summer 1982), pp. 105 ff.

50. Mike Knight, 'When Owning Becomes a Nightmare', ROOF, 8 (November/December 1982), p. 25.

51. Shelter, Facts on Council House Sales, p. 15.

52. Bernard Kilroy, 'The Financial and Economic Implications of Council House Sales', in English (ed.), The Future of Council Housing, pp. 65 ff.

53. Roger Critchley and Nigel Lee, 'Massive Losses on Council House Sales', ROOF, 8 (July/August 1983), p. 9.

54. House of Commons Environment Committee, Council House Sales, Vol. III, Appendices, pp. 26-52. Cf. Vol. I, Report, p. xlvii.

55. Kilroy, 'The Financial and Economic Implications of Council House Sales', p. 62.

56. Statement by Michael Heseltine as Secretary of State for the Environment, quoted in Forrest and Murie, Right to Buy?, p. 6.

Chapter Four

WEST GERMANY: UMWANDLUNGEN IN EIGENTUMSWOHNUNGEN AND THEIR EFFECTS

West German Housing Policy: Main Characteristics and Tenure Aspects

West Germany came out of the Second World War with 25 per cent of its housing stock in ruins; the major cities were, of course, even worse off. During the first postwar decade, West Germany furthermore had to accommodate 12.5 million refugees; they poured into the larger cities where jobs were most easily found. (1)

No wonder, then, that the First Federal Housing Act of 1950 called for a system of massive government subsidies for the construction of housing which 'by size, standard and rent is destined and appropriate for wide sectors of the population'. (2) The goal was to build as many units as quickly as possible. The 1953 objective of building 2 million units up to 1956 was exceeded; no fewer than 3.1 million dwellings were produced, of which 1.8 million were Sozialwohnungen. This 'social rental housing' production was directly subsidised by the governments at Federal and State levels, and was also 'purpose-bound' with respect to which households were allowed to rent. Only households up to a certain income limit were eligible, in contrast to the other types of housing called for under the 1950 Act, i.e. tax-privileged and privately financed housing. (3)

This feeling of urgency prevailed for most of the 1950s. Social rental housing made up more than 50 per cent of housing production, adding about 250,000 units to the housing stock annually. However, the Second Federal Housing Act of 1956 started the process of gradual reorientation of the housing policy towards what was dubbed more 'normal, market-like' conditions. Rent-setting regulations had been lifted from the tax-privileged housing already in 1953; now, the Federally determined 'guideline rent' system was changed into a so-called 'cost-renting' system, which is said to practically guarantee landlords to have their costs covered at the same time as renters' expenditures are kept low. (4) The 1956 Act furthermore changed the objectives of housing policy. Apart from the goal of producing social housing to put an end to the housing shortage, efforts should also be directed towards helping broad strata in the population to become home owners. This was seen by Christian Democrats as an important way of spreading wealth. (5)

The 1960s witnessed Christian Democratic efforts for further liberalisation of the housing market, but also some moves that increased governmental involvement. Rent controls in the pre-1948 stock were lifted. The Lücke Plan of 1960 called for abandoning rent controls as well as all regulations on tenure security. This would be done area by area as soon as the local housing market showed an excess demand of 3 per cent or less. Causing much social hardship, the market rent system forced the Christian Democrats to introduce a housing allowance programme in 1965, thus transferring governmental money to eligible households (the so-called Subjektförderung). In the same year, legislation was promulgated which actually strengthened the position of social renters by making the strings attached to social housing (cost rents, income eligibility rules) a matter of public law and control. (6)

Public support to housing production (the so-called Objektförderung) had so far been directed mostly towards social rental housing under the First Subsidy Programme. Reacting to the decrease in housing production, the Grand Coalition in 1966 introduced the Second Subsidy Programme, which widened the circle of eligible households. However, the new programme was also meant to help medium-income families to home ownership. What happened was that the share of Sozialwohnungen whose production received support through the First Subsidy Programme gradually decreased, from 90 per cent of directly supported units in 1966 to 48 per cent in 1970 (cf. Figure 4.1). In fact, the production of publicly supported Sozialwohnungen for rent decreased from 121,000 in 1970 to 33,000 a decade later. The publicly assisted production of owner-occupied housing increased its share of all supported new dwellings - that is, of both the First and Second Subsidy Programmes - from 42 per cent in 1970 to 71 per cent in 1980. (8) The 1970s thus witnessed an increasing emphasis on owner occupation. Single- and

Figure 4.1: Housing Production in West Germany, 1966-81.

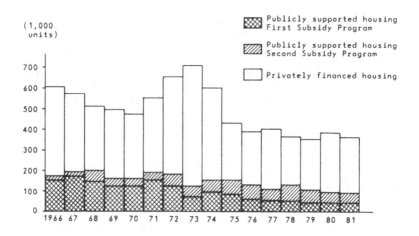

Source: Hellmut Wollman, 'Housing Policy in West Germany – Between State Intervention and the Market' p. 142 in Klaus von Beyme and Manfred G. Schmidt (eds.), <u>Policy-Making in the Federal Republic of Germany</u> (Gower Farnborough, 1984).

two-family housing became dominant in new production after 1975 (see Figure 4.2). Income-related support to social housing production and to housing consumption gradually lost their earlier dominance in the system of governmental support. The growing share of owner-occupied units in new production, and the 1977 widening of tax privileges to acquisition of home ownership in the existing rental stock - see below - caused the indirect support to grow in importance (see Figure 4.3). During the 1970s, the capacity of the social housing sector to provide housing for low-income households was diminished not only by lower production but also by an increase in what is termed 'wrong occupancy' (<u>Fehlbelegung</u>). By this is meant that as the household income level

Figure 4.2: Housing Production in West Germany, 1970–83. Shares of One- and Two-family Houses and Multi-family Housing. Percentage of completed dwellings.

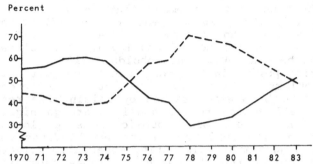

Sources: Renate Petzinger and Marlo Riege, <u>Die Neue Wohnungsnot-Wohnungswunder Bundesrepublik</u> (Hamburg: VSA-Verlag 1981), p.144; <u>Wirtschaft und Statistik</u> 4/1982, p. 299; ibid., 4/1983, p. 337; ibid., 4/1984, p. 326.

Figure 4.3: The Development of Housing Subsidies in West Germany, 1955–80. In billion DM.

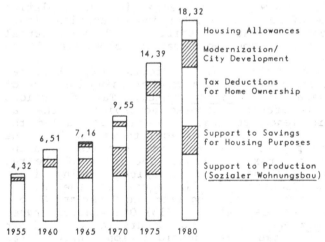

Source: Renate Petzinger and Marlo Riege, <u>Die Neue Wohnungsnot-Wohnungswunder Bundesrepublik</u> (Hamburg: VSA-Verlag 1981), p. 96.

moves upward, an increasing share of households in Sozialwohnungen will be way above the income eligibility rules they met when they first moved into such housing. It has been estimated that by the beginning of 1983, almost one third of the renters of social housing had incomes that exceeded the eligibility limits by 20 per cent or more. (9) By the early 1980s, a new housing shortage became evident as the waiting lists for social housing in metropolitan areas went beyond 250,000 households. (10)

Housing policy in the 1980s has tried to tackle these problems in two ways. In 1981, the 'wrong occupancy' problem was attacked by raising the rent levels in all social rental housing through higher interest rates on 'old' public housing loans. Provisions in the 1982 law on purpose bindings for social housing aim at stimulating especially private owners of social rental housing to repay subsidies prematurely. Having done that, they can have the full benefit of a 'free' rental unit; they can convert it and sell it at market prices, or they can charge market rents. On the other hand, the Christian Democratic-Liberal coalition has inaugurated a massive programme of direct subsidies to construct new rental Sozialwohnungen. In 1982 and 1983, half a billion DM was spent annually for this purpose. (11) Figure 4.2 shows an increase in the relative importance of multi-family housing production. There are indications that the shift towards more rental units in social housing began to show already in 1981. (12)

However, the main efforts of Christian Democrats are directed towards increasing the rate of home ownership (Eigentumsquote). Tax deductions additionally granted increase according to the tax rate. This leads to what in German is called the Mitnehmer - free rider - effect; those who have the ability to pay are also enjoying subsidised housing through income tax deductions. The value of the tax deductions for new owner-occupied housing in a typical production year is equal to the direct subsidies to social housing from the First and Second Subsidy Programmes combined. (13) One scholar argues that the Mitnehmer phenomenon occurs in 90 to 95 per cent of all cases of subsidisation through tax deductions. (14)

The wealth-creating element in West German housing policy thus seems to be as central as ever. In his 1983 Governmental Declaration, Chancellor Helmut Kohl said it would be the policy of his government to increase the possibilities of many citizens to acquire a home of their own. The Liberals are also committed to Eigentumsförderung, and both parties see conversions as a means to this end. (15) In the words of the incoming Christian Democratic Minister for Housing, support for individual home ownership should be at the forefront of governmental housing policy:

> In this endeavour, we must consciously work within a family policy perspective. Support to the purchase and maintenance of private home ownership serves as a necessary correction against the distribution of home ownership brought about by the market forces if left alone. The objective of widespread individual home ownership thus can not be realized without state support and tax privileges. This is especially true for families with children. (16)

The conversions of rental housing into owner occupation has thus taken place in a context where housing policy objectives have become gradually more geared towards treating housing as a source of wealth, the issue being its distribution among the households. In the following analysis of conversions, the effects on wealth distribution will thus be of central importance along with the effects on the distribution of housing standards and costs.

Umwandlung in Eigentumswohnungen: The Political, Legal and Economic Framework

After the Second World War, homelessness was a serious problem in West Germany. To find shelter for themselves, many households used their savings as a capital input in new rental housing, hoping that this would guarantee them a rental contract. Rental legislation provided a very insufficient security of tenure for such households, who thus ran the risk of losing their money without getting a flat. In March 1951, the Bundestag therefore enacted a law on condominiums (the Wohnungseigentumsgesetz). The desperate situation in the housing market is evidenced by the fact that this was the first - and for some time the only - law enacted unanimously by the West German Parliament.

In terms of housing policy the new law had several aims. It was to give households which had put their savings into the construction of new multi-family housing a stronger security of tenure. It would also provide the households with forms of saving secured against inflation; this was expected to influence housing production in a positive way. The restoration of the inner cities destroyed during the war would be quickened by giving the households a stake in the process. Furthermore, the new act was to provide 'nomadic renters' with new possibilities of getting into owner-occupied housing. (17)

The main content of the 1951 legislation for owner-occupied flats is as follows. A flat in a multi-family building can be individually owned, and the owner has a wide-ranging freedom of disposal of that flat. He can sell it at prevailing market prices. He can rent it to someone else, and he can mortgage his flat. The flat owner also owns the common parts of the building and the ground area together with the other flat owners. When he sells the flat, he automatically loses his right in the commonly owned property. A flat owner must take such care of his flat that he causes no harm to other flat owners. He must also accept the encroachments stemming from activities necessary to keep the common property in good condition. If he causes damage to common property, he must pay compensation. The maintenance and care-taking of the common property is a common responsibilty for all flat owners, while each flat owner is fully responsible for maintenance and care of his own flat. All rights and duties are, however, not regulated by law. Flat owners can make arrangements on such things as the right to let or sell the flats. To be binding on successive owners, such agreements must be noted in the real estate register's entry for the flat or flats concerned in the agreement. (18)

All flat owners are members of the flat owners' association - Wohneigentümerversammlung - where decisions are taken concerning such things as regulation of behaviour, budgets, plans for care-taking and maintenance, and so on. The association also decides the hiring or dismissal of a special administrator, the Verwalter, who runs commons business in accordance with the association's decisions. At least once a year, the administrator convenes a meeting with the association members to decide on his proposal for next year's management budget. Decisions are taken according to the principle of one man, one vote. Only a simply majority is needed if the members have not agreed otherwise, and provided the decision does not concern extra-ordinary repair and renovation. In this case, unanimity is required. As for the contributions to common management purposes, each flat owner pays according to the value of his flat in relation to the common property as recorded in the official real estate register. (19)

Legislation affecting conversion may be separated into the following categories: (1) tenant protections; (2) preservation of the publicly supported stock of rental housing for low- and moderate-income households; and (3) buyer protections. When conversions concern Sozialmietwohnungen, regulations under (1) and (2) combine to give a very strong security of tenure for the renter.

In the privately financed rental sector, the general rule states that a purchaser of a converted flat cannot claim the flat immediately upon purchase, even if he wants to use it as his own home. This is because present renters in buildings undergoing conversions have a legally guaranteed right to stay on in their apartments for a period of three years following the notification of the purchase in the real estate register. To this is added the usual period of notice in cases of non-renewal of rent contracts. In West Germany, the length of the notice period varies with the duration of the renter's stay in the flat. The minimum period is three months; if the renter has had a contract for the flat for ten years or more, he has a legal right to stay for another year after the contract is ended. Together with certain other regulations, the renter may enjoy his tenure for as long as five years after the flat was converted and sold to another person. (20) In comparison to the rules prevailing in most US states, this is an extremely long security of tenure period.

As noted earlier, West German multi-family housing can be divided into two sectors, depending on the system of finance for new production. Publicly suported rental housing - the Sozialwohnungen - is legally bound to serve the purpose of providing housing for those households which satisfy income and other criteria for 'social' renters. These bonds hold for as long as the subsidies are not fully paid back to the public purse. Now, an owner or converter has the possibility of repaying - prematurely - the subsidies. This does not, however, immediately release the flats or the building from the binding social rent purpose. According to the 1980 legislation, the bond is not lifted until eight years after the repayment of the subsidies, or until the end of the year in which it would have been fully repaid under normal amortisation schedules, whichever period is shorter. To enjoy security of tenure for this period, the renter is obliged to show proof of his right to the dwelling within four months after the owner/converter asks him to do so. If the renter does not provide such proof, the date ending the bond on the flat's use may be determined six months after the owner made his request to the renter. If a renter buys his present flat, or if the flat is not rented at the time of repayment, or if the repayable subsidy is less than DM 3,000, the bond on the flat's use is lifted immediately. In cases where the full eight-year period is applicable, the earlier-mentioned regular period of notice in cases of ended rent contracts also comes into effect. Altogether, rental legislation covering the Sozialmietwohnungen provide the present renter with a security of tenure that may last for as long as ten years after the conversion. (21)

The 1980 legislation also contains other clauses to protect renters. Owners of social multi-family housing must notify the appropriate authority about the intent to convert the building, and provide this authority with the names of the renters affected by the conversion. If the owner is selling the flats, he must also provide the names of the prospective buyers. Then the public authority notifies renters as well as purchasers about the legal terms and effects of the conversion. The authority must also inform the renter about his right of first purchase. According to the 1980 legislation, the renter of a converted dwelling purchased by another person has the right to first purchase of the dwelling within six months of the notice. If he uses this right, he is entitled to the same conditions of purchase as those enjoyed by the initial buyer. (22)

In addition to this legislation, the Länder have issued guidelines for conversions of Sozialmiet-wohnungen. These guidelines often require that (1) a substantial share of the converted flats are purchased by the present renters; (2) the public authority subsidising the housing gives its consent to the conversion; and (3) conversions do not concern dwellings whose location, standard, and rent level make them specially important for the provision of low-income rental housing. (23)

Because of frequent instances of fraudulent behaviour on the part of builders or sellers of Eigentumswohnungen, legislation was enacted in 1975 to protect the rights – and the money – of buyers of such dwellings. A builder or converter may accept and use money given to him by buyers only if (a) there is a legally valid contract between buyer and seller, which has been registered by the notary public upon checking that all necessary permits have been issued; (b) the buyer's property title has been noted in the real estate register and there are no encumbrances or easements superseding the buyer's title to the property; and (c) the intention to convert, and the terms of conversion, are appropriately noted in the real estate register. The builder/converter is only allowed to accept custody of certain parts of the contracted sum for the dwelling according as the production or renovation process develops in different stages. The money paid must be put into separate accounts and explicitly linked to the name of the buyer. (24) Point (b) is of course very important. The buyer must be informed about the status of the flat - that is, about whether there are any bindings on its use which would make it impossible for the buyer to take over and use the dwelling immediately.

The economic framework of conversions and ownership of flats is set by property and income tax regulations, and by different incentives given to households saving for housing purposes. In West Germany, a tax is levied on the purchase price of real estate. Earlier, Eigentumswohnungen were exempt from this tax under certain conditions. The flat must be used as a home by the buyer, his spouse or children for at least one year during the first five years after purchase. At least two-thirds of the flat must be used for the purpose of living. Furthermore, the taxable value of the flat must not exceed DM 100,000. In 1982/83, the exemption was lifted and a general tax of 2 per cent of the purchase price is levied on every flat purchase. (25)

Owner-occupied flats are also favoured by the regular property taxation. New or heavily renovated and modernised Eigentumswohnungen which are used by the owner are taxed only on the value of the flat-owner's part in the commonly owned ground of the property. Thus, the property value of the flat itself is not subject to taxation. This favourable taxation prevails for the first ten years after purchase, provided also that the flat meets certain size limits spelled out by law. (26)

Since 1977, the income tax regulations covering home ownership are also valid for converted flats. The owner who uses at least two-thirds of his flat for housing purposes can deduct 5 per cent of the acquisition cost from his taxable income during the first eight years of ownership. After this period, he may deduct 2.5 per cent of the remainder every year.

However, this deduction can be enjoyed only by flat owners who rent their flats to others. The eight year, 5 per cent deduction covers an acquisition cost of up to DM 200,000. If the purchase price was higher, the owner can deduct only 2 per cent of the value above that limit. Furthermore, he can do so only if he rents the flat to someone else. (27) The tax laws evidently favour flat ownership as an investment rather than as a form of shelter.

Saving for owner occupation enjoys favourable treatment in either of two ways. Part of the money put into a house savings bank may be deducted from the taxable income of the saver, or the saver may receive a premium amounting to 14 per cent of the sum saved, plus 2 per cent for each child in his household. These premiums can also be enjoyed when the saver has set up a savings plan with other credit institutions. (28)

To finance the purchase, West German buyers provide a large amount of own capital. According to a 1981 survey, the average share of own capital was 42 per cent for all purchases made between 1977 and 1981. The average buyer had saved intensively for about seven years before the purchase. One third of the households sampled said their saving had forced them to limit their consumption substantially, and that they continued to do so after the purchase. The rest of the purchase is financed in equal parts through primary and secondary mortgages, running for about 25 and 11 years respectively. At least for the secondary mortgages, savings premiums or limited tax deductions help reduce the financial burden. Almost 90 per cent of the purchasers enjoyed public support during their savings phase, either through house savings premiums or through the possibility of limited deductions from taxable income mentioned earlier. Immediately after the purchase, the average housing cost/net income ratio was 30 per cent, but it fell to 20 per cent within seven years after purchase. (29)

Private converters of non-subsidised rental housing are in principle free to sell at whatever price the market may allow. For converters of Sozialwohnungen, and especially for public housing companies, there have been some local regulations. In Bremen, Sozialwohnungen may not be sold at a price exceeding the replacement value of the converted apartment. Housing expenditures following purchase should not exceed 30 per cent of household income, and the buyer's capital input may be as low as 10 per cent of the purchase price. (30)

Processes and Procedures of Umwandlungen

West German conversions are usually initiated by the seller by way of registering a partition declaration – Teilungserklärung – with the real estate office. The declaration divides the property into individual parts, each comprising one Eigentumswohnung. When the declaration is registered, the seller can begin marketing the flats. To make it possible for the buyers to get legal title to the flats they buy, the seller must also register a partition plan and a delimitation description. The latter – called the Abgeschlossenheitsbescheinigung – consists of a drawing acknowledged by the local building authority and showing the exact location and limits of each individual flat in the building. For every flat, a separate entry is made in the real estate register, noting the flat's share of the common property as well as all easements, contracts or encumbrances pertaining to that flat. (31) Thus, the social bindings caused by governmental subsidies should be noted here.

The initiative in the conversion process is thus with the seller. He may be the property owner himself, but there could also be a special converter. In the latter case, a property owner sells the whole building to a person or company specialising in conversions, and this person or company in turn converts the flats and sells them to individual buyers. Table 4.1 shows private individuals to be the owner category most involved in conversions, followed by public housing companies. These two seller categories differ with respect to what type of flats are converted. Not surprisingly, private sellers mostly deal in privately financed flats, while public housing companies convert and sell mostly Sozialwohnungen. There is also a marked difference in the conversion strategy. Private individual owners sell to converters in 4 cases out of 10, and private housing companies in as many as 6 cases out of every 10 units converted. On the other hand, public housing companies convert and sell directly themselves to buyers in the majority of all conversions in their stock. This is especially marked in the case of conversions of Sozialwohnungen.

Given the very strong security of tenure for sitting tenants written into West German law, one would expect a rather prolonged conversion process from the Abgeschlossenheitsbescheinigung and the Teilungserklärung to the final issuance of a property title to the flat buyer. In his study of conversions in Hannover, however, Veser finds a surprisingly

Table 4.1: Different Property Owner Categories' Share of Conversions, and Shares of their Conversions Done Through Converters, West Germany, 1978.

Owner category	Share of converted			Share of earlier owner's stock sold to converter and not directly to buyers		
	Flats	Sozial-wohnungen	Privately financed flats	All flats	Sozial-wohnungen	Privately financed flats
Private individuals	41	28	54	41	43	37
Public housing companies	27	42	14	13	10	27
Private companies	10	11	10	62	54	68
Others	15	14	15	46	63	38
No answer	7	4	7			
	100	100	100	36	34	38
				(averages for all owners)		

Source: Infratest, Folgen der Umwandlung und Veräusserung von Mietwohnungen als Eigentumswohnungen (Infratest GmbH, Munchen, 1980, pp. 21 ff.

quick process. Six months after the process began, 53 per cent of the flats in question were converted. After two and a half years, as many as 91 per cent were converted. When it came to actual sales, as many as 68 per cent of the converted flats had been sold after two and a half years. The fastest sales were made in the pre-1918 stock, where there was an over-representation of private company owners who sell quickly but also make a lot of repairs before conversion and sale. Private individual owners were fairly active in converting and selling their pre-1918 and post-1948 stocks. The public housing companies emerge as slow sellers in Hannover. Based upon his findings, Veser concludes that

> if one assumes that flats are not mainly bought by people who only invest in the flat but not move in, quick sales imply a high degree of tenant eviction. There is a clear connection between modernization and sales activities; large investments by the owner/converter force quick sales because of liquidity needs. Furthermore, modernization can be used as a motive to force tenants out. One may thus expect to find different degrees of forced tenant moves among different owner and converter categories. (32)

The national Infratest study found that 44 per cent of the earlier tenants had moved out within three years after the conversion process started. (33) As it turns out, both sellers/converters and buyers/owners of converted flats develop techniques of getting the tenants out quicker than the law permits. Renters are notified of eviction, the grounds very often other than those spelled out in the law. Barely camouflaged threats of eviction are sounded, often in combination with rather aggressive sales promotion campaigns. Money is offered to cover the costs of moving out for tenants who seem unwilling to buy their flats. Extensive modern-isation is allowed to drag on for months, thus making the building difficult to live in. Such modernisation is often preceded by notification of rent hikes, combined with offers of financial assistance to those willing to move out. As many as 37 per cent of the tenants who had moved out mentioned that they had been offered such financial assistance. One quarter of those who moved out said they had been notified of rent hikes. Another quarter said they had been offered to buy their flats but added that they had to decide within four weeks. (34)

Some very intricate methods seem to have been used by certain sellers/converters. By gradually packing empty flats with foreign guest workers, landlords try to force German renters to move. At a certain stage, the landlord announces his intention to thoroughly modernise his building, and forces the guest workers out. In this way, he can begin selling the flats immediately, using the argument that buyers can move in right after modernisation is finished. (35) One method involves selling the property to a front man. When the front man stops paying his debt to the seller, the latter may step in and legally demand a forced take-over of the building. Now, the legal security of tenure does not apply, and the original property owner is free to evict the tenants and start converting the flats. (36)

German public housing companies have a special responsibility for providing social rental housing. In 1978, they owned 24 per cent of the total rental stock, and as many as 59 per cent of all its dwellings were Sozialwohnungen – being built with public support. (37) How do they act in the process of conversion?

In Bremen, the public housing company sells only to sitting tenants. The sales offer is valid for one year, and the tenant has the right to stay in the flat, even if he does not buy it. With the offer tenants are given full information about their security of tenure under the law. The sales price cannot be more than the replacement cost of the flat. The long-term costs to the buyer cannot be more than 30 per cent of total household income. If the building contains more than seven flats, two-thirds of the tenants must agree to buy before the conversion can be implemented.

When the sales offer has been sent out to the tenants, the public housing company calls a tenant meeting. At this meeting the details of the conversion process are presented. In particular, the company makes sure to provide information about the legal and financial conditions attached to the purchase of flats. It is not until after such tenant meetings that the formal procedure starts with the Teilungserklärung and formal sales offers. In most cases, the public housing company continues as the manager of the building during the first five years after conversion. The whole process from the first tenant meeting to the final partition and the establishment of a flat owner association is said to take twelve months. The company asserts that by going about conversions in this manner, it has succeeded in developing a conversion process that does not intrude on the rights of sitting tenants. (38)

If the pattern found by Veser, and to some extent corroborated by the national study, is true, we may expect changes in the socio-economic and demographic profile of households in conversion areas. These changes may be most pronounced in areas with a large share of older dwellings being converted.

The Volume of Umwandlung in Eigentumswohnungen

The West German conversions of rental housing to owner occupation take place in a housing market characterised by a much lower share of home ownership than the US and British markets. The first decades after the war witnessed a rapid increase in rental dwellings, which made up two-thirds of the total housing stock in 1960. Since then, dwellings for home ownership have gradually come to dominate new housing production, thus leading to an increase in owner occupation's share of the total stock reaching 40 per cent in 1982.

The rental sector has three main landlord categories. Private individuals and private companies owned 11 million rental dwellings in 1978, or about three-quarters of the rental stock. Their share of the privately financed rental stock was as high as 90 per cent in 1978. The public housing companies had one quarter of the rental stock, but dominated in the publicly supported rental stock where it owned nearly six out of every ten Sozialwohnungen. Altogether, this part of the rental stock - with bindings on its use as long as the support is not paid back to the government - accounted for 28 per cent of all rental housing in 1978. All Sozialwohnungen were built after 1948, so that all 'older' dwellings referred to later on belong to the privately financed rental stock.

Several reasons combine to make it very difficult to ascertain the volume of tenure conversions, and hence their importance in this development towards more home ownership. First and foremost, there are no nationwide figures for the total volume of conversions. Second, available figures on the volume of conversions in the publicly supported rental sector are being disputed. Third, actually available figures on conversions in both rental sectors from some of the larger cities reveal no generalisable pattern in terms of how the

Table 4.2: Ownership and Size of the Rental Housing Stock in West Germany in 1978. Total figures (in millions) and percentage shares.

Owner category	All rental dwellings		Privately financed dwellings		Publicly supported dwellings (Sozialwohnungen)	
	total	%	total	%	total	%
Private individuals	9.1	63	7.9	77	1.2	29
Public housing companies	3.4	24	1.0	10	2.4	59
Other companies	1.9	13	1.4	13	0.5	11
Total	14.4	100	10.3	100	4.0	100

Source: Knut Gustafsson, 'Mietenniveau - Mietenstrukturen. Nachlese zur Wohnungsstichprobe 1978', Bundesbaublatt, XXXII (April 1983), p. 200

Table 4.3: Conversions of Publicly Supported Rental Dwellings into Eigentumswohnungen in the Länder of West Germany, 1977-82.

Land	Conversions up to 1979	1980	1981	1982	Total number converted end of 1982
Schleswig-Holstein	679	317	147	17	1,160
Hamburg	609	291	199	916	2,015
Nidersachsen	-	89	244	119	452
Bremen	2,007	108	979	432	3,526
Nordrhein-Westfalen	2,510	1,280	342	725	4,857
Hessen	-	-	-	-	-
Rheinland-Pfalz	386	172	97	345	1,000
Baden-Württemberg	7,012	537	611	473	8,633
Bayern	1,578	473	314	612	2,927
Saarland	-	-	-	-	-
Berlin (West)	2,360	1,146	1,370	n.a.	4,876(a)
West Germany total	17,141	4,413	4,303	3,639(a)	29,496(a)

Note: (a) Without West Berlin.
Sources: Rolf Kornemann, 'Umwandlung von Miet- in Eigentumswohnungen', Der Langfristige Kredit, Heft 15 (1983), p. 485; Ude Jens Frerics, 'Umwandlung - nach Zuversicht und Routine ein Stillstand?' Wohnungseigentum, 34, Heft 2 (1984), pp. 3 and 6.

conversions are distributed between the two rental sectors. An estimate of the total volume of conversions must thus rest on indirect rather than direct evidence.

To begin with, Table 4.3 presents nationwide figures on conversions in the publicly supported rental stock. According to the sources, these figures have been made available by federal housing authorities. For most of the regions, conversions of Sozialmietwohnungen began in 1977. This would point to an annual volume of 4,000 to 5,000 conversions in this sector. However, more intensive city studies cast some doubt on the accuracy of the Länder data. As can be seen from Table 4.4, there were as many as 1,575 conversions of publicly supported rental dwellings in the city of Hannover between 1980 and 1982. This should be compared to the 452 conversions reported for the whole region of Niedersachsen during the same period (cf. Table 4.3). Evidently, the overall national figures may contain some underestimations of the actual volume of conversions of Sozialmietwohnungen. In the words of one scholar, the differences between the figures for one city - Hannover - and the whole region - Niedersachsen - should 'serve as an example of the substantial lack of knowledge for estimating the quantity of conversions.' (39)

Table 4.4: Conversions from Rental Dwellings to Eigentumswohnungen in Hannover, 1980-2.

Year	Number of conversions				
	Total	Privately financed rentals		Publicly supported rentals	
		Number	%	Number	%
1980	1,267	656	51.8	611	48.2
1981	1,796	1,160	64.6	636	35.4
1982	1,638	1,310	80.0	328	20.0
Total 1980-2	4,654	3,126	66.5	1,575	33.5

Source: Jürgen Veser, Umfang und Struktur der Umwandlung von Miet- in Eigenteumswohnungen in Hannover, Institut für Stadtforschung, Berlin, 1984 p,18f.

The Hannover figures indicate that roughly one third of the flats converted between 1980 and 1982 came from the publicly supported rental stock. Data from

West Berlin indicate that about 42.5 per cent of all flats converted between 1979 and 1981 had been in the publicly supported sector. In Hamburg, the corresponding figure for the conversions between 1978 and 1982 was 21.2 per cent. Of the 1981 conversions in Munich, 33 per cent occurred in the publicly supported rental stock. (40) A nationwide survey published in 1980 indicates that this share of all 1978 conversions was 39 per cent. (41)

Although these figures reveal no stable pattern, they do provide the range within which one should find the respective shares of privately financed and publicly supported flats of the total conversion volume. It would seem, then, that a quite probable distributive pattern is twothirds and one third, respectively. According to Table 4.3, this would mean a total annual volume of 15,000 conversions. However, Table 4.4 indicates that the volume of conversions in the publicly supported rental stock may be more than three times higher than governmental figures. If so, the total annual volume could be estimated to 45,000 to 50,000 dwellings.

Another piece of indirect evidence is found in total stock and total production figures for the 1970s. According to the 1968 housing survey, there were 381,000 Eigentumswohnungen in West Germany. At the end of 1973, this number had increased to 700,000. (42) The 1978 housing survey - which was done in the spring - showed that new production of Eigentumswohnungen amounted to 346,000 for the period 1972-8. (43) If 1978 is counted as only one quarter, this gives an annual average of 55,000 newly produced Eigentumswohnungen. New production from January 1974 until the first quarter of 1978 should thus have been about 235,000 units. At the same time, however, the 1978 housing survey showed that there were 1,215 million Eigentumswohnungen in West Germany, (44) indicating a total growth from the end of 1973 of 515,000 units. Conversions from January 1974 until the first quarter of 1978 may thus have been 280,000, indicating an average annual volume of conversions of 65,000 dwellings.

Another line of circumstantial reasoning concerns the development of both the total occupied stock, the owner-occupied stock, and new production from 1978 onwards. Table 4.5 shows some results from the housing surveys and microcensuses taken in West Germany since 1972. Although the surveys and the microcensuses are by no means totally comparable, they together seem to indicate an interesting development.

Table 4.5: Development of the West German Housing Stock, 1972-82: Increases in the Total Stock, and in Owner Occupancy (in thousands).

	1 per cent survey 1972	1 per cent survey 1978	Microcensus 1980	Microcensus 1982
Total occupied stock	20,080	22,255	22,801	23,232
Home ownership stock	7,244	8,365	8,890	9,322
Owner occupation's share of total increase, in %		52.5	96.1	100.2

Source: Rolf Kornemann, 'Zur Umwandlung von Miet- in Eigentumswohnungen: Günstige Konstellation für kaufwillige Mieter', <u>Der Langfristige Kredit</u>, <u>Heft 7</u> (1984), p. 222; (percentages computed by me).

Table 4.6: <u>Eigentumswohnungen</u>: Additions from Multi-family Housing Production and from <u>Conversions</u> of Existing Rental Housing in West Germany, 1979-83.

Year	Multi-family housing starts (1,000 units)				Conversions to Eigentumswohnungen	
	Total (1)	Rentals (2)	Eigentums-wohnungen (3)	(3) as percentage of (1)	Total (a) (4)	(4) as percentage of (3)
1979	109	58	52	47.7	53	102.0
1980	122	63	59	48.4	54	91.5
1981	130	63	67	51.5	54	80.6
1982	149	74	75	50.3	55	73.3
1983	192	86	106	55.2	56	52.8

Note: (a) Estimates - see text for comments.
Sources: <u>Wirtschaft und Statistik</u> (4/1984), p. 323.

154

Between 1972 and 1978, owner occupation represented slightly more than half of the growth in the total occupied stock. If we are to believe the microcensuses, close to 100 per cent of the growth in total stock after 1978 has come in the owner-occupied sector. However, we know that at least 430,000 flats were completed in new multi-family housing production between 1978 and 1981. (45) Given the percentage distribution between Eigentumswohnungen and rental flats in housing starts (see Table 4.6), there is reason to believe that around 215,000 rental flats were added to the housing stock during this period. Consequently, owner occupation's share of the total stock increase should have been less than 100 per cent. It is tempting to conclude that the explanation for this discrepancy lies with conversions; the additions to the rental stock are cancelled out by conversions to home ownership in the existing rental stock. If this is true, we arrive at a total annual volume of conversions of about 55,000 dwellings.

By pursuing different lines of circumstantial reasoning, we arrive at an estimated range of conversions of 45,000 to 65,000 dwellings. In Table 4.6, a conservative estimate of slightly over 50,000 units annually is made. Given the figures for new production, and completions up to 1983, there should now be around 1.75 million Eigentumswohnungen in West Germany, representing 13 per cent of all occupied multi-family housing. The largest additions to the stock of Eigentumswohnungen probably come from new production. Till there are reliable nationwide figures on conversions this is, however, only an estimate; some would even call it a very conservative one. (46)

Consequences for the Level and Distribution of Housing Quality

Just like the situation in the United States, the West German legislation does not regulate who has, or who has not, the right to buy a flat for owner occupation. Any multi-family building can be converted, and any households can become the owner of an Eigentumswohnung. The following analysis will therefore try to establish what kind of housing is converted and what the consequences may be for the rental supply. Furthermore, the characteristics of buyers and non-buyers among pre-conversion tenants will be analysed together with the profile of buyers from the outside. Finally, the post-conversion quality of housing enjoyed by the tenants who moved out from the converted buildings will be discussed.

As can be seen from Table 4.7, nearly two-thirds of the West German rental housing stock in 1978 was built after the Second World War. More than six out of every ten flats had four rooms or more, and just about as many had such quality characteristics as bath, wc, and central heating. According to the nationwide Infratest survey, the age distribution of the converted flats was roughly the same as that of the whole rental stock, given the differences in age classification between the 1978 national housing survey and the Infratest study. It is notable that two-thirds of all conversions took place in buildings with seven flats or more.

As for dwelling size, small flats are heavily over-represented among the converted flats. The share of flats with three rooms or fewer in the converted stock is almost twice as high as that for the whole rental stock. On the other hand, the average size - in square meters - of converted flats is higher than for rental apartments in general. The equipment standard seems to have been somewhat higher in converted flats. The fact that converted flats seem to be somewhat more troubled by traffic noise than the total housing stock may indicate that a large share of the converted stock is located in central city areas with heavy traffic. Another indication of this is that a majority of the conversions covered by the Infratest survey were in densely built blocks in city centres. (47)

This is borne out by the data on Hannover conversions. Six out of every ten conversions occurred in the central city. But the Hannover data also indicate another pattern. Two out of three conversions occurred in the privately financed rental stock. This stock has the older dwellings, and is predominantly located in the inner city area. Furthermore, the buildings converted are mostly smaller than those converted in the publicly supported stock. The latter was built after the war and is mostly situated in the suburban areas or the outer city ring.

The clearly shown preference for older central city dwellings is furthermore revealed in the geographical pattern of conversions within the central city area. Ten neighbourhoods - or census areas - accounted for more than two-thirds of all inner city conversions. On the average, 3.7 per cent of their multi-family housing stock was converted between 1980 and 1982. In their 1918-48 rental stock,

Table 4.7: Selected Characteristics of the Housing Standard in West Germany, 1978; Total Stock, Rental Housing, and Convered Flats. In percent.

Building or dwelling characteristic	All inhabited dwellings	Rental dwellings		Converted flats
Year structure built				
-1918	21	21		30
1919-1948	15	14		
1949-1964	35	38		33(a)
1964-	27	25		35(a)
	100	100		98
Building size				
1 Dwelling	24	6		
2	22	19		
3+	54	75	(3-6)	34
			(7-12)	42
			(13-)	24
	100	100		100
Dwelling size				
1-2 Rooms	8	11		29
3	20	27		44
4	31	37		17
5+	41	25		8
	100	100		100
(Average Dwelling Space, m2)	(80)	(68)		(74)
Equipment standard				
Bath, wc, central heating	59	56		64
Bath, wc	27	29		30
wc	6	8		5
No wc in dwelling	8	8		1
	100	100		100
Housing Environment				
Heavy, persistent traffic noise	32			40
Intermittent traffic noise	34			39
Little or no traffic noise	29			19
No answer	5			2
	100			100

Note: (a) 1960 used as dividing year.
Sources: Ingrid and Ulfert Herlyn, Wohnverhältnisse in der Bundesrepublik (Campus Verlag, Frankfurt/New York, 1983), pp. 43, 68; Wirtschaft und Statistik 5/1980), pp. 283 ff.; Albert Schröter, 'Ergebnisse der 1%-Stichprobe 1978 - Ein erster Überblick', Bundesbaublatt, XXIX (July 1980), p. 437; Infratest 1980, pp. 15 ff. Where percentages do not add up to 100, it is because of 'no answers'.

Table 4.8: Selected Characteristics of Converted Flats in Hannover, 1980-2.

Building characteristics	All converted flats		Privately financed rentals converted		Publicly supported rentals converted	
	Total	%	Total	%	Total	%
Year Structure Built						
-1918	858	19	858	28		
1919-1948	1,085	23	1,085	35		
1949-1968	2,473	53	965	31	1,508	96
1968-	238	5	171	6	67	4
	4,654	100	3,079	100	1,575	100
Building size						
3-15 Dwellings	2,878	62	2,390	78	488	31
16-	1,776	38	689	22	1,087	69
	4,654	100	3,079	100	1,575	100
Location						
Central city	2,758	59	2,146	69	612	39
Suburban areas	1,896	41	933	31	963	61
	4,654	100	3,079	100	1,575	100

Source: Jürgen Veser, Umfang und Struktur der Umwandlung von Miet- in Eigentumswohnungen in Hannover, pp. 20 ff.

the conversion rate was as high as 13.1 per cent. (48)

Reports of conversions in Cologne seem to confirm this pattern. Of all the conversions taking place there between 1976 and 1980, nearly 30 per cent occurred in the core of the inner city. The sales were concentrated in four particular neighbourhoods, accounting for 54 per cent of all inner city conversions. These areas are characterised by older, prestigious high-quality housing. If one takes into account only the sales of converted flats built before 1948, these four neighbourhoods accounted for over 70 per cent of the conversions of old housing in the inner city area. It is estimated that as many as 10 per cent of all flats in the inner city area were converted in the latter half of the 1970s. (49)

One may thus conclude that there is a specific pattern for West German conversions. They occur first and foremost in central city areas, and they concern older dwellings, preferably in prestigious surrounding and of good quality. The rental stock in these areas is mostly privately financed and owned. According to the 1978 national survey this stock has so far functioned as an important provider of low-cost rental housing for low income housing. Average rents have been lower than in the post-war stock, thus allowing 56 per cent of the 1978 renters of older dwellings to pay less than 15 per cent of their net income for rent. Insofar as this supply of low-cost rental housing is diminished through conversions, it may affect the chances of lower-income households to get into such housing. (50)

Moderately priced but qualitatively good housing in attractive areas thus represents a significant share of the rental flats converted into Eigentumswohnungen. Since buyers of converted flats can come from many groups beside sitting tenants, one may expect a considerable change in the socio-economic and demographic profile of households in converted buildings and areas. Given what was just said about the kind of housing most frequently involved in conversions, this could in turn indicate a considerable shift in the distribution of housing quality among residential groups.

But first, let us look at the general characteristics of West German home owners and renters, as shown by the 1978 sample census. Table 4.9 shows that the typical home owner household comprised two persons or more. The head of household was older than the average for all households. There were relatively few low-income earners among home

Table 4.9: Tenure Profile of West German Households According to Different Household Characteristics, 1978.

Household characteristics	Percentage share of households in different tenures, 1978			
	All households	Owner occupiers	Renters	Buyers of converted flats
Socio-economic position of head of household				
Own account professional managerial	8	15	4	not comparable
White-collar employees				
- upper	6	7	6	
- middle and lower	21	20	22	
Blue-collar workers	26	25	27	
Economically inactive, or not gainfully employed	38	33	41	
	100	100	100	
Monthly net income of household				
-2,000 DM	57	44	64	27
2,000-2,500	16	17	16	29
2,500-3,000	10	12	9	17
3,000-4,000	11	16	8	16
4,000-	6	11	3	8
	100	100	100	96(a)
Household Size				
1 person	30	15	38	11
2	28	28	29	34
3	18	21	16	27
4	15	20	11	22
5+	9	16	6	6
	100	100	100	100
Age of head of household				
-30	13	3	18	10
30-40	18	16	20	29
40-65	42	56	34	52
65-	27	25	28	9
	100	100	100	100

Note: (a) No answers from 3 per cent.

Sources: Wirtschaft und Statistik (3/1982), p. 207; Herlyn and Herlyn, Wohnverhältnisse in der Bundesrepublik, pp. 51, 70; Infratest 1980, passim.

owners, but relatively many heads of households with high-status occupations. Among renters, single-person households were quite frequent. Renter households were frequently found in the lower-age and lower-income brackets. They were also more often found outside the regular labour force than owner occupiers.

If anything, the table also indicates that buyers of converted flats are more like owner occupiers as a whole than they are renters. This is particularly evident for household size. Buying households as a rule consist of 2 to 4 persons; only one tenth are singles. Buyers are even more seldom found in the lower income brackets than are owner occupiers in general. Households who are in their 40s and 50s dominate among buyers just as they do among owners in general.

For this pattern to constitute a major socio-economic and demographic shift in the distribution of housing quality, some important conditions must be fulfilled. Buyers from the outside must dominate over tenant buyers. Furthermore, outside buyers must actually move into their purchased flats.

Table 4.10: Distribution of Tenant and Outside Buyers According to Type of Finance of Converted Dwelling, West Germany, 1978. In percent.

Buyer category	All dwellings	Sozial- wohnungen	Privately financed dwellings
Tenant buyers	37	46	28
Outside buyers	63	54	72
Total	100	100	100

Source: Infratest, 1980, pp. 28 ff.

As Table 4.10 shows, the first condition is fulfilled. Households outside converted buildings constitute almost two-thirds of all buyers. This pattern is even more pronounced for privately financed dwellings, while sitting tenants have bought their flats more often in the conversions of Sozialwohnungen. As already noted, it is the privately financed stock that dominates in the attractive inner city areas and the one which is more aggressively marketed to outside buyers. However, nearly one third of the buyers interviewed in the nationwide sample said they had no intention of

Table 4.11: Socio-Economic Characteristics of Households Involved in Conversions in West Germany, 1978.

Household characteristics	Percentage share of households			
	All pre-conversion tenants	Non-buying tenant movers	Buying tenants	Outside buyers moving in
Occupation status of head of household				
- gainfully employed	64	65	80	83
- not gainfully employed	36	35	20	17
	100	100	100	100
Head of household's position in present or earlier occupation				
- managerial	12	7	14	17
- qualified	52	56	61	58
- manual and other	34	35	25	24
	98	98	100	99
Monthly net income of household				
-2,000 DM	47	48	24	34
2,000-2,500	26	26	39	26
2,500-3,000	12	13	16	19
3,500-4,000	11	8	16	14
4,000-	3	1	4	5
	99	96	99	98
Household size				
1 person	21	20	6	13
2	37	32	43	28
3	21	29	23	28
4	14	13	22	26
5+	6	6	6	5
	99	100	100	100
Age of head of household				
-30	12	8	8	14
30-40	17	20	19	42
40-65	48	49	64	37
65-	23	22	8	7
	100	99	100	100

Source: Infratest, 1980, passim. (Percentages do not always add up to 100 because of no answer. Tenants who have not yet bought or moved are included in all 'pre-conversion tenants').

moving into the flats they had purchased. They had either bought it as a capital investment or for some relative. (51) Taking this into account, there were still as many as 40 to 50 per cent of the converted flats that had new residents within two or three years after the conversions began.

A closer look at the socio-economic and demographic characteristics of different groups involved in or affected by conversions confirms that there is indeed a considerable change in household composition in converted buildings and areas. The pre-conversion profile is shown in Table 4.11. What is remarkable is that the profile of non-buying tenant movers from the converted buildings almost exactly resembles that of all pre-conversion tenants.

This is not the case with buying tenants. They are more often found among the gainfully employed, in leading or qualified positions, and in the middle-income brackets than the pre-conversion tenants as a whole. Young and elderly households as well as singles and low-income earners are much more seldom found among buying tenants than their share of all pre-conversion tenants would have us believe.

A similar pattern occurs among outside buyers who move into their purchased flats. Almost all are gainfully employed, a majority of them in leading and qualified positions. A considerable share might be termed high-income earners. There are very few elderly households among the buyers. On the other hand, the share of outside buyers with heads younger than 40 is remarkably high.

There are thus strong indications that a considerable change in the composition of households does occur as a consequence of conversions. Low-income, elderly, and single-person households will be less often found in buildings and areas that have undergone conversion. Households with managerial jobs, and comprising 2 to 4 persons are quite conspicuous among buying tenants and outside buyers moving in. Middle-aged households dominate among tenant buyers, while nearly half of the outside buyers who move in are under 40 years of age. We may thus conclude that a shift towards middle-aged, middle-class, and larger households follows with the conversion of rental housing and that the decent quality housing in attractive inner city areas is increasingly enjoyed by such groups.

This is borne out by Table 4.12. Tenant buyers have bought more often in the post war-stock. Their flats are medium-sized and with modern standard of

Table 4.12: Selected Characteristics of Dwellings for Different Categories of Buyer of Converted Flats, West Germany, 1978.

Standard characteristic of converted dwelling	Buyer category			
	All buyers	Tenant buyers	All outside buyers	Outside buyers moving in
Year structure built				
-1948	25	13	32	40
1949-1960	36	43	32	27
1960-	37	42	34	31
	98	98	98	98
Dwelling Size				
1-2 Rooms	25	21	27	21
3	46	48	45	44
4	19	21	18	21
5+	9	8	9	13
	99	98	99	99
Equpiment Standard				
Bath, wc, central heating	66	70	64	62
Bath, wc	30	28	32	34
wc	2	2	2	3
No wc in dwelling	1	-	-	-
	99	100	99	99

Source: Infratest, 1980, pp. 30 ff. Percentages do not add up to 100, because of 'no answer'.

equipment. Outside buyers moving in are most often found in older flats with somewhat higher space standard. Given what we already know about the geographical distribution of older and newer dwellings, we may conclude that conversions cause an influx to the attractive inner city areas of 2- to 4-person households in their 30s and 40s with higher incomes than previous tenants.

Table 4.13: Housing Standard for Moving Tenants Before and after Conversion, West Germany, 1978-80.

Standard characteristics of dwellings	Converted dwelling	New dwelling
Year structure built		
-1948	34	25
1949-1960	47	27
1960-	19	42
	100	94
Dwelling size		
1-2 Rooms	48	42
3	37	36
4	8	14
5+	7	7
	100	99
Equipment standard		
Bath, wc, central heating	48	75
Bath, wc	27	17
wc	13	4
No wc in dwelling	12	3
	100	100
Housing Environment		
Street or crossing with heavy traffic noise	37	22
Intermittent traffic noise	49	49
No traffic noise	13	26
	99	97

Source: Infratest, 1980, pp. 65 ff. Percentages do not always add up to 100 because of 'no answer'.

What happens to the non-buying tenants? What housing standard do they enjoy after moving from their earlier, now converted flats? As Table 4.13 shows, they very frequently move to flats in the post-war rental stock, thus getting a somewhat larger and definitely more modern dwelling. On the other hand, moving to such flats mostly means moving away from the central city to the modern large estates in the suburbs or the outer city ring. This is evidenced by the figures given for noise disturbances; many renters are now living on large estates with traffic separation. As many as 61 per cent of the non-buying movers said they had been able to improve their standard of housing. However, many movers, especially among the elderly, complained about the subjective loss in standard caused by having to move from their old and well-known neighbourhood. (52)

To sum up, it seems clear that West German conversions in the late 1970s and early 1980s tended to be concentrated in attractive areas in the inner city, where privately financed older dwellings dominate. Publicly supported rental housing is more concentrated outside the inner city, and conversions of such housing consequently occur in suburban areas. It is also evident that conversions cause a change in the socio-economic and demographic profile of converted buildings and neighbourhoods. There is an influx into converted inner city flats of 2- to 4-person households with higher incomes and high-status occupations. Buying tenants tend to be middle-aged with medium incomes. Among those moving out are many single-person households, low-income earners, and elderly households. They often seem to be moving to the newer housing estates in the suburban areas.

Buyers thus resemble traditional home owners more than they do renters. They have the resources necessary to buy converted flats. They may also have had specific expectations about the economic consequences of their purchase. The question, then, is what these consequences have been and how they are distributed among different groups of households affected by conversions.

Effects on the Level and Distribution of Housing Costs

As may be recalled from the first part of this chapter, West Germany's housing policy has become increasingly enmeshed in the more general governmental policy of wealth distribution. Opportunities should be created for diffusing wealth among the citizens. An important such opportunity is the one of acquiring a home of one's own. In this perspective, the conversion of rental dwellings to Eigentumswohnungen is a means of redistributing wealth, since home owners become part of those enjoying the increase in wealth created by the dual processes of gradually repaid mortgages and increasing property values.

As we have seen, this opportunity has been more intensively used by certain groups in the conversion process; buyers do not represent a cross-section of all pre-conversion renters. It would seem that the principle of equality of opportunity has not been working in the process. Renters who have taken the opportunity to buy resemble traditional home owners in terms of income and socio-economic position more than they do all other renters.

This does not, however, allow us to immediately dismiss the argument that the conversion process may still lead to an equality in outcome. Groups affected by conversions may experience changes in housing costs which correspond to both their ability to pay and to the quality of housing they enjoy after conversions. To find out, we would need short-term and longer-term data on both gross and net housing costs for comparable groups. The long-term perspective is necessary because differing legal and economic tenure conditions will affect the (net) level of housing costs differently for home owners and renters. The only truly comparable groups are tenant buyers and continuing renters, because they inhabit dwellings of roughly the same quality before and after conversions and live in the same buildings. Unfortunately, the West German data available on conversions do not allow such a close comparison, since they do not give any detailed data on housing cost developments for continuing renters.

The following analysis focuses on (1) changes in buyer and renter outgoings as a direct result of conversions; (2) more long-term net effects of the conversion for those two groups, and (3) effects on the distribution of wealth.

Putting the cost effects in perspective is somewhat difficult, since the West German data available give almost no information on the owner-occupied sector. Between 1978 and 1982, the average rent increased by 27 per cent. There are indications that rents increased faster than renters' disposable incomes. (53) As Table 4.14 shows, the rent burden increased during this period. The share of renters paying less than 10 per cent of their net household income for rent was cut in half. At the same time, the share paying between 20 and 30 per cent increased markedly, and the share of renters paying more than 30 per cent almost doubled. If a rent-income ratio of more than 25 per cent is considered as 'burdening', then 17 per cent of all West German renters were burdened by their housing costs in 1978. The weight of the rent burden was particularly high among the elderly, the very young, and among the single-parent households. (54)

Table 4.14: Rent-Income Ratios for West German Renters, 1972-82 (percentages across)

Year	Percentage of households with a rent-income ratio				
	-10	10-20	20-30	30+	Total
1972	26	49	17	8	100
1978	20	49	21	10	100
1982	12	47	27	15	100

Sources: Herlyn and Herlyn 1983, p. 77; Hans Gerd Siedt, 'Wohnverhältnisse und Mieten im April 1982. Ergebnisse der Mikrozensus-Ergänzungserhebung', Wirtschaft und Statistik (12/1983), p. 966.

Developments within the owner-occupied sector in the late 1970s were also characterised by rising costs. Between 1977 and 1980, monthly costs for families bulding new homes increased by one third. Just between 1978 and 1980, the average monthly costs for families in new single-family homes increased from 1,825 to 2,655 DM in metropolitan areas. Some authors conclude that 'the clearly visible shift in the social composition of households building new homes since the 50s and 60s - fewer blue collar workers, more upper and middle class white collars employees - is an expression of this rise in production costs' and that many low- and middle-income earners now saving for owner occupation 'will never see their dreams fulfilled'. (55) While the average home buyer in 1970 paid 154,000 DM for his home, his counterpart in 1980 had to pay 227,000 DM - 50 per cent more. Two-thirds of buyers interviewed about the financial burden of purchase said they had had to limit their other expenditures substantially to be able to save enough for their own capital input. This input was as high as 43 per cent among home buyers in the late 1970s. (56) The effects on the socio-economic distribution of home ownership is shown in Table 4.15.

Table 4.15: Home Ownership Rates among Households Under and Over the Median Income Line, West Germany, 1972-82

Households with incomes	Home ownership rate in			
	1972	1978	1980	1982
Under the median	24.8	28.2	28.6	28.9
Over the median	39.1	43.9	47.2	49.5

Source: Rolf Kornemann, 'Zur Umwandlung von Miet- in Eigentumswohnungen: Gunstige Konstellation für kaufwillige Meiter', Der Langfristige Kredit, Heft 7 (1984), p. 222.

As many as one third of the renters in buildings undergoing conversions said they had already thought of buying an Eigentumswohnung. To them, the offer seemed an advantageous way of realising dreams of home ownership. Many had been shopping around but thought their own flat was the best value, not the least because of investments they had made while renting the flat. Among the 'unprepared' buyers, calculations based on their expectations about future rent increases - in many instances influenced by the converters' explicit or implicit threats of rent hikes - was a very important factor in the decision to buy rather than continue to rent.

The development during the 1970s thus led to a situation where 'only households with higher than average incomes would be able to become owners of single family homes without public support, this being even more pronounced in metropolitan areas'. (57) Under such circumstances the conversion of rental flats to Eigentumswohnungen could be seen as an opportunity for many households to become home owners without having to pay a price way beyond what they could afford. In effect, conversions could thus lead to more equal outcomes in terms of housing costs and wealth distribution. Interviews with buyers of converted flats do indeed reveal that economic expectation was an important motive for purchase.

What immediate changes in housing costs are experienced by households affected by West German conversions? Unfortunately, there is no way of comparing the two key groups - buying tenants and continuing renters. They remain in the same flats and buildings as before, and are thus comparable also in terms of housing quality. The only indication of changes for continuing renters is that 52 per cent of them have experienced rent increases after the conversion. However, the actual size of the increase is not known. (58)

Table 4.16: Factors Most Important in Households' Decision to Buy a Converted Flat, West Germany, 1978-80.

Motive for purchase	Household category		
	'Prepared' tenant buyers	'Unprepared' tenant buyers	Outside buyers
Advantageous way of getting into owner occupation	100	56	55
Flat of better value than other offers	36	18	78
Future rent increases as heavy as increases caused by purchase	33	52	–
To capitalise on earlier investments in the flat	29	31	–

Source: Infratest, 1980, pp. 41 ff. Percentages do not add up to 100 because of multiple answers.

What remains possible is to compare the changes experienced by tenant buyers and non-buying tenants moving out. Table 4.17 shows that buying tenants suffered an immediate surge in monthly outlays of 100 per cent. Their gross outlays thus took 24 per cent of their income after conversion; before, the rent-income ratio was 12 per cent. Since moving tenants now live in a somewhat larger flat, the comparison should concern pre- and post-conversion rent per square metre. This leads to a rent increase of 25 per cent after moving from the converted flat.

Available data do not provide any information about the changes in housing costs for outside buyers. One indication is that only 18 per cent in this group decided to buy the particular converted flat because their earlier dwelling was too expensive. (59) This could mean that the majority of outside buyers do experience cost increases as a result of conversions. If so, we may conclude that West German conversions have a tendency to drive the costs of housing upward for most households affected by conversions. Those who stay and buy see their outlays doubled, while continuing renters probably do not experience such a dramatic increase. Moving tenants change their standard upward, but also incur higher rents.

Table 4.17: Housing Cost Consequences for Buying Tenants and Non-buying Tenant Movers in West Germany, 1979-80.

Aspects of housing costs	Household category	
	Buying tenants	Non-buying tenant movers
Net average pre-conversion rent		
- DM per month	291	252
- DM per square metre	3.73	3.68
Average pre-conversion rent-income ratio, %	12	13
Average post-conversion housing expenditures		
- DM per month	583(a)	333
- DM per square metre	7.47	4.61
Average post-conversion rent-income ratio, %	24(a)	17

Note: (a) Gross outlays
Source: Infratest, 1980, passim.

However, these conclusions refer to short-term effects. They concern gross outlays. If one includes the effects of tax regulations and value appreciation, the actual - and long-term - costs of buyers may well turn out to be quite different from gross expenditures. In the longer run, buyers may be better off than renters in terms of actual costs for the same standard of housing. Also in the longer run, a redistribution of wealth in favour of buyers may occur as a result of conversions.

First of all, the buyer repays his mortgage in constant annuities. Thus, his outgoings are the same year after year, while the renter may suffer annual rent increases. As was said earlier, average West German rents increased by 7 per cent annually in the

late 1970s and early 1980s. Second, flat owners are
entitled to deduct 5 per cent of the purchase price
of their dwelling annually during the first eight
years of ownership. Given the average purchase price
for tenant buyers of 65,000 DM and a tax rate of 25
per cent, the buyer's actual monthly cost is lowered
by 68 DM, or 12 per cent. However, the buyer's costs
still exceed those of the non-buying mover by 55 per
cent.

Table 4.18: Changes in Wealth for the Average West
German Buyer of a Converted Flat, 1978-82. In DM,
nominal prices.

End of year	Property value	Repayable mortgage	Net value of wealth
1978	80,000	48,000	32,000
1979	82,400	46,600	35,800
1980	84,900	45,000	39,900
1981	87,400	43,400	44,000
1982	90,000	41,700	48,300

(See note 60 for comments about assumptions
underlying these calculations.)

When the increase in property value is taken into
account, this difference is reversed. (60) Even at
the low annual increase rate of 3 per cent, the net
value of wealth for the average tenant buyer is
almost double that of the average renter already in a
few years after purchase. The renter suffers annual
rent increases, which gradually diminish the
difference between rent payments and net outgoings of
the buyer. This in turn diminishes the annual amount
a renter could 'save' from not having the high
outlays of the owner. Consequently, the wealth
increase from his savings becomes slower, and the gap
to the wealth increase enjoyed by the property owner
widens year by year.

Admittedly, these figures are the result of an
analysis of averages based on certain assumptions.
However, they allow us to pinpoint the general
direction of the effects on the distribution of
housing costs. It seems difficult to retain the
position that conversions do indeed provide for
equality of outcome. Buyers are unproportionally
found among middle and higher income households and
in more prestigious occupations. In many ways they
resemble the average home owner more than the average
renter. Households who continue as renters are more
often found among the elderly, the very young and the

lower-income households. Since the longer-term development of housing costs after conversions tend to favour buyers, the final result is inequality of outcome; the economically resourceful have greater opportunities to buy, and they fare much better in terms of final outcome.

Table 4.19: Changes in Wealth for the Average West German Renter Staying as Renter after Conversion, 1978-82. In DM, nominal prices

End of year	Annual rent payment	Difference between owner net outlays and rent, or amount 'savable'	Net value of wealth
1978	-	17,000	17,000
1979	4,365	1,755	19,600
1980	4,670	1,450	22,000
1981	5,000	1,120	24,300
1982	5,350	770	26,230

(See note 60 for comments on the assumptions made for these calculations.)

In 1978, a commission of housing experts wrote that

(I)t is only possible to achieve a higher home ownership rate and the broadest possible distribution of wealth from real estate through conversions of rental flats into Eigentums- wohnungen. Conversions will increase the supply as well as the demand, since the price of old flats is far lower than that of newly produced dwellings. (61)

It is true that the conversion process has resulted in an increased number of home owners. In this respect, the objective of more home ownership is reached. If, however, the goal is to reach new socio- economic and demographic strata, the result is less comforting. Measured in such terms, conversions do not seem effective in broadening the benefits of home ownership or the distribution of wealth.

Umwandlungen, Housing Markets and the Availability of Rental Housing

West German conversions in the late 1970s and early 1980s were taking place in a housing market characterised by growing imbalances in certain parts of that market. On the supply side, it is true that there was a good match between total stock and total household figures. However, new production of rental housing decreased from about 400,000 dwellings in 1973 to only 60,000 at the end of the 1970s. The decrease was especially marked in metropolitan areas. Investments were increasingly directed towards the existing stock, where modernisation, conversion and other measures led to a continuing decrease in the supply of centrally located, priceworthy rental housing. Furthermore, the supply of Sozialwohnungen - which are especially produced to provide housing for less resourceful households - decreased. This happens when the number of Sozialwohnungen freed from the social housing policy bonds by repayment of public support exceeds the annual volume of new social housing production. In fact, the number of pre-1964 Sozialwohnungen dropped by 20 per cent between 1972 and 1978.

On the demand side, problems have increased for low-income households in their search for decent priceworthy rental housing. Their ability to pay has decreased in relative terms. More higher-income households are directing their demand towards the supply of housing which would seem best suited to the purses of low-income families. This is an important factor behind the particular direction of Umwandlungen described earlier. (62)

With this shrinking base of low-rent decent housing in central cities a particular West German rental policy problem becomes more accentuated. The long waiting lists for Sozialwohnungen become even longer because an increasing share of such dwellings is occupied by households which did qualify under the income rules when they moved in, but now earn far more than these income rules for social renting allow. Since such households quite naturally won't move, there is an increasing Fehlbelegung - 'wrong occupancy' - in the social housing stock; it is estimated at 30 per cent in 1983. Households who do qualify under the income rules thus find their way into low-rent social housing blocked by these 'wrong' households. (63)

Those who argue for conversions hold that Umwandlungen would help in solving the rental market problems. The premature repayment of public subsidies connected with conversions of Sozialwohnungen would help towards financing new such dwellings, especially because public housing companies are obliged by statute to reinvest in such housing. Furthermore, much of the problem of Fehlbelegung would disappear because the resourceful households now 'wrongly' occupying social housing would be the first to buy their flats. All in all, conversions would bring more money into the housing sector, something that would increase the capacity for investments in new production. Low-income earners would thus be better off in terms of housing chances than if conversions were brought to a halt. (64)

All converted flats which are occupied by the owner are of course lost to the rental market. They constitute between 80 and 90 per cent of all conversions. The 1978 national conversion survey found that 12 per cent of the converted flats were bought by investors without any intention of own use. These apartments are probably rented to others, since investors can make certain tax deductions that way. Still, 45,000 rental dwellings are removed from the rental market annually. As was noted earlier, the increase in inhabited dwellings since 1978 has occurred almost totally in home ownership; the rental sector has not changed in absolute terms. Since demolitions could not be responsible for this development, (65) the only explanation left is that of conversion. Given the earlier description of the West German rental market it would seem that conversions have aggravated the situation.

On the other hand, all converted flats would not have become immediately available to the rental market even if they had not been converted. A large proportion of the renters – especially in Sozialwohnungen – would have no motive for moving out to another flat because they pay such low rents. The West German discussion indicates that the expected length of tenancy in social housing is close to 20 years. As will be recalled from the British debate, the loss of relets should be based on that figure. Assuming a similar length of tenancy in the privately financed rental stock, we thus arrive at an estimated annual loss of immediately available rental housing of 2,500 flats if the volume of sales is around 50,000 dwellings. As one author argues, selling to resourceful social tenants could hardly be seen as 'dissipation of rental housing', especially when the volume of empty or difficult-to-let flats is increasing. (66)

However, this argument concerns only the 'wrong occupancy' problem in Sozialwohnungen. Several analyses of the West German rental market stress the importance of the privately financed stock of old rental housing in inner cities as a reservoir of good value rental housing for households with moderate incomes. In his study of Umwandlungen in Hannover, Veser tries to estimate the rental markets effects in inner city areas with high conversion activity. Assuming the same rate of old flat conversions up to 1992 as the one actually occurring in 1980-82 he concludes that by 1992, the pre-1948 rental stock in high conversion areas will have diminished by 23 per cent. In the 1949-68 stock, about 16 per cent would disappear from the rental market. Even if the conversion rate dropped by a third, the losses up to 1992 would be 19 and 13 per cent, respectively. (67) Could this loss be compensated for by new production financed by income from sales and from repaid subsidies? As noted earlier, public housing companies are obliged to use the replacement value as the basis for determining the sales price of Sozialmietwohnungen. They are also obliged to use the income from sales for housing purposes. One could thus argue that conversions in fact free capital for new production. On the other hand, two factors combine to make such new production less in volume than the conversions. First, the replacement value is among other things based on the age of the dwelling. The older the flat the larger the depreciation factor, and the lower the replacement value. A company selling many flats from the 1950s and 1960s would thus not get enough income to finance new production of the same number of flats as those converted. Furthermore, the sales price must be set in such a way as not to exceed a 'reasonable' housing cost/income ratio. This may at times lead to prices even below the already depreciated value of the unit. In Bremen, the public housing company Neue Heimat sold Sozialmietwohnungen in 1980 at prices that were 10 per cent below the replacement value. Under such circumstances, new production filling the rental housing gap created by conversions will not be possible. (68)

Conversions in West Germany thus strengthen the tendency for construction of new Sozialmietwohnungen to go down at the same time as construction for ownership goes up. Umwandlungen may free some resources, but the overall result will be a dwindling supply of good value rental housing. In the longer run, this leads to diminishing chances for new households to find accommodation in such housing.

Umwandlung in Eigentumswohnungen and Residential Influence

West German renters have a comparatively strong influence over their housing situation. Their security of tenure is strong; most renters can stay at least three years after the notification of conversion. Their freedom of disposal is also comparatively great; West German renters themselves determine the interior standard of the flat since they are responsible for carpeting, wall-papering, and kitchen equipment. Furthermore, they have a legally guaranteed right to take their furniture and equipment with them when they move out of the flat. (69) And according to the 1978 housing survey, at least 10 per cent of the renters had invested in modernising their flats between 1973 and 1978. Another survey showed that 16 per cent of the renters planned to make such investments in the near future. One fifth of surveyed renters are reported to have made investments of 5,000 DM or more. (70)

As was shown earlier, an important motive for purchase among tenant buyers was the desire to protect the investments made in their dwelling. Many may not have known about their right to take such investments out when moving. Generally, renters affected by conversion activities seem to have known very little about their rights and possibilities of influencing their own situation. About 40 per cent of all renters, and more than half of all tenants moving out said they did not know about their security of tenure - about their right to stay. Only a third reported common tenant meetings, common visits to Tenant Unions, or contacts with lawyers or public agencies to try to assess - and assert - their rights. Nowhere was there any formation of a tenants' interest organisation. In fact, only 5 per cent of the tenants reported that they had been able to prolong the security of tenure to the legal three or five years through negotiations with the landlord or converter. (71)

When tenants buy their flats, they get the strongest possible security of tenure. They also get larger freedom of disposal. Now, they can sublet the flat, redecorate or make other investments without having to worry about possible losses at the time of moving. Flat owners also have a say in the running maintenance and care of the building through membership and participation in the flatowner association.

As it turns out, most buyers are satisfied with the purchase; 80 per cent say they are happy with

177

their decision. About 90 per cent are satisfied or very satisfied with the flat and the housing environment. There is, however, also a group of not so satisfied buyers. Among the outside buyers, a sixth were unable to get into the purchased flat because of the security-of-tenure regulations protecting the sitting tenant. In this group of less satisfied buyers, as many as 22 per cent regretted their decision to buy. As was the case with tenants, these outside buyers seem to have been badly informed about the legal and economic framework of conversions. As many as 19 per cent did not know about the rental bindings of the Sozialwohnung they bought. Of these unknowing buyers, 43 per cent said they would not have bought had they known they would not be able to take over the flat immediately upon purchase. As a result of this lack of knowledge, many buyers of purpose-bound flats will not be able to utilise the possibilities of exemption from the property purchase tax (cf. above, p.143) (72)

In conclusion, conversions lead to an increase in residential influence for buyers who are able to get into their purchased flats. In the process as such, however, neither buyers nor non-buyers seem to be able to exert a decisive influence unless they are well informed about their rights. That influence lies where the initiative is, that is, with the seller/converter.

Umwandlung and the Public Purse

Insofar as buyers of converted flats are new owners – that is, did not earlier enjoy tax privileges from their housing situation – conversions mean that tax incomes will be foregone by the public sector. As may be recalled, a German home owner can deduct 5 per cent of the purchase value of his home from taxable income during the first eight years of ownership. This he can do as long as the value does not exceed certain limits.

Some figures indicate that sales prices in 1978 averaged around 1,200 DM per square metre, at least for Sozialwohnungen converted by public housing companies. (73) Assuming an average flat size of 70 square metres, and a tax rate of 30 per cent, and further assuming annual sales of 50,000 flats, the tax deductions over the following eight years would amount to 500 million DM. If prices of converted flats have increased by 5 per cent annually between 1978 and 1984, and conversion volumes have been 50,000 flats annually, the value of the tax deductions for the 1984 conversions over eight years comes to 675 million DM. Put together, the eight year deductions for each of the conversion years 1978 to 1984 amount to a total sum of 4.1 billion DM. Flats converted before 1983 were exempt from the purchase price tax, which also adds to the loss of tax revenues. Of course, some tax money could flow in from property taxes, especially if property values are adjusted upwards in assessments subsequent to the conversion. On the other hand, Eigentumswohnungen are very favourably treated by property tax regulations for the first ten years after purchase - (cf. above p. 143) - which means that the possible inflow would be but a trickle.

A central argument in the conversion debate has been that the money flowing in from sales and repayments of subsidies would be used for new production of rental housing. How tenable is that argument? As was said earlier, West German public housing companies cannot sell at prices higher than the replacement value of the converted unit. Furthermore, this value includes depreciation according to the age of the flat. Judging from the 1980 report of an independent expert commission, the 1978 replacement value of flats in the pre-1968 stock was 25 per cent lower than that of a new 1978 flat. (74) As indicated by Table 4.8, converted Sozialmietwohnungen in a city like Hannover are predominantly found in the pre-1968 stock. Selling such flats at replacement value thus seems a losing proposition, especially if the company is committed to building new rental flats to replace the ones being converted. As the years pass, the depreciation factor drives the replacement down. At the same time, the costs of producing new flats increase. Just betwen 1979 and 1981, the production costs of new rental flats supported through the First Subsidy Programme increased from 132,000 to 173,000 DM, or by 31 per cent. (75)

In turn, this could be taken as an indication that the more pre-1968 Sozialmietwohnungen are converted, the more government support is needed - particularly through the First Subsidy Programme (cf. above p. 135) - if the volume of sales is to be replaced by new rental dwellings. Just between 1979 and 1981, the volume of support from this programme to new Sozialmietwohnungen in multi-family housing increased from 1.75 to 2.82 billion DM. However, the volume of rental units stayed the same, or about 35,000 annually. (76)

All in all, conversions thus seem to strain the

public purse in two ways. First, they increase the volume of tax income foregone by bringing more households into the circle of tax-privileged home owners. Second, the need for replacement production increases the demand for public subsidies which are already rapidly increasing as a result of increasing production costs.

Conclusion

West German Umwandlungen from tenancy to owner occupation seem to be a result of both conscious governmental policy and market developments. The legal and economic framework for new Eigentumswohnungen was extended in 1977 to provide tax privileges also for the acquistion of such dwellings in the existing rental stock. The motive for this was to promote the political goal of spreading wealth to more and more households. Subsequent policy statements make it clear that West German conversions are seen as part and parcel of a supplementary shift in governmental policy. At the same time, increasing prices for single-family housing, favourable rent/income ratios for large numbers of social renters - the Fehlbelegung phenomenon - and an increasing demand for housing in inner cities combined to create a dynamic market for conversions.

Several features combine to make the context of West German tenure conversions quite unique. The initiative to conversions lies with the seller, just like in the USA. But unlike the American scene, several seller categories operate; private landlords sell directly to buyers, or sell to converters who in turn sell to households, and public housing companies sell to buyers. As in the USA, buyers are not only sitting tenants but also outside households. However, West German protection of sitting tenants' security of tenure is remarkably strong compared to in the USA. Furthermore, it differs with respect to submarkets; tenant protection is stronger in publicly subsidised than in privately financed housing. This latter stock suffers no limitations in terms of sales prices; sellers may charge whatever price the market allows. The sale of publicly supported dwellings by public housing companies is guided by the replacement value of the unit being converted, at least when sales are directed towards sitting tenants. Finally, the privately financed and publicly supported rental stocks differ with regard to age and location. The former contains both prewar and postwar units, and dominates in inner city areas.

The latter is wholly postwar and is predominantly found in the new neighbourhoods built since the 1950s.

All these variations in the context suggest that the effects of conversions to Eigentumswohnungen will be highly dependent on the strategies used by sellers. What units they select and what strategies they pursue towards sitting tenants will have a very strong impact on the socio-economic outcome of conversions. In all likelihood, converters are drawn to the most attractive and qualitatively best segments of the rental housing stock. Sellers with a large share of Sozialmietwohnungen may prefer to sell as many units as possible to the sitting tenants, while converters of privately financed dwellings may be more aggressively marketing to outside buyers, all because of differences in tenant protection and price regulations.

This is the picture emerging from our account here. West German conversions have occurred most frequently in larger cities, particularly in attractive areas with good housing. Conversions of Sozialmietwohnungen occur more often in suburban neighbourhoods, while older, inner city dwellings dominate among conversions in the privately financed stock. In this latter stock, conversions are frequently done via a special converter; this is much less prominent in conversions from the stock of public housing companies. Such companies also sell much more frequently to their sitting tenants, while the majority of privately financed flats being converted are sold to outside buyers.

The socio-economic profile of pre-conversion tenants did not differ significantly from that of all West German households in 1978, except for a slight tendency towards fewer single-person and low-income households. These differences were somewhat more pronounced if one compares only with all West German renters. Still, there would indeed be a socio-economic spread of home ownership if a cross-section of pre-conversion tenants formed the majority of buyers of converted flats.

There is, however, a rather high degree of movements following conversions. As many as 55 per cent of the pre-conversion tenants move out within a couple of years after conversions. Furthermore, movers and buyers have very different profiles. Non-buying movers represent a cross-section of all pre-conversion tenants, while tenant buyers have more qualified jobs, somewhat higher incomes, are very frequently middle-aged, but seldom found among singles, the very young or the elderly. The same is true for outside buyers moving in. Over time, West German conversions thus seem to lead to a concentration of households with good ability to pay in the more attractive areas of multi-family housing.

Good ability to pay seems to be a prerequisite for households who want to use the opportunity of home ownership offered through conversions. The short-term effect of buying one's rented flat is to drive the monthly gross outlays on housing dramatically upward; buying tenants see their outlays doubled. Continuing tenants also suffer cost increases, as do non-buying tenant movers. Over time, however, buyers enjoy a favourable accumulation of wealth compared to renters.

The economic outcome thus seems to be one of more inequality; those who have a good ability to pay and can afford to buy, enjoy a favourable growth of wealth compared to those who lack the resources necessary to use the opportunity provided by conversions. To a considerable extent, this unequal development is brought about by the differences in legal and economic policy measures towards the different tenures. In sum, conversions do increase the number of households in owner occupation. But the West German experiences so far cast some doubt on the proposition that conversions also mean a spread of home ownership to new socio-economic strata.

Proponents argue that conversions will have a positive effect on the public purse. Where subsidised housing is converted, the government no longer has to pay subsidies. Housing authorities will have resources freed for housing production without additionally burdening the taxpayer. Our analysis of the West German situation does not seem to corroborate this proposition. Subsidies repaid and money earned from sales do not match the costs of replacing converted units through new production. More governmental subsidies are needed at the same time as governmental incomes decrease because of the increasing number of households in tax-privileged housing.

Notes
1. Uwe Wullkopf, 'Wohnungsbau und Wohnungs-baupolitik in der Bundesrepublik Deutschland', Politik und Zeitgeschichte, Band 10 (1982), p. 11.
2. For the background of the 1950 Act see Hellmut Wollman, 'Housing Policy in West Germany – Between State Intervention and the Market', in Klaus

von Beyme and Manfred G. Schmidt (eds.), Policy-making in the Federal Republic of Germany (Gower, Farnborough, 1984) p. 138f.

3.   Wullkopf, p. 11 f.

4.   Ruth Becker, 'Grundzüge der Wohnungs-politik in der BRD seit 1949', in Klaus Habermann-Niesse et al. (Hrsg.), Alternativen in der Wohnungspolitik (Alternative Kommunalpolitik, e.V., Bielefeld, 1983), p. 12 f.

5.   Wollkopf, p. 12.

6.   Becker, p. 14 f.; Wollman, p. 000 (15 ff.).

7.   Wullkopf, p. 15. Cf. Becker, p. 17.

8.   Wollman, p. 145.

9.   Wullkopf, p. 14. Cf. below, p. 000

10.   C.H.M Hass-Klau, 'The Housing Shortage in Germany's Major Cities', Built Environment, 8, (1983), p. 60. Cf. Wullkopf, p. 20.

11.   Wollman, p. 000 (25 ff.).

12.   'Sozialer Wohnungsbau 1981' Wirtschaft und Statistik (9/1982) p. 675.

13.   Knut Gustafsson, 'Strukturfragen der Wohnungseigentumspolitik', Bundesbaublatt, XXIX (July 1980), p. 426, f.

14.   Wullkopf, p. 23.

15.   Rolf Kornemann, 'Mehr Wohneigentum durch Umwandlungen?', Der Langfristige Kredit, Heft 20 (1983), p. 630.

16.   Oskar Schneider, 'Die soziale Erneuerung der Wohnungspolitik - politische Losungsalter-nativen', Politische Studien, 33 (1982), p. 567.

17.   Deutsches Volksheimstättenwerk, Das Wohn-ungseigentum (Deutsches Volksheimstättenwerk, Köln, 1981), p. 8.

18.   Gesetz uber das Wohnungseigentum und das Dauerwohnrecht (Wohnungseigentumsgesetz), Sections 5-6, 10-15.

19.   Ibid., Sections 16, 21-29. See also Heinz Peters, Die Verwaltungsbeirate im Wohnungseigentum. Praktische Tips für die Besitzer von Eigentumswohn-ungen (Bauverlag GmbH, Wiesbaden und Berlin, 1977), pp. 31 ff. The association may also elect a Board from among the flat owners, to assist the Administrator in the management of common property.

20.   Deutschen Mieterbund, Mieterschutz '82 (Deutschen Mieterbund, e. V., Kohn, 1982), p. 24 f.; Hans Häring, 'Fragen bei der Umwandlung von Mietwohnungen in Eigentumswohnungen', Zeitschrift für gemeinnütziges Wohnungswesen in Bayern, 72 (1982), p. 351 f. According to Haring, the government plans to increase the legally guaranteed period of stay from three to five years. See also Deutsches

Volksheimstättenwerk, Zweckbindung von Sozialwohn-ungen (Deutsches Volksheimstattenwerk, Köln, 1981), pp. 72 ff.

21. Deutschen Mieterbund, p. 25ff.; Haring, p. 351 ff.; Deutsches Volksheimstättenwerk, Zweckbin-dung von Sozialwohnungen, p. 71.

22. Deutschen Mieterbund, p. 26 ff.; Deutsches Volksheimstättenwerk, Zweckbindung von Sozialwohn-ungen, pp. 68ff.

23. Deutschen Mieterbund, p. 27 f. See also Taschenbuch fur den Wohnungswirt (Hammonia Verlag, Hamburg, 1981), p. 45 ff.

24. Deutsches Volksheimstättenwerk, Das Wohn-ungseigentum, p. 45 ff.

25. Ibid., p. 47. See also Jürgen Veser, Umwandlung von Miet in Eigentumswohnungen. Die Folgen fur den Betroffenen und die Auswirkungen auf den Wohnungsmarkt (Institut fur Stadtforschung, Berlin, 1982), p. 7.

26. Deutsches Volksheimstättenwerk, Das Wohn-ungseigentum, p. 47 ff.

27. Ibid., p. 49. Cf. Veser 1982, p. 7.

28. Deutsches Volksheimstattenwerk, Das Wohn-ungseigentum p. 48.

29. Anonymous, 'Erwerb von Eigentum fällt sich oft leichter als bedacht Folge des intensiven Sparens', Bundesbaublatt, XXXI (August 1982), p. 532. Cf. Ernst-Gunter Schmidt, Die Eigentumswohnung hat viele Vorteile (Bauverlag GmbH, Wiesbaden und Berlin, 1977), on the methods of financing an Eigentumswohnung, as seen from the viewpoint of prospective buyers.

30. Alfred Wappler, 'Und sie ist doch eine gute Sache. Die Umwandlung von Mietwohnungen', Gemeinnutziges Wohnungswesen, 33 (1980), p. 246.

31. Deutsches Volksheimstättenwerk, Das Wohn-ungseigentum, p. 18 ff.

32. Jürgen Veser, Umfang und Struktur der Umwandlung von Miet- in Eigentumswohnungen in Hannover (Institut für Stadtforschung, Berlin, 1984), pp. 38 ff.

33. Infratest, Folgen der Umwandlung und Veräusserung von Mietwohnungen als Eigentumswohn-ungen (Infratest GmbH, Munchen, 1980), p. 24 ff.

34. Ibid., pp. 70 ff.

35. Ibid., Anhang, p. 21 ff.

36. Karl-Heinz Seyfried, 'Zugzwang', Capital, 20 (Heft 9/1981), p. 128.

37. Knut Gustafsson, 'Mietenniveau - Mieten-strukturen. Nachlese zur Wohnungsstichprobe 1978', Bundesbaublatt, XXXII (April 1983), p. 200.

38. Wappler, pp. 244 ff.
39. Veser 1984, p. 3.
40. Ude Jens Frerics, 'Umwandlung - nach Zuversicht und Routine ein Stillstand?' Wohnungs-eigentum, 34 (Heft 2/1983) pp. 3 ff.
41. Infratest, p. 20.
42. Norges Offentlige Utredninger, NOU 1980:6, Eierleiligheter (Universitetsforlaget, Oslo, 1980), p. 34.
43. Lothar Herberger et al., 'Bestand und Struktur der Gebaude und Wohnungen. Ergebnis der 1%-Wohnungsstichprobe 1978', Wirtschaft und Statistik, (5/1980), p. 176.
44. Ibid.
45. Cf. figures given under 'Bautätigkeit' in Wirtschaft und Statistik (5/1981), p. 348; (4/1982), p. 299; (4/1983), p. 337 ff. It should be noted that losses from demolition, etc. were about 12,000 annually after 1978; cf. ibid. (10/1981), p. 724; (11/1982), p. 819. Cf. note 65.
46. According to the 1982 microcensus, about 122,000 Eigentumswohnungen with completion years 1979 and earlier had been added to owner occupation in the multi-family housing stock from early 1980 to early 1982. Even if some of these were new production from 1978-9, one arrives at a conversion rate of 50,000 dwellings annually; cf. Wirtschaft und Statistik (12/1983), p. 962. Veser estimates a volume of at least 70,000 after 1978 (communication to the author May 1985).
47. Infratest, p. 16.
48. Veser 1984, ch. 5.
49. Hartmut Meuter, 'Eigentumsbildung im Wohnungbestand - Die Betroffenheit von Altbauquar-tieren durch Umwandlung von Mietwohnungen', in Adalbert Evers et al. (Hrsg.) Kommunale Wohnungs-politik (Birkhäuser Verlag, Basel/Boston/Stuttgart, 1983), pp. 192 ff.
50. Ibid., p. 182 ff.
51. Infratest 1980, pp. 30, 44.
52. Ibid., p. 68.
53. Hans Gerd Siedt, 'Wohnverhältnisse und Mieten im April 1982. Ergebnisse der Mikrozensus-Ergänzungserhebung' Wirtschaft und Statistik, (12/1983), p. 961; Manfrer Euler 'Wohnungsmieter und Wohnungsmieten im Januar 1983. Ergebnis der Einkommens- und Verbrauchsstichprobe', Wirtschaft und Statistik, (5/1984), p. 467.
54. Uwe Wullkopf, 'Ist der Abbau sozialer Disparitaten in der Wohnungsversorgung noch lohnendes Ziel der Wohnungspolitik?', in Institut

Wohnen und Umwelt (Hrsg.), <u>Wohnungspolitik am Ende?</u>
<u>Analysen und Perspektiven</u> (Westdeutscher Verlag
GmbH, Opladen, 1981), p. 17 ff.
55. Renate Petzinger and Marlo Riege, <u>Die neue</u>
<u>Wohnungsnot. Wohnungswunder Bundesrepublik</u> (VSA-
Verlag, Hamburg, 1981), p. 14 ff.
56. Lisa Höflich-Häberlein and Reinhold
Weissbarth, 'Ohne Fleiss kein Preis', <u>Bundesbau-</u>
<u>blatt</u>, XXXI (September 1982), p. 621.
57. Gustafsson, 'Strukturfragen der Wohnungseigentumspolitik', p. 428.
58. Infratest, 1980, p. 60.
59. Ibid., p. 45.
60. The figures in Tables 4.18 and 4.19 are
based on the following assumptions. The average
tenant buyer in 1978 paid 65,000 DM for his flat,
enjoying a rebate on the usual purchase price of
15,000 DM. He put in about 17,000 DM of his own. His
48,000 DM debt was divided into annuity loans. Two-
thirds carried an interest of 8.5 per cent, and a 1
per cent repayment. One third of the debt carried an
interest of 5 per cent and a 7 per cent amortisation.
This latter loan is repaid in 12 years. The property
value increase is calculated at 3 per cent of the
unrebated price. Buyers have an average tax rate of
25 per cent. Their outlays on housing include payment
to the common maintenance; the average net monthly
outlays amount to 510 DM. Renters experience an
annual rent increase of 7 per cent, and enjoy an
interest on their savings amounting to 4 per cent.
Staying rents are assumed to have an increase in rent
of 20 per cent immediately upon conversion. This way
of modelling the development is also used in GEWOS,
<u>Verkauf von Gebrauchtwohnungen - Empfehlungen einer</u>
<u>unabhängigen Kommission des GEWOS e.V. an den</u>
<u>Gesetzgeber</u>, (GEWOS, e.V., Bonn, 1979), p. 46.
61. Ibid., p. 2.
62. Veser 1982, pp. 31 ff.
63. Wullkopf, 'Wohnungsbau und Wohnungsbaupolitik in der Bundesrepublik Deutschland', p. 14.
64. GEWOS, <u>Wohnungseigentum aus dem Mietwoh-</u>
<u>nungsbestand. Überlegungen, Hinweise und Anregungen</u>
<u>einer unabhangigen GEWOS e.V.-Fachkommission</u> (Ham-
monia-Verlag GmbH, Hamburg, 1980), pp. 15 ff.
65. Anonymous, 'Abgänge von Gebauden, Gebaudeteilen und Wohnungen 1981', <u>Wirtschaft und</u>
<u>Statistik</u> (11/1982), p. 818 f. The article indicates
that only about 12,000 dwellings in multi-family
housing were demolished annually around 1980. It is
notable that this figure represents the difference
between new production and estimated conversion in

1980; this seems to support our conclusion that conversions are the main cause of the zero-growth of the rental market.

66. Kornemann, 'Mehr Wohnungseigentum durch Umwandlungen?', p. 628 ff.

67. Veser 1984, pp. 86 ff.

68. Wappler 1980, pp. 246, 250. These practices also govern sales of privately financed flats owned and managed by these companies.

69. Wolfgang Kröning, 'Alternativen zum gewohnlichen Wohnungsbau. Motive, Tendenzen, Beispiele fur veränderte Formen des Massenwohnungsbaus', in Institut Wohnen und Umwelt (Hrsg.), Wohnungspolitik am Ende? Analysen und Perspektiven, p. 76.

70. Rudolf Halberstadt, 'Rechtsprobleme der Wohnungsmodernisierung durch Mieter', in Institut Wohnen und Umwelt (Hrsg.), Wohnungspolitik am Ende? Analysen und Perspektiven, p. 136 ff.

71. Infratest 1980, p. 74 ff.

72. Ibid., pp. 49 ff.

73. GEWOS 1980, p. 53.

74. Ibid., p. 29.

75. 'Sozialer Wohnungsbau 1979' Wirtschaft und Statistik (9/1980), pp. 624 ff.; 'Sozialer Wohnungsbau 1981' ibid., (9/1982), pp. 675 ff.

76. Ibid., pp. 625 and 676, respectively.

Chapter Five

THE EFFECTS OF TENURE CONVERSIONS: A COMPARATIVE EVALUATION

In the opening chapter, I presented the main arguments for and against tenure conversions. On most issues raised in connection with such conversions, I found two distinct opinions about the possible effects. Furthermore, it was shown that in arriving at these differing judgements, proponents and opponents alike are heavily biased by their opinions on government's role in housing, as well as by their views on the vices and virtues of different housing tenures. Thus, it was possible to link the two main lines of argument over tenure conversions to two principal schools of thought on government's role in housing. In line with earlier comparative housing studies, we named these schools 'supplementary' and 'comprehensive'.

In the chapters that followed, the effects of conversions have been studied in the United States, Great Britain, and West Germany. The mode of presentation could be characterised as configurative description; for each country, the presentation follows the outline presented in Chapter 1 (cf. p. 25f). As far as available data allow, I have shown the volume and spatial pattern of conversions, and tried to assess the effects on the availabililty of rental housing. Furthermore, I have described what is known about the pre- and post-conversion socio-economic profile of households in converted buildings and areas, to allow an assessment of conversions' effects on housing segregation. In a similar way, data on pre- and post-conversion housing costs for different groups of affected households have been presented, to enable us to judge the distributive effects of conversions. The possible consequences for the public sector economy have been estimated on the basis of available data from empirical studies.

What such configurative descriptions enable us to do is to confront the arguments of supplementarists and comprehensivists with empirical findings and to assess their tenability country by country. But we want to carry this analysis one step further. The aim is to find out if there are any generalisable patterns occurring in each country regardless of differences in the political, legal, or economic context. If the same pattern of consequences is found despite differences in the 'social relations of housing provision' existing in each country, then we are in a much stronger position when it comes to assessing the validity of the different views on tenure conversions. Furthermore, we may be in a better position to assess the effects of the broader housing policies proposed by supplementarists and comprehensivists.

Conversion Volumes and Rates and the Availability of Rental Housing

In brief, proponents of conversions hold that there will be only limited consequences of conversions in the rental market. Conversions will free money for new housing, and production will substitute for dwellings lost to owner-occupation. Besides, many of the units sold would have continued to be occupied by the present renters for many years, and would not have been on the market anyway. Opponents fear there will be substantial effects at least on certain segments of the rental stock. Low-cost but decent rental housing in inner cities will be particularly hit by conversions. Capital flowing from conversions will not suffice as a substitute for converted units because of differences in historic production costs. Besides, such capital will more probably flow into other types of housing production, thus inflicting considerable losses to the rental sector.

General patterns are difficult to discern in the volumes of conversions of the three countries studied here. Studies are made at only one point in time, as in the United States, or not at all, as in West Germany. In the British case, exact figures for annual sales are available. However, it should be remembered that they concern council house sales only; information about the substantial number of conversions from the private rental sector would add to the British picture.

Absolute numbers in themselves do not carry much information. They are much more interesting when put in relation to other data about the housing sector.

In Table 5.1, the average annual volumes of conversions - as they can be determined by existing data or estimated with some credibility - are related to national rental stocks, and to volumes of rental housing production.

Table 5.1: Average Annual Conversion Volumes in Relation to Rental Stocks and New Rental Housing Production in the United States, Great Britain and West Germany, around 1980

Country (and period)	Average Annual Volume of conversions	Average Annual Volume as a percentage of the rental stock (in a given year)	Average Annual Ratio of volumes in conversions/ new rental housing production
United States (1976-9)	71,000	0.3 (1977 stock)	0.2
Great Britain (1980-3)	137,500	1.4 (1980 stock)	2.7
West Germany (1978-83)	55,000(a)	0.4 (1978 stock)	0.8

Note: (a) Estimate - see discussion, pp. 152-5.
Sources: Statistical Abstracts of the United States 1979, p. 785; HUD, The Conversions of Rental Housing to Condominiums and Cooperatives. A National Study, p. IV-6; Central Statistical Office, Social Trends 13 (1983), p. 111; DoE, Housing and Construction Statistics, December 1983, Parts 1 and 2; Wirtschaft und Statistik 4/1984, p. 323.

As can be seen, tenure conversions make the smallest dent in the US rental housing stock. This is all the more so since annual conversions - at least in the late 1970s - amounted to only one fifth of the volume added to the rental stock through new production. In West Germany, there were four units converted for each five new rental ones produced during the early 1980s. The greatest impact seems to be felt in Great Britain. The annual average volume of conversions in the years after the Right to Buy exceeded that of new rental production by almost three to one. As a result, the British public rental sector experienced a net loss of about 350,000 units between 1980 and 1983, just because of conversions.

These differences reflect contextual differences between the three countries. It comes as no surprise that the largest volumes, and the largest relative impact on rental housing, appear in Great Britain, where the most favourable policy towards conversions is found. The large discounts on sales prices has no doubt helped in enlarging the volume of sales. Nor is it surprising that conversions have the least relative importance on rental housing in the United States. No particular subsidies for purchasing condominiums exist. The size of the rental stock is such that conversions would have to reach very large numbers to make any particular inroad into the stock. Furthermore, new rental production was quite high during some of the years in the late 1970s. As for West Germany, there might have been more conversions than rental production had it not been for the policy-induced increase in new rental production beginning in 1982.

What then about the argument that new production will compensate for losses due to conversion? This is clearly not the case for Great Britain, where the ratio of conversions/new rental production rose from 1/1 in 1980 to 5/1 in 1983. In West Germany, new rental housing production outgrew conversions after 1982. As for the United States, rental production increased up to 1979, but then began a downward turn as a result of surging interest rates. On the other hand, production of new condominiums held steady. In West Germany, the production of new Eigentumswohnungen doubled from 1979 to 1983. Given that the West German increase in rental housing production was induced by new governmental subsidies, there is no discernable pattern of substitute production in the wake of conversions.

In terms of which parts of rental housing are most often subject to conversions, a clear and general pattern can be found. Dwellings of good quality or having attractive forms, and located in attractive areas and estates have been most popular. In Great Britain, conversions have predominantly concerned houses, not flats. Especially in West Germany, conversions are most frequent in inner city areas with low-cost decent rental housing, thus contributing to longer waiting lists for rental housing in metropolitan areas. In the United States, certain very popular suburban areas have been experiencing high conversion rates. However, the main impression is one of high activity in inner cities of the large metropolitan areas.

This general pattern seems to occur regardless

of differences in the legal, economic or political contexts of conversions. This can be explained by pointing to the fact that when converted dwellings come under a totally different set of constraints regarding their use. They now become <u>marketable</u>; they can be bought and sold, mortgaged and re-mortgaged, all the time in line with market valuations. What happens is that values lying dormant in rental housing - perhaps because of rent control or rent regulations, or other constraints - suddenly are freed - that is, become exploitable in the housing market. (1) Quite naturally, the interest will focus on those segments of the convertible rental sector where the discrepancy between the value under rental use and the value in the owner-occupied market is expected to be the highest. Hence the concentration of conversions to specifically attractive parts of cities in terms of prestige, location, and housing standards. In Great Britain, there is also another factor at work - the historical fact that such a large segment of public rental housing consists of detached, semi-detached, or terraced housing. Such housing forms correspond to the seemingly universal ideal of an owner-occupied home.

It would thus seem as if the opponents' arguments have been more accurate and valid than those of the proponents. The capital freed through conversions does not seem to have flown directly back into production of new rental housing. On the contrary, production for home ownership, be it houses or flats, has shown a more positive trend in the three countries than has rental production. Except for Great Britain, one should admit that the overall effects on rental housing availability have been limited. However, the effects have been more substantial for certain segments of rental housing. At least in West Germany, the reservoir of low-cost but decent rental housing in inner cities suitable for lower-income households has been tapped to such an extent that it is possible to talk about a shortage of housing for such groups. In Great Britain, the concentration on houses in the public rental sector means that the freedom of choice for households within that sector will be severely limited in the future.

However, proponents may still argue that losses are exaggerated. What counts is the loss of relets - that is, the rate of losses should be determined as the number of converted dwellings that would have been free to let in the year of conversion. If moving rates are low in the converted stock, it follows that very few of the converted units would have come out on the rental market anyway. With high moving rates, the conversions would be more immediately felt as losses to the market.

It is true that moving rates in the popular house segment of British public housing are very low. Households who manage to get into such housing usually stay for the rest of their lives. In West Germany, moving rates seem to be low in attractive inner city areas. US conversions do take place in attractive areas, where the moving rates are lower than the average for all rental housing. All this supports the proponents' view that the effects on rental housing availability will be quite limited.

Still, all units converted will ultimately be lost to the rental market. Furthermore, the concentration on certain segments of the rental stock indicates that the loss of freedom of choice to prospective tenants is far greater than the calculated numerical loss of relets. This is in line with the opponents' view of what will happen to the rental market after conversions.

In sum, our analysis points to the opponents as having the most valid arguments about the effects of conversions on the rental stock. They are more accurate in their view on the probability of substitute production. They are able to predict the concentration of conversions in certain segments of rental housing. When it comes to the effects on the rental market, each school seems to have a point. As the proponents have argued, the loss of units from the actual supply of rental dwellings is limited. But just like the opponents have feared, the concentration of conversions in certain segments results in a diminished freedom of choice for those demanding rental housing. What is somewhat surprising, or perhaps ironic, is that conversion proponents – who are otherwise so prone to point to the goal of equal opportunity – fail to recognise these possible effects of tenure conversions. The explanation may well be that to them, freedom of choice is equal to increased opportunities for home ownership rather than preserving a broad spectrum of choice in the rental sector.

Tenure Conversions and the Distribution of Housing Quality

Proponents argue that conversions will widen the opportunities of home ownership; a broader spectrum of the population will be able to take part in the growth of wealth that follows when house prices increase. They tend to play down the possibilities of increased housing segregation; more home ownership implies a greater mobility in the housing market and will lead to a social mix on housing estates that prevents segregation. The emphasis is thus on opportunity; conversions will provide more opportunities to more people, and market mechanisms will work towards an outcome acceptable in terms of social mix.

Opponents argue that conversions will lead to a more unequal distribution of housing quality. Attractive rentals will be converted at prices far above the ability to pay of many present renters, at least among those at the lower end of the income spectrum. Large rebates may have a modifying effect on this process, but the need for capital inputs will still exclude many households from becoming home owners while at the same time favouring better-off households. The emphasis is thus on outcome; the mechanisms of what some call 'commodification' (2) will inevitably lead to a more pronounced socio-economic segregation in housing than existed before conversions took place.

A comparative analysis of these distributive effects must keep in mind the differences in context between the three countries studied here. In the United States and West Germany, conversions do not restrict the opportunities of home ownership to the tenants presently living in the units to be converted. In principle, all households could buy a unit and move in. In such cases one is allowed to talk in terms of changes in social mix as a result of conversions. In the British case, only sitting tenants can participate as buyers. The analysis must thus concentrate on who buys and who does not, that is, on what types of households use the opportunity to become home owners. The change in social mix in an area experiencing conversions would actually come from the reletting of the rental units still existing in that area. A comparison of all three countries should thus concentrate on the issue of opportunity. Any conclusions concerning the actual outcome in terms of segregation must be limited to the US and West German cases. As for Great Britain, effects on segregation should be analysed in a longer time perspective.

One clearly generalisable pattern coming out of our analysis of the three countries relate to the issue of equal opportunity. Households who did buy the converted units offered for sale do not represent a cross-section of the socio-economic spectrum. Neither does their socio-economic profile indicate that conversions have spread home ownership to new strata in the populations of the three countries.

In the United States, pre-conversion tenants in conversion areas differ from all renters in terms of income, their median income being 2.5 times higher than that of all renters. Within this group of previous renters, those who actually bought their dwellings came disproportionately from the highest income brackets; they did so even more than all home owners. Outside buyers moving in were less often low-income households, less often from racial minorities, and more often young, single, and well-educated than their share of all American households would have predicted.

In the first four years of British conversions under the Right to Buy, about 8 per cent of the council house tenants took the opportunity of purchasing their home. The socio-economic profile of this group differs substantially from that of all public tenants, at least for the cities from which we have data. There is a clear over-representation of households whose heads have managerial or professional jobs, as well as of skilled manual labourers. Semi-skilled and unskilled manual labour is particularly under-represented in the buyer category. The income of the principal earner in buying households tends to be much higher than the average for all public tenants. Small families and large adult households are over-represented, as are households with heads 45 to 54 years of age.

The West German pattern is one of under-representation of low-income earners among buyers. Especially middle-income households seem over-represented. Furthermore, buyers of converted flats are much more often gainfully employed than all pre-conversion tenants taken together. In demographic terms, flat buyers are more similar to the home owners than they are to the renters. The exception seems to be age; flat buyers seem somewhat younger than home owners in general. As is the case with both the United States and Great Britain, older households are more seldom found among buyers of converted flats.

The conclusion is obvious. Tenure conversions have not contributed to a more equal distribution of opportunities for home ownership. True enough, conversions have increased the <u>number</u> of home owners. However, the argument that conversions will widen the opportunities of home ownership cannot be interpreted as meaning only an increase in the number of home owners. It must also be taken to mean that conversions will draw hitherto under-represented – or unrepresented – socio-economic strata into the owner-occupied sector. In other words, we take the argument to include a distributive aspect. What this study does is to refute the validity of such assertions. The general pattern in all the three countries is quite clear. Households with an above-the-average ability to pay are over-represented among buyers in comparison to their share of all households or of all pre-conversion renters. When there is manna from heaven, access to it becomes crucial. If such access is unequally distributed, so will be the manna. (3)

What we are referring to here is, of course, households' ability to pay. The unequal use of the opportunity for home ownership provided by tenure conversions that is found to be the general pattern in these three countries may be explained by the generally applicable relationship between the costs of tenure provision and the households' ability to pay. Home ownership requires a capital input from the buyer; during the first years of owner occupation high mortgage interest rates require good and predictable incomes for the household. This 'front-loading' is partly cushioned by tax deductions, but still represents a challenge to the household economy that may be insurmountable by households with a low ability to pay. (4) The general pattern found here thus refutes the sometimes aired view that tenure conversions – by offering the possibilities of home ownership at costs lower than those of traditional home ownership – will spread home ownership to new social groups. If anything, those using the opportunity are socio-economically more similar to traditional home owners than they are to non-owners. Whether they are initiated through political will or not, and regardless of such frills as substantial rebates, tenure conversions do not seem capable of breaking through the general relationship between tenure costs and ability to pay.

But does unequal ability to use opportunities lead to housing segregation in the sense that the attractive housing being converted is more and more enjoyed by certain socio-economic groups, while others move out? As we have pointed out before, some conditions must be fulfilled for this to be so. First, a substantial share of the pre-conversion tenants must move out and be replaced by households moving in. Second, households moving out and households moving in must differ from each other to such an extent and in such directions that the end result is a homogenisation of the socio-economic structure in the converted buildings and areas. Third, the households moving out should end up in buildings and areas dominated by the same socio-economic stratum that characterize the out-moving group, leading to a homogenisation of the socio-economic structure in the areas subject to an influx of pre-conversion tenants.

The first condition is near for both the United States and West Germany. The share of pre-conversion tenants moving out within a couple of years after conversion is 58 and 45 per cent, respectively. As for the second condition, certain tendencies can be found in the US case. Outside buyers moving in are more often high-income earners, more often having professional/managerial jobs, less often from an ethnic minority, and more often young singles than was the case for all pre-conversion tenants. The same is true for tenant buyers, at least with regard to income and occupational status. Non-buying movers show considerable variations as to income, family size, and age. However, there is an over-representation of large households, and an under-representation of very young ones. Especially prone to move out are elderly low-income households. As a result, the socio-economic structure is converted buildings has changed. There are relatively fewer low-income earners, and relatively more high-income households. There is also a higher share of managerial/professional people, while the share of retired people has diminished. The share of ethnic minorities has decreased in central city buildings, but held steady in suburban ones after conversion. All in all, there is a discernible tendency towards a homogenisation of the socio-economic structure, the direction being towards <u>gentrification</u>.

The socio-economic characteristics of West-German non-buying movers are very similar to those of all pre-conversion tenants. We have just shown that buyers of converted flats are more similar to all home owners in demographic terms than they are to the group of all pre-conversion tenants. Buyers are relatively more often found in economically better-off strata than all pre-conversion tenants taken as a group. All in all, this leads to a post-conversion pattern where there are relatively fewer low-income, elderly, or very young households. Instead, there is now a relatively larger share of high-income households, people with managerial/professional jobs, households with two to four persons, and households of middle age than before. Also in West Germany, there is thus a tendency towards gentrification as a result of conversions.

In both countries where the right to buy converted dwellings is not confined to sitting tenants only, there is thus a general pattern. In converted buildings and areas, there is a change in household structure; it becomes more homogenised towards the middle- and upper-class end of the continuum. The attractive housing of good quality often subject to conversion is increasingly enjoyed by people with an adequate ability to pay. In this sense, it seems relevant to talk of increasing segregation in housing areas subjected to tenure conversions.

But what happens to those moving out in terms of housing quality? Do they predominantly end up in housing areas of lower quality, and dominated by households with a lower ability to pay for housing? Data are too scant to allow any firm conclusions. In the United States, about two-thirds of the pre-conversion tenants moving to another rental unit managed to get the same or better housing standards. One third suffered a loss in housing quality; low-income and elderly movers were particularly dissatisfied. Still, there is no evidence justifying the conclusion that our third condition of segregation is at hand. In the West German case, there is evidence implying that a large part of the non-buyers have moved out from inner-city areas to modern multi-family housing estates located at the outer areas of the cities, thus improving their housing standard. Given the social composition of the movers, one may assume that there will be a higher share of low-income and elderly households in such areas. The main impression is, however, that there are too few data to warrant any conclusions on the segregation effects of conversions outside the buildings and areas subjected to conversions.

The British case is special. With only sitting tenants acknowledged as buyers, the pre-conversion match of socio-economic household structure and housing types and quality is crucial for the analysis of conversions and their segregational consequences. As we have shown earlier, there is a systematic pattern in British council housing. Households with better incomes and higher status (at least in the eyes of housing allocation officers) tend to be allocated to the attractive houses, while low-income and low-status households tend to be concentrated in

tower blocks and in low-status, low-quality estates.
Since the overwhelming majority of the British sales
concern houses and thus involve households with a
higher ability to pay, the result is residualisation;
the low-status, low quality dwellings taken an
increasing share of the remaining council house
stock. (5) With the prevailing socio-economic and
quality match, this also leads to categorisation;
public housing becomes the tenure for low-income
people. This categorisation will be all the more
visible as conversions proceed to a point where the
public sector has run out of housing attractive
enough to lure tenants into buying, and where the
number of sitting tenants having an adequate ability
to pay is too low to sustain further conversions
under the present conditions for council house sales.

What we find is a general tendency that
conversions of rental housing are accompanied by a
more pronounced housing segregation, albeit that in
the British case this is to a large extent the result
of specific historic, physical, and administrative
circumstances. Once some part of the housing stock is
shifted from one set of regulations on its use to
another, relations of housing provision specific for
the new tenure come into play. When ability to pay
becomes the distributive principle rather than need
or some other restriction on the interplay between
supply and demand, there seems to be a general
tendency for the better-quality segment of housing to
end up being enjoyed predominantly by households with
a high ability to pay. The final outcome of
conversions in terms of distribution of housing
quality is thus one of increased socio-economic
segregation.

Again, our analysis points to the opponents as
having the most accurate views of conversion effects.
Not only do proponents tend to play down the risks of
a more unequal distribution of housing quality as a
probable consequence of conversions, but their
obsession with opportunity makes them unable to
foresee that the existing inequal distribution of
opportunities among socio-economic groups will
overtake any policy intentions concerning a more
equal distribution of housing quality. (6) The
general outcome shown here tends to justify
opponents' fears; a pattern of gentrification occurs
in areas undergoing conversions. Those who could
barely make it under the rental system move out when
owner occupation is introduced, while those who could
make it under any system of housing provision move in
or prevail. In Britain, those renters who can afford

to become home owners also happen to live in that segment of the stock thought of as most suitable for home ownership.

Tenure Conversions and the Distribution of Housing Costs

Proponents of tenure conversions carry their opportunity argument also to the issue of conversion effects on housing costs. Since prices are lower for converted housing than for traditional single-family housing, the economic benefits of home ownership can be enjoyed by a larger share of households. More households will have the opportunity to improve their economy through home ownership; they will enjoy value appreciation 'to beat' inflation, tax relief through mortgage interest deductions, and have their home as a security for loans. In short, conversions will provide more households with the economic security that home ownership is said to promote.

Opponents again argue in terms of equality of outcome rather than in terms of diffusion of opportunity. Buyers are already better off, and they have to be; down payments and mortgage payments, compounded by wider responsibilities for running and maintenance costs will in the short run increase outlays on housing beyond what can be afforded by lower-income households. Tax benefits and value appreciation will increasingly be enjoyed by those who are already better off in terms of ability to pay for housing. Furthermore, it is possible that rents will increase in converted buildings as a result of modernisation, and in neighbourhoods experiencing conversions because of increasing demand for housing in these attractive areas. Such processes would make continuing renters worse off in terms of housing costs. In sum, tenure conversions may lead to more inequality in the distribution of housing costs and economic wealth.

We have already found how the first of these two lines of argument fares in comparison with actual experience; everywhere, households with good ability to pay are more often than others found among the buyers of converted housing. However, this is not enough to conclude that conversions also generally lead to a more unequal distribution of housing costs. First, one must find out whether prices of converted units, and the immediate costs of living in them are such as to be beyond the reach of certain household strata. Here, several national peculiarities may come into play, such as the conditions and size of rebates, restrictions on sellers and seller categories, and so on. Second, it is necessary to assess the generality of long-term developments in housing costs and wealth accumulation for buyers and continuing renters. These are the only truly comparable groups, since they inhabit dwellings of similar quality. Here, individual countries may provide different contexts of possibilities and restrictions; mortgage deductions, capital gains, and appreciation rates apply differently, thus leading to different outcomes.

Unfortunately, available data are not totally adequate for such a systematic comparison. The US material provides the fullest picture. On average, US tenant buyers in the late 1970s experienced an immediate increase of 44 per cent in gross outlays on housing. The corresponding figure for continuing renters in converted buildings was a 7 per cent increase. As many as 37 per cent of the tenant buyers suffered an increase of more than 50 per cent. This happened to only 1 per cent of continuing renters. The share of households spending more than 30 per cent of their income on housing after conversions was 40 per cent among tenant buyers and 27 per cent among continuing renters. The share was especially high among tenant buyers who were elderly, low-income earners, or came from racial minorities. It is notable that no group affected by US conversions experienced an average decrease in gross housing expenditures following conversions. Quite naturally, this is felt most among renter groups with low ability to pay and with no possibilities of reaching a considerably lower net cost of housing.

This picture is completely reversed when the effects of tax deductions and value appreciation are taken into account. According to the data and the assumptions presented in Chapter 2, 91 per cent of tenant buyers then enjoyed a decrease in net housing costs, averaging 57 per cent of their earlier rent payments. Still, however, 49 per cent of continuing renters experienced an average increase in rents amounting to 7 per cent. Since more continuing renters are low-income earners, and fewer have high incomes than is the case among tenant buyers, the conclusion is obvious: the favourable long-term effects of home ownership have been primarily enjoyed by exactly those households who were in a better position than others to make use of the economic opportunities offered by tenure conversions.

West German data do not allow a direct comparison of the effects on tenant buyers and continuing renters. While there are indications that slightly more than half of the continuing renters experienced rent increases after conversions, the size of these increases is not known. For tenant buyers, the immediate increase in housing expenditures was 100 per cent. Tenants who chose to move to another rented flat suffered an average rent increase of 25 per cent. The pattern is thus much the same as for US conversions.

When tax deductions and value appreciation are taken into account, the picture becomes rosier for the tenant buyer. As was shown in Chapter 4, the net value of wealth for the average tenant buyer is almost double that of the average renter as soon as five years after purchase (assuming that the renter puts the difference between net owner outlays and actual rent into a savings account). Since this long-term development favours tenant buyers over continuing renters, the final result is inequality. Buyers who were already better off, enjoy a very positive development of individual wealth, while continuing renters - dominated by elderly, very young, and lower-income households - have a much less favourable economic outcome from housing.

Insofar as West German conversions concern Sozialmietwohnungen in the public housing company stock, they involve a transfer of wealth from the public sector to individual households. This is the most important aspect of British conversions, and one that is a central aim of official policy. The first four years of council house sales witnessed such a transfer of wealth - in the form of rebates to buying households - amounting to £3.7 billion, provided buying households do not resell until after five years. Also in the British case, we have found that buying tenants do not represent a cross-section of all households. Most buying households are above average in terms of ability to pay; a substantial share would probably have been able to buy a house at market value, thus enjoying only the wealth accumulation stemming from value appreciation.

Unfortunately for our comparison, this study has not come across any long-term British data on housing cost developments for buying tenants and continuing renters living in comparable types of council housing. It seems clear, however, that governmental policy towards council house rents tends to favour buyers. Through direct governmental involvement, local housing authorities are forced to increase rents in public housing at a rate that implies an increase also in real terms. At the same time, buyers both see the value of their loan repayments falling in real terms and enjoy tax relief on their mortgage interest payments. Given what we already know about the socio-economic character-istics of buyers and continuing renters, the British council house sales also are a clear case of more unequal distribution of housing costs as a consequence of conversions.

We thus find that buyers of converted housing tend to have a more favourable long-term development in terms of actual housing costs than continuing renters. Since buyers – on the average - already have a better ability to pay than continuing renters, the outcome is a general pattern; conversions lead to inequalities in the distribution of housing costs. Of two households with the same need for housing, the one with better ability to make use of the opportunities provided by conversions will enjoy the possibility of substantial future benefits from housing while the one which could not - for economic reasons - use this opportunity, will face only economic sacrifices from the use of housing. So far, we must thus conclude that conversion opponents have been more accurate in their analysis than have proponents, although the latter have a good point; conversions do spread the economic benefits of home ownership to a larger <u>number</u> of households.

In all three countries, conversions fundamen-tally change the meaning households attach to their dwellings. As households change from renting to owning their dwellings, they go from a simple <u>use value</u> relationship to housing to a two-fold one of both <u>use and exchange value</u>. Renting households get used to seeing a high rate of house price inflation as inevitably leading to higher rents. As owners, however, they may welcome such a high rate as representing potential capital gains - increases in their unit's exchange value. (7)

This accumulative potential of home ownership is a major factor in distinguishing the economic outcome of buying from that of continuing to rent a unit in converted housing. But value appreciation is in turn dependent on other factors. Housing quality is important. High-standard units in attractive areas are likely to increase more and faster in value than other units - if a second factor is working, i.e. if the sales price is lower than the assumed market value of the units. As we have seen, rebates are a common feature in tenure conversions. Third, value appreciation is influenced by the regulatory context. If taxation principles are such as to allow home owners to pocket the value increase with little or no tax being due, then the accumulative potential will be viewed as larger, and value increases will probably be more accentuated.

However, the benefits of value appreciation can be enjoyed only if there are buyers, and demand for high-priced owner-occupied housing is very much dependent on regulations which bring down the actual costs of home ownership. As we have seen, the tax deductibility rules of our three countries are such as to bring about a substantial difference between gross outlays and net costs of housing.

Altogether, these tenure-related factors influence long-term actual housing costs in a way which is advantageous to tenant buyers rather than to continuing renters. (8) Specific regulations of conversion prices and rebates do not change the fundamental fact that owner-occupied units have an exchange value, thus demanding a capital input from prospective buyers. Such capital is more easily raised by economically resourceful households, who can then enjoy the favourable long-term development of value appreciation and low net housing costs thanks to taxation rules. Tenure conversions do not change the inequitable 'housing rates of return' that emanate from owning and renting. (9) That this general pattern is - to a considerable extent - the result of governmental subsidy systems affecting the housing sector is sometimes overlooked. Ironically enough, this is most often done by those who favour conversions as a method of de-subsidising and privatising the housing sector.

Tenure Conversions and the Economy of the Public Sector

Conversion proponents argue that where heavily subsidised rental housing is converted - such as council housing in Great Britain and Sozialmietwohnungen in West Germany - the immediate effect on the public purse will be positive. The state no longer has to pay subsidies to these units. Housing authorities receive money from buyers' down payments. A major argument in favour of British sales was that mortgage payments would probably exceed future rent income, since rents were expected to decrease in real terms. Sales from the public sector will free resources for new rental housing production without burdening the taxpayer. In the United States, where local taxes are heavily based on property, the increase in property value following from tenure conversions will have a positive effect on local tax revenue.

Opponents take a totally different view. They say that with present systems of tax relief and subsidies to different tenures, the costs to the public sector will over time be higher for owner-occupied housing than for publicly supported renting. The tax relief on mortgage interest, and the almost non-existent taxation on capital gain, will cause losses to the public purse. They also argue that tenure conversions result in increasing amounts of loan capital being tied up in unproductive exchange and circulation of dwellings, because of the privileged position of investment in ownership of housing compared to investments in industrial production.

Assessing the actual 'subsidisation' effects of tenure conversions is no easy matter. First of all, tax deductions are made by individual households. Their incomes and thus marginal tax rates vary, as does the size of their mortgages. Every analysis based on average data is therefore bound to be at best incomplete, and at worst misleading. Second, converted dwellings vary with respect to pre-conversion subsidy status. If conversions primarily take place in unsubsidised private rental housing – as in the US case or the West German freifinanzierte dwellings – and all buyers take mortgages, then there is a direct increase in the number of subsidised units, and the amount of tax relief to buyers can be counted directly as an increase in housing subsidy. However, if conversions mostly concern rental housing that is publicly subsidised, the assessment is more complicated. Building age is evidently important. Newly produced dwellings draw more subsidies than older ones because of differences in production costs and differences in the size of remaining mortgages. Rent-setting principles complicate the picture even further. If cost-pooling and rent-averaging is applied, older low-cost units 'subsidise' the rent of newly produced more expensive dwellings, thus being an economic asset to the public housing sector. When converted and mortgaged by the tenant buyer, they burden the public purse because of the tax relief to the owners.

Without detailed empirical studies of individual households and converted units, there is no adequate solution to these analytical difficulties. What is possible here is to hint at the trends and directions of effects on the public purse rather than pretending to provide the full picture.

In the US case, we found that there was an increase in local tax revenue following from increased property values of converted units. On the other hand, local property taxes are deductible from state and federal income tax, thus leading to a loss of revenue at these levels. The most important decrease in tax revenue, however, concerns mortgage interest deductions from taxable income. Using the averages derived from the HUD national study, we estimated the 'subsidisation' effect of the 366,000 US conversions in the 1970s to be more than half a billion dollars just for the fiscal year 1979. Since these units were not subject to any governmental subsidy before, the amount of revenue foregone could be seen as a net effect of conversions. However, one should not forget that a substantial number of buyers were earlier owners, already enjoying tax benefits from home ownership. We know that nearly two-fifths of all buyers were former owners. We can thus estimate the net 'subsidisation' effects to be at least $300 million for fiscal year 1979.

In West Germany, around two-thirds of all converted rental units around 1908 were privately financed. For the publicly supported dwellings being converted there are no indications of the size of subsidies or the length of the remaining subsidy period in comparison to the eight-year period of tax deductions allowed to the buyer of converted units. Using average figures found in the national Infratest study, and assuming an annual volume of 50,000 sales at prices increasing five per cent annually over the 1978 level, we arrive at an estimated DM 600 million loss of tax revenue for the year 1985 as a result of conversions between 1978 and 1985. The total loss for the whole period would be about DM 2,500 million. How much the repayment of Förderungen (production subsidies) on subsidised dwellings may reduce this gross estimate is impossible to ascertain. What we do know, however, is that the average buyer of an average-price converted unit in 1978 got DM 10,000 in tax relief during his first eight years of ownership. We also know that the tax relief enjoyed by the two-thirds buying non-subsidised units represents a direct loss to the public purse insofar as buyers did not enjoy any tax reliefs before.

The substantial rebates on sales prices enjoyed by British tenant buyers represent an important transfer from the public sector. Local authorities lose money because of this systematic under-estimation of the exchange value of converted units. If buyers are smart, they will not resell their units

within the first five years after purchase. In this
way, they evade repaying whole or part of the rebate
to local authorities. Income tax benefits following
mortgage interest deductions totalled £450 million
for the sales between 1980 and 1983. It should be
remembered, though, that governmental subsidies to
public housing were lowered by £1,200 million during
the same period. It is worth noting how this
development has affected continuing renters and
tenant buyers. The former have seen their average
housing subsidy fall from £270 to £100, while the
latter have enjoyed an increase to £360. Furthermore,
it should be noted that a large part of the sales
concerns older council housing, which until
converted used to contribute a 'subsidy' to newer,
more costly public rental housing.

Although it is difficult to assess the final net
effect of conversions in cases involving units or
households already subsidised in one way or another,
it seems safe to conclude that there is indeed a
visible tendency. Far from lifting the burden of
subsidies from the public purse, tenure conversions
extend subsidies to net groups, thus straining the
public sector. How much more this is the case after
conversions is more easily assessed where
conversions take place in earlier non-subsidised
housing.

We are again forced to conclude that conversion
opponents have the more adequate and valid arguments
concerning the effects of conversions. Admittedly,
there are many proponents who seem to think that tax
relief on mortgage interest is not truly a subsidy to
housing, but rather an example of a more general
principle underlying taxation policy. But the fact
remains that buyers of converted dwellings can lower
their housing costs through tax deductions, while
continuing renters can not. Tenure conversions –
extending home ownership – do not rid public budgets
of housing subsidies; they make subsidies appear in
new forms, and shift their incidence to other groups
than before. It should be clear from the preceding
pages that this incidence shift has profound
distributive effects.

This development will have important, and
possibly contradictory effects on the relationships
between the public sector and the increasing number
of home owners. Extending home ownership through
tenure conversions means giving more households a
stake in the existing system of tax relief. A larger,
and potentially powerful, constituency will
anxiously guard the present regulatory system, aware

as they are of its importance for the development of exchange values, annual housing expenditures, and so on. But at the same time, the conversions increase the number of households who depend on public spending for the long-term development of their investment in housing. Schools, streets and public amenities all demand public expenditures, and are important to the value appreciation of housing as they make neighbourhoods more or less attractive. Obviously, home owners will be very reluctant to accept any infringements on their tax privileges as a way of securing the money necessary for public investment. How governments will be able to manoeuvre in this situation with an increasingly powerful home owner lobby at once demanding public investments and defending their tax privileges is outside the context of this analysis. It is, however, worth pointing out this possible effect of increasing the rate of home ownership.

Conclusion

Some generalisable patterns emerge from our comparative evaluation of tenure conversion effects. Conversions are concentrated in housing of good quality in attractive areas. Households with good ability to pay are over-represented among buyers, while those with less ability are under-represented. Whereas all households affected by conversions seem to experience short-term increases in housing expenditures, the long-term development is generally more favourable to buyers than to continuing renters. The overall result is thus a redistribution of housing quality and economic wealth favouring households that were already better off before the conversions.

Even if there are some variations related to differences in national contexts, this general pattern seems to verify the arguments of opponents, and refute those of proponents of conversions. The final outcome seems to be one of increased inequality in housing, both in terms of housing quality and housing costs. The diffusion of opportunity – so much hailed by proponents – may have been true in a numerical sense, but certainly not in a socio-economic. Conversions do not change the distribution of ability to utilise opportunities prevailing at the time such conversions are initiated. A tendency to further marginalisation of households already living at the margin is discernible in the wake of conversions. In the first chapter, we tried to show

how the pros and cons of tenure conversions are linked to much broader views on government's role in welfare provision. The fact that opportunity-centred proponents have been so far from adequate in their assessment of possible consequences of conversions compared to outcome-centred opponents makes us wonder about the implications of their approach to the distribution of welfare in housing.

Notes

1. Cf. R. Forrest and P. Williams, 'Commodification and Housing: Emerging Issues and Contradictions', Environment and Planning A, 16 (1984), p. 1168 ff.

2. According to the usual connotations of the concept, only the British council house sales and the West German conversions of Sozialmietwohnungen could be viewed as commodification in a strict sense; cf. Forrest and Williams, p. 1167 and the literature cited here. On the other hand, the partition and sale of units from hitherto privately owned rental buildings and estates does increase the volume of totally commodified housing by taking units out of rent controls and other regulations limiting their character as commodities.

3. Cf. the discussion in Le Grand, The Strategy of Equality, pp. 72 ff.

4. Cf. the discussion by Michael Ball, Housing Policy and Economic Power. The Political Economy of Owner Occupation (Methuen, London, 1984), pp. 287 ff.

5. This is sometimes referred to as the stigmatisation of public rental housing; cf. Kemeny, The Myth of Homeownership, pp. 141, 144.

6. In so doing, proponents seem to be victims of the ideological power of equal opportunity's 'prospect-regarding variant, in the wish and hope that the children of yesterday's losers may become tomorrow's winners'. In effect, setting up the same rules for all tenant buyers (as in the British case) is a policy of means-regarding equal opportunity. Still, the 'talents' (in this case, the ability to pay) are unequal. As Douglas Rae has shown, every such policy must violate equality of prospects, given strictly unequal talents. In Rae's terminology, proponents thus behave as if both converted housing and ability to pay are within the 'domain of allocation'. In fact, only converted housing is; cf. Douglas Rae, Equalities (Harvard University Press, Cambridge, Mass., and London, 1981) pp. 62, 67, 75.

7.   Ray Forrest, 'The Meaning of Homeowner-ship', Environment and Planning D: Society and Space, 1 (1983), p. 211.

8.   Cf. the arguments by Ball, Housing Policy and Economic Power, p. 341.

9.   Cf. Headey, Housing Policy in the Developed Economy, p. 27 ff.

Chapter Six

FROM TENANCY TO HOME OWNERSHIP: GOVERNMENT, HOUSING,
AND THE DISTRIBUTION OF WELFARE

Tenure Conversions and Government's Role in Housing

This study began by outlining two different views on
government involvement in housing. They differ with
respect to the proper scope of involvement, as well
as in their position on what kind of equality
governments should strive for in housing. Converting
rental housing to owner occupation was presented by
its proponents as a way of limiting the role of
government, and allowing the interplay of supply and
demand to allocate housing quality. Many
commentators and debaters have seen conversions as a
practical example of the trend towards 'privatisation', 'commodification', or 'de-socialisation'
visible in housing sectors in many industrialised
countries.

   As its point of departure, the study relied on a
commonly used dichotomy in housing policy research -
that is, the one between 'supplementary' and
'comprehensive' housing policies, where the former
was seen as identical to the political view that
government's role in housing should be limited to
supporting only those in real need. Implicitly, the
study assumed that tenure conversions are an example
of moving closer to this 'supplementary' line of
governmental policy.

   One evident conclusion is that these categories
are too imprecise and thus inadequate to throw much
light on the role of government. Since they seem pre-
occupied with <u>direct</u> interventions in the production
and consumption of housing, they leave out features
crucial for determining the precise scope of
governmental involvement. Furthermore, they are too
broad to allow for analyses of shifts in types of
governmental support, shifts which in turn may be
crucial to an understanding of the effects of housing
policy on equality. It just is not possible to say

that simply because a policy is comprehensive, there will also be more equality in housing.

Neither is it possible to say that because rental housing is converted into owner occupation, the governmental role in the housing sector will be more limited. Several factors contribute to make such a statement very difficult to make. First of all, one must take into account the preconversions subsidy status of converted dwellings and affected households. If the dwellings were subsidised – for example, through interest subsidies – and these are paid back at the time of conversion, this would seem to imply a diminishing role for government. However, buying households may be receiving housing allowances under regulations allowing them to continue to do so. In other words, a limitation of governmental involvement as a result of conversions presupposes that whatever support buying households received before conversions is no longer forthcoming as a result of changing to owner occupation.

Even if this were the case, we know that buying households become eligible for a new form of support once they buy a converted flat. Provided they take a mortgage, they are entitled to a deduction of mortgage interest from taxable income or – as in the West German case – a deduction of a certain percentage of the purchase price from that income. Insofar as buyers take mortgages, and insofar as they were not owners with a mortgage before, tenure conversions actually lead to an <u>increase</u> in governmental involvement. But if the buyers become owners outright, or had a mortgage before, the effects on involvement are more difficult to judge. Only in the case of conversions of non-subsidised private rental housing in the United States and West Germany does it seem possible to assume a clear-cut effect on the scope of governmental involvement. If buyers are tenants with no earlier mortgage interest deductions, such conversions signify an increase in that involvement. It is <u>comprehensive</u> in nature, since <u>all</u> owners with a mortgage can make deductions, regardless of income or other criteria.

True enough, tenure conversions may be paralleled by changes in governmental housing policies which imply a more rigorous application of means tests as the method of determining eligibility to assure that 'direct' support goes to those 'who really need' it. But this should not obscure the fact that tenure conversions constitute a step in the opposite direction. By making 'indirect' state support – here, tax subsidies – dependent on <u>tenure</u>, public sector involvement is potentially widened in comparison to a strategy of support based strictly on <u>socio-economic</u> or <u>demographic</u> criteria since need is <u>not</u> made part of the eligibility for tax deductions.

What we are trying to say here is that governmental housing policies in the countries studied are organised on a principle of 'segmental equality'. Individual households are assorted into segmented subcategories to receive support according to such criteria as family size, income, health and age. Any pair of households may find they are receiving quite different aid streams, depending on their particular combination of such characteristics. (1) Along this line, it is quite possible to successively narrow the segment of households eligible for support, that is, to have a supplementary policy of housing support. However, along with segmental equality based on household characteristics, housing policies pursue such equality by distinguishing between housing tenures and treating them differently. In all the countries studied here, conversions mean that tenant households becoming home owners move from a subcategory where support is dependent on income criteria to one where no such means test is necessary before they can enjoy tax deduction for housing purposes. Tenure conversions thus involve moving households from one subclass of tenure, where they are segmented according to means-test criteria to another, where they are not. In all likelihood, this has the potential of increasing governmental involvement in housing.

Tenure Conversions and Equal Opportunity
The proposition that tenure conversions actually increase governmental involvement in housing may seem very much at odds with the commonly held view that such conversions - particularly those involving the sale of hitherto publicly owned and managed rental housing - are a practical example of the trend towards marginalism in many welfare states. 'Marginalism' is here taken to mean a concentration of governmental intervention to specific aspects of welfare, and to narrowly defined groups of recipients. Aspects and groups falling outside the specifications are basically left to the distributive mechanism of the marketplace. In contrast, globalism is more like what we have earlier referred to as comprehensive policies. Many aspects of social welfare are seen as within the realm of

governmental intervention, and the groups of recipients are broadly defined.

It may, however, be argued that the 'privatisation' of public rental housing through conversions is an example of marginalism at work. This becomes clear when we consider the issue of equal opportunity, raised by several proponents of tenure conversions. Especially the British Tories, but also the West German Christian Democrats and US Republicans, have seen conversions as an instrument for increasing the freedom of choice in housing, and for promoting opportunities of home ownership to groups lacking such opportunities in the past.

In a formal sense, the British Right to Buy provides <u>all</u> public tenants with equal possibilities of buying their house, of getting a rebate, and of obtaining a mortgage from the seller. On the other hand, Tory policy does not take into account the unequal distribution of ability to pay among public tenants. In this way, tenants are provided with the same tools for acquiring home ownership, but left with quite different capacities for using these tools. (2) In the words of a Tory spokesman: 'We propose to create a climate in which those who are able will prosper ...' (3)

This is a perfect example of what Douglas Rae calls 'means-regarding equal opportunity', where 'subjects have the same opportunity for X if each has the same instruments for achieving X'. (4) Through the Right to Buy, every British council house tenant has the formal legal instruments for becoming a home owner. However, ability to pay is the key to success in becoming a home owner. Since this capacity is unevenly distributed among public tenants, they will have different <u>real</u> prospects of fulfilling their dreams of home ownership, despite the <u>formal</u> means-regarding equal opportunity provided by the Right to Buy.

The means-regarding equal opportunity provided by such a programme as the Right to Buy is typical of marginalist programmes. Status quo is changed by providing an equal instrument for all. At the same time, aspects of great importance to the recipient's prospects of success are left out of the programme. The Right to Buy thus produces an end-state which Rae calls marginal egalitarianism. (5) The changes caused by the reform leave households with the same inequalities of resources as before. Whereas A now has both the right to buy and the ability to pay, B only has the right to buy. While seemingly global in character, a means-regarding reform effectively marginalises those who lack the capacity or talent to use the means provided.

Means-regarding equal opportunity is perfectly consistent with the logical of market societies. It provides politicians so inclined with a means for legitimising unequal prospects of success. By making people formally equal in relation to market mechanisms, those who can prosper and those in 'real need' will sort themselves out in a seemingly 'natural' way. Yet, and somewhat surprisingly, this form of equal opportunity is seldom as bluntly promoted in political debates as in the Tory spokesman's statement just quoted. More often it is glossed over by general reference to the prospect-regarding variant of equal opportunity - that is, to the belief - or hope - that regardless of ability, households will have the same probability of achieving such things as home ownership, once they are given the formal instruments entitling them to go for it.

As Rae has shown, prospect-regarding equal opportunity is impossible to attain without violating the means-regarding variant if subject ability relevant to its achievement is unequally distributed. (6) In other words, equal prospects of home ownership through tenure conversions pre-supposes equal ability. In turn, this presupposes governmental intervention the form of general redistributive policies, treating people unequally by extracting money from some households and giving it to others, provided of course that home ownership in its present form is at the core of official housing policy.

Such massive and comprehensive direct governmental intervention is ideologically inconsis-tent and politically difficult to promote for politicans bent on seeing the general redistribution of income and wealth as mainly a function for the market under conditions of means-regarding equal opportunity which legitimises marginalisation of those unable to prosper. But why do proponents of conversions accept a massive redistribution of wealth through governmental involvement in the form of tax deductions to all home owners regardless of need? The explanation is that they consider owner occupation - not global equality in the distribution of housing quality - as the social good to be promoted in this sector. (7) By this, mechanisms towards inequality are built into the final distribution of housing quality.

Tenure Conversions and Equality of Outcome

Throughout this book, we have been concerned with the final outcome of tenure conversions, with the distribution of housing quality and housing costs among households after conversions. It is high time now for a more thorough consideration of the conceptual underpinnings of this concern. What is meant, more precisely, by equality of outcome in housing? What principles of welfare distribution in the housing sector are used when judging the final outcome of conversions?

Again, it may be instructive to consult Rae's discussion of equality. We remember that segmental subject structures of equality are defined by the division of subjects into two or more mutually exclusive subclasses where pair-by-pair equality is required within, but not between sub-classes. What happens in tenure conversions is that tenant purchasers move from one subclass – tenants – to another – owner occupiers. In so doing, they also move from an exclusive to an inclusive subject class of equality. As tenants, they qualify for support according to means-tested income, or age or health criteria. As home owners, they are entitled to tax deductions regardless of such features. All they need to qualify is a mortgage. (8)

Conversions are thus an example of a segmental subject structure where subdivision is done along tenure lines. However, this is not the kind of segmental structure used here as a criterion of equal outcome. Rather, we have thought of household size and dwelling standard as the main lines of subdivision of the class of equals. Equality of outcome is related to housing quality and housing costs. An equal outcome is one where housing quality is distributed according to household size. Any pair of households within the same size class will enjoy the same space standard, regardless of income, race, age, or any other subdivision. Another measure of equal outcome concerns housing costs. Any pair of dwellings with the same space and equipment standard should cost the same in net terms, regardless of tenure. In short, dwellings of equal use value should have equal costs. (9)

Thus, our standards for judging whether or not tenure conversions lead to equal outcome in housing are examples of what Rae would call segmental subject structures with inclusive classes. Once households are subdivided according to size, that is all there is to it. No other subdivision, such as income, is relevant. This would instead be the case in an exclusive strategy of welfare distribution, where subjects are divided into subclasses until only a few remain eligible according to all criteria. Once dwellings are classified according to space and equipment standards, there is no more subdivision. Tenure is not regarded as a relevant criterion of use value.

Now, it may be argued that it is unfair to judge the outcome of tenure conversions by other principles than those guiding such a reform. Some may even suspect they are chosen because the author thinks they are inherently 'better' or 'more worth achieving' than the kind of means-regarding equality of opportunity found to be the underlying principle for tenure conversions as a conscious policy strategy. However, this standard of judgement is used to illustrate a competing set of distributive principles which can be distilled from the arguments put forth by the opponents of conversions. As I see it, the logic of their argument leads to a subdivision of subject classes along the inclusionary lines of household size and dwelling standard. Further segmental divisions along such lines as household income and dwelling tenure would be only secondary to the main principles of welfare distribution. (10)

It is easily shown that tenure conversions cannot result in an equality of outcome in housing so defined. The basic principles of subdivision are different from those of household size and dwelling standard. By subdividing according to the principle of tenure, and by treating tenure subclasses unequally regardless of equality in standard, tenure-based housing measures inevitably provide for different costs of dwellings with equal use value just because of their different tenures. And as long as access to a certain housing tenure is made dependent on ability to pay the distribution of housing standards within that tenure will reflect the distribution of household income, not household size.

Again, one should not use this to conclude that conversions are identical to national 'supplement-ary' housing policies, as these were defined at the beginning of this book. The British experience is a case in point. It shows that it is perfectly possible to have a strategy of segmental and exclusionary equality for the remaining public sector, while at the same time pursuing a segmental and inclusionary one for owner occupation. If we take the first strategy to be roughly equivalent to

'supplementary', and the second to 'comprehensive' -
still in the sense in which these were defined in
Chapter 1 - we find that it is very difficult to
uphold the classification of national housing
policies as being either 'supplementary' or
'comprehensive'. Means-tested housing allowances to
'needy' renters and tax deductions to all home owners
regardless of income or wealth do occur side by side
in many modern housing policies, regardless of the
overall size and scope of these policies in relation
to the housing sector as a whole.

Tenure Conversions and Comparative Housing Policy: Are There Lessons To Drive Home?

What was just said points to one of the lessons to
drive home from this comparative study of tenure
conversions. The 'supplementary-comprehensive' dichotomy does not seem fruitful for the analysis of this
recent development in housing. At the outset, we
linked it to two distinct sets of political ideas
about the distribution of housing standards and
costs, and to even more general ideas about welfare
distribution. We have found, however, that it is not
possible to conclude that tenure conversions are
typical of 'supplementary' housing policies, but not
forthcoming in 'comprehensive' ones. Instead, we are
left with the insight that while these categories may
have had some meaning in historical analyses of
policy developments in industrialised countries,
present-day national housing policies pursue
'supplementary' and 'comprehensive' measures at the
same time. We are also forced to conclude that this
is the case regardless of the relative size or scope
of governmental involvement in the housing sector as
a whole. There may be limited overall involvement by
the government, as in the United States, but with
'comprehensive' techniques such as tax deductions to
all home owners with mortgages regardless of such
criteria as income or wealth. The British and West
German cases of tenure conversions from public
renting to home ownership make it clear that
conversions may indeed involve moving households
from what would traditionally be called 'supplementary' to 'comprehensive' methods of delivering
housing support.

The problem is that the 'supplementary-
comprehensive' dichotomy has come to be politically
loaded. Historically, 'comprehensive' has been
associated with 'progressive' and 'reformist'
governmental programmes aiming at large-scale

reforms of the housing sector in the direction of what is sometimes referred to as a 'classless' provision of housing. 'Supplementary' policies, on the other hand, have come to be associated with a more limited governmental role where the emphasis is less on the inclusiveness and more on the incidence of support. In this political interpretation of 'supplementary' policies, the role of government is not seen as providing 'classless' support but rather as concentrating it to those whose need can be firmly established by means-test criteria.

Admittedly, we tended to build this bias into our analysis by linking the dichotomy to two different sets of ideological beliefs and political strategies concerning government and housing. In so doing, we joined earlier researchers in the tendency of obscuring the fact that 'progressive' and 'reactionary' governments alike have been using 'comprehensive' and 'supplementary' techniques for delivering housing support ever since this pair of concepts first appeared in the literature on housing policy. The lesson of this is that the 'supplementary-comprehensive' dichotomy should be moved from the level of <u>wholesale</u> national <u>policy</u> to that of different policy <u>techniques</u>. For what we have seen here is that tenure conversions lead to the use of comprehensive tax subsidies for a whole class of households which were earlier subject to supplementary means-tested types of support. Furthermore, we have learned that comprehensive techniques can be used to discriminate between groups of households based on their tenure as easily as they may be used in 'classless' policy strategies.

If that is true, what then about the possibilities of classifying national housing policies in terms of their overall aims and effects? In this respect, our study points to one further lesson to drive home. A promising way of comparing national housing policies would be to look for the principles which guide decisions of how to subdivide groups that should or should not be given support. As the discussion earlier in this chapter indicates, there are several such principles. Once the groups are identified, one should establish whether support is given through 'comprehensive' or 'supplementary' techniques, that is, whether all members of a subject class are included, or whether some are excluded because of additional criteria for eligibility. In this way, comparative housing policy studies could achieve three things. First, it would be possible to classify housing policies according to dominant principles of selecting target groups for governmental intervention and dominant techniques of providing support. Second, such analyses would clarify what kinds of equality in housing are sought by different policies. Third, this would in turn provide criteria for evaluating policy outcomes, and force debaters of the merits and demerits of different courses of action to specify their criteria for judgement. To state that tenure conversions do not lead to equality of outcome necessitates making explicit the criteria for such a judgement, and the kind of comparative analysis outlined here enables us to do just that.

A third lesson to drive home is that there is more to tenure conversions than the 'privatisation' so often hailed by political proponents of the dismantling of governmental involvement. If 'privatisation' is taken to refer to 'those elements of state-provided facilities which are being returned to the market', (11) then conversion of privately owned rental buildings to condominiums in the United States or <u>Eigentumswohnungen</u> in West Germany do not qualify as examples of 'privatisation'. It is furthermore doubtful whether such conversions could even be seen as examples of what many housing policy analysts refer to as 'commodification'. Privately owned rental buildings are commodities which can be sold in the market for rental buildings. If there are no rent regulations before conversions, individual flats are commodities to be rented at going market prices. The lesson for comparative analyses along these lines seems to be that 'commodification' should be reserved for such cases where the use value and the exchange value of a housing unit can be enjoyed by the same subject.

The most important lesson, however, is that although tenure conversions in some cases involve selling out publicly owned and/or supported housing, this does not necessarily imply a decreasing governmental involvement in the housing sector. That involvement is only shifted from one set of policy criteria and techniques to another. As the study clearly shows, this shift has everywhere had far-reaching implications for the final distribution of housing standards and housing costs.

Notes
1. Rae, <u>Equalities</u>, pp. 29 ff.
2. Cf. Christine M.E. Whitehead, 'Privatis-ation and Housing', in Julian Le Grand and Ray

Robinson (eds.), <u>Privatisation and the Welfare State</u> (George Allen & Unwin, London, 1984), p. 131.

3. Cf. above, Chapter 1, p. 2f.

4. Rae, p. 66.

5. Ibid., p. 50.

6. Ibid., p. 69.

7. Cf. Whitehead, p. 127.

8. Cf. Rae, pp. 22 ff., 29 ff.

9. I consider this definition of equality of outcome much more meaningful than the notoriously vague one by Le Grand, <u>The Strategy of Equality</u>, p. 15. His definition does not make clear how it is related to his other types of equality, i.e. use and cost.

10. Cf. the discussion of how basic principles enter – or should enter – policy judgement by Charles W. Anderson, 'The Place of Principles in Policy Analysis', <u>The American Political Science Review</u>, <u>73</u>, (1979), pp. 716 ff.

11. Cf. Whitehead, who defines 'privatisation' as 'private market provision and allocation'; p. 117. See also Forrest and Williams, 'Commodification and housing: emerging issues and contradictions', p. 1167, where they state that 'recommodification' and 'reprivatisation' in essence refer to 'those elements of state-provided facilities which are being returned to the market'.

BIBLIOGRAPHY

'Abgänge von Gebäuden und Gebäudeteilen 1980', Wirtschaft und Statistik (10/1981), pp. 724-6.

'Abgänge von Gebäuden, Gebaudeteilen und Wohnungen 1981' Wirtschaft und Statistik (11/1982) pp. 818-21.

Adams, Carolyn T., 'Housing Policy', pp. 88-121 in A. Heidenheimer, H. Heclo, and C.T. Adams, Comparative Public Policy. The Politics of Social Choice in Europe and America, 2nd edn. (St Martin's Press, New York, 1983).

Anderson, Charles W., 'The Place of Principles in Policy Analysis', The American Political Science Review, 73, (1979), pp. 711-23.

Baber, Asa, 'The Condominium Conspiracy', Playboy (November 1979), pp. 140-2, 172, 204, 252, 254.

Ball, Michael, Housing Policy and Economic Power. The Political Economy of Owner Occupation (Methuen, London, 1983).

Bassett, Keith, 'The Sale of Council Houses as a Political Issue', Policy and Politics, 8 (1980), pp. 290-307.

Bassett, Keith, 'Council House Sales in Bristol, 1960-79', Policy and Politics, 8 (1980), pp. 324-33.

'Bautätigkeit 1981' Wirtschaft und Statistik (4/1982), pp. 295-9.

'Bautätigkeit 1982' Wirtschaft und Statistik (4/1983), pp. 335-8.

'Bautätigkeit 1983' Wirtschaft und Statistik (4/1984), pp. 323-6.

Beazley, M. et al., The Sale of Council Houses in a Rural Area - A Case of Study of South Oxfordshire (Oxford Polytechnic/Department of Town Planning, Oxford, Working Paper No. 44, 1980).

Becker, Ruth, 'Grundzüge der Wohnungspolitik in der BRD seit 1949', pp. 10-22 in Klaus Habermann-Niesse et al. (Hrsg.), Alternativen in der Wohnungspolitik

(Alternative Kommunalpolitik, e.V., Bielefeld, 1983).

Beren, Jack, 'The Condominium Corner', Journal of Real Estate Taxation, 3 (Winter 1975), pp. 221-6.

Building Societies Association, BSA Bulletin, No. 27 (July 1981).

Burke, Gill, Housing and Social Justice. The Role of Policy in British Housing (Longman, London, 1981).

Central Statistical Office, Social Trends 13 (HMSO, London, 1983).

Challen, Philip C., The Sale of Council Houses (Leeds Polytechnic, School of Town Planning, Leeds, BA Dissertation, May 1980).

Charles, S.T., 'Council House Sales', Social Policy and Administration, 16 (Summer 1982), pp. 104-14.

Critchley, Roger, and Nigel Lee, 'Massive Losses on Council House Sales', ROOF, 8 (July/August 1983), p.9.

Department of the Environment (DoE), Housing Policy - A Consultative Document (HMSO, London, Cmnd. 6851, 1977).

Department of the Environment (DoE), The Right to Buy. A Guide for Council, New Town and Housing Association Tenants (DoE Welsh Office, Housing Booklet No. 2, Cardiff, March 1980).

Department of the Environment (DoE), Appraisal of the Financial Effects of Council House Sales (Welsh Office, Cardiff, 1980).

Department of the Environment (DoE), 'Sales of Council Houses and Flats and Disposal of Land', (DoE, London, 2 September 1980, mimeo).

Department of the Environment (DoE), Council House Sales: The Government's Reply to the Second Report from the Environment Committee, Session 1980-81, HC 366 (HMSO, London, Cmnd, 8377, October 1981)

Department of the Environment (DoE), Housing and Construction Statistics (quarterly).

Deutschen Mieterbund, Mieterschutz '82 (Deutschen Mieterbund, e.V., Köln, 1982).

Deutsches Volksheimstättenwerk, Das Wohnungseigentum (Deutsches Volksheimstattenwerk, Köln, 1981).

Deutsches Volksheimstättenwerk, Zweckbindung von Sozialwohnungen (Deutsches Volksheimstattenwerk, Köln, 1981).

Dinkenspiel, John R., Joel Uchenick, and Herbert L. Selesnick, Condominums, The Effects of Conversion on a Community (Auburn House, Boston, Mass., 1981).

'Displacement Foes Try to Stop Condo Conversions', Savings & Loans News, 99 (10/1978), pp. 120-1.

'DoE's first Annual Report', Housing Review 33 (January/February 1984), p. 3.

Donnison, David, and Clare Ungerson, Housing Policy (Pengiun Books, Harmondsworth, 1982).

English, John, 'The Choice for Council Housing', pp. 181-95 in John English (ed.), The Future of Council Housing (Croom Helm, London, 1982).

Ernst, Klaus, 'Die Umvandlungen von Mietwohnungen in Eigentumswohnungen', Der Gemeinderat, 23 (9/1980), pp. 17-18.

'Erwerb von Eigentum fällt sich oft leichter als bedacht Folge des intensiven Sparens', Bundesbau-blatt, XXXI (August 1982), pp. 532, 575.

Euler, Manfred, 'Wohnungsmieter und Wohnungsmieten im Januar 1983. Ergebnis der Einkommens- und Verbrauchsstichprobe', Wirtschaft und Statistik (5/1984), pp. 460-7.

Feins, Judith D., and Terry Saunders Lane, How Much for Housing? New Perspectives on Affordability and Risk (Abt Books, Cambridge, Mass., 1981).

Fielding, Nick, 'Who is Subsidising Whom?', ROOF, 9 (March/April 1984), pp. 11-14.

Forrest, Ray, 'The Social Implications of Council House Sales', pp. 97-114 in John English (ed.), The Future of Council Housing (Croom Helm, London, 1982).

Forrest, Ray, 'The Meaning of Homeownership', Environment and Planning D: Society and Space, 1 (1983), pp. 205-16.

Forrest, Ray, and Alan Murie, Council House Sales and Council Housing in Birmingham. Summary of Research Findings (University of Bristol, School of Advanced Urban Studies, Bristol, 1982, mimeo).

Forrest, Ray, and Alan Murie, 'The Great Divide', ROOF, 7 (November/December 1982), pp. 19-21.

Forrest, Ray, and Alan Murie, 'Residualization and Council Housing: Aspects of the Changing Social Relations of Housing Tenure', Journal of Social Policy, 12 (October 1983), pp. 453-68.

Forrest, Ray, and Alan Murie, Right to Buy? Issues of Need, Equity and Polarisation in the Sale of Council Houses (University of Bristol, School for Advanced Urban Studies, Working Paper 39, 1984).

Forrest, Ray, and Peter Williams, 'Commodification and Housing: Emerging Issues and Contradictions', Environment and Planning A, 16 (1984), pp. 1163-80.

Frerics, Ude Jens, 'Umvandlung - nach Zuversicht und Routine ein Stillestand?', Wohnungseigentum, 34 (Heft 2/1983), pp. 3-8.

Friedman, Joseph, and Daniel H. Weinberg, The Economics of Housing Vouchers (Academic Press, New York, 1982).

Friedman, Joseph, and Daniel H. Weinberg (eds.), The Great Housing Experiment (Sage, Beverly Hills, Urban

Affairs Annual Review Vol. 24, 1983).

Friend, Andrew, A Giant Step Backwards. Council House Sales and Housing Policy (Catholic Housing Aid Society, London, CHAS Occasional Paper/5, 1980).

Gallagher, Pam, 'Ideology and Housing Management', pp. 132-53 in John English (ed.), The Future of Council Housing (Croom Helm, London, 1982).

Gesetz über das Wohnungseigentum und das Dauerwohnrecht (Wohnungseigentumsgesetz), SS5-6, 10-15.

GEWOS, Verkauf von Gebrauchtwohnungen - Empfehlungen einer unabhängigen Kommission des GEWOS e.V. an den Gesetzgeber (GEWOS, e.V., Bonn 1979).

GEWOS, Wohnungseigentum aus dem Mietwohnungsbestand - Überlegungen, Hinweise und Anregungen einer unabhangigen GEWOS e.V. - Fachkommission (Hammonia Verlag, GEWOS Schriftenreihe, Neue Folge 31, Hamburg, 1980).

Greater London Council, Housing Committee, 'Right-to-Buy: Progress' (GLC, Housing Committee, HG 187, Report (11, 12.81) by the Controller of Housing and Technical Services, London).

Gustafsson, Knut, 'Mietenniveau - Mietenstrukturen. Nachlese zur Wohnungsstichprobe 1978' Bundesbau-blatt, XXXII (April 1983), pp. 195-201.

Gustafsson, Knut, 'Strukturfragen der Wohnungseigen-tumspolitik' Bundesbaublatt, XXIX (July 1980), pp. 427-30.

'Haack stoppt Spakulation mit Sozialwohnungen', Bundesbaublatt, XXVII (1978), p. 523.

Halberstadt, Rudolf, 'Rechtsprobleme der Wohnungs-modernisierung durch Mieter', pp. 136-53 in Institut Wohnen und Umwelt (Hrsg.), Wohnungspolitik am Ende? Analysen und Perspektiven (Westdeutsches Verlag GmbH, Opladen, 1981).

Häring, Hans, 'Fragen bei der Umvandling von Mietwohnungen in Eigentumswohnungen', Zeitschrift für gemeinnütziges Wohnungswesen in Bayern, 72 (1982), pp. 351-4.

Harloe, Michael, and Maartje Martens, 'Comparative Housing Research' Journal of Social Policy, 13 (1984), pp. 255-77.

Hass-Klau, C.H.M., 'The Housing Shortage in Germany's Major Cities', Built Environment, 8 (1983), pp. 60-70.

'Haushalte von Wohngeldbeziehern im Vergleich mit Gesamtheit der Haushalte. Ergebnis der 1%-Wohnungsstichprobe 1978', Wirtschaft und Statistik (3/1982), pp. 206-13.

Headey, Bruce, Housing Policy in a Developed Economy - The United Kingdom, Sweden, and the United States

(Croom Helm, London, 1978).

Herberger, Lothar, et al., 'Bestand und Struktur der Gebäude und Wohnungen. Ergebnis der 1%-Wohnungs-stichprobe 1978', Wirtschaft und Statistik (5/1980), pp. 283-91.

Herlyn, Ingrid and Ulfert, Wohverhältnisse in der Bundesrepublik (Campus Verlag, Frankfurt/New York, 1983).

Höflich-Häberlein, Lisa, and Reinhold Weissbarth, 'Ohne Fleiss kein Preis', Bundesbaublatt, XXXI (September 1982), pp. 621-3.

Horowitz, C.F., 'Conversion Controls', Society, 21 (March/April 1984), pp. 58-65.

House of Commons Environment Committee, Session 1980-81, Council House Sales Vol. I, Report; Vol. 11, Minutes of Evidence; Vol. III, Appendices (HMSO, London HG 366 I-III, 1981).

Howenstine, E. Jay, Attacking Housing Costs: Foreign Policies and Strategies (Rutgers University/Center for Urban Policy Research, New Brunswick, NJ, 1983).

Infratest, Folgen der Umwandlung und Veräusserung von Mietwohnungen als Eigentumswohnungen, (Infratest GmbH, Munchen, 1980).

Jackson, F. Scott, 'The ABCs of Commercial Co-ownership', Real Estate Review, 10 (3/1980), pp. 43-9.

Jacobs, Barry G., et al., Guide to Federal Housing Programs (The Bureau of National Affairs, Inc., Washington, DC, 1982).

Jacobs, Sidney, 'The Sale of Council Houses; Does it Matter?', Critical Social Policy, 1 (1981), pp. 35-53.

Jones, Colin, 'The Demand for Home Ownership', pp. 115-31 in John English (ed.), The Future of Council Housing, (Croom Helm, London, 1982).

Jones, Maggie, 'Choice in Housing Tenure in Britain', pp. 177-217 in Hans Kroes and Fritz Ijmkers (eds.), Buitenlandse vormen van woningbeheer (RIW-instituut voor volkhuisvestingsonderzoek, Delft, 1982).

Kamer, Gregory J., 'Conversion of Rental Housing to Unit Ownership - A Noncrisis', Real Estate Law Journal, 10 (1982), pp. 187-209.

Karn, Valerie, 'Class, Race and Gender Stratific-ation in the Allocation of Council Housing', pp. 79-90 in Lennart J. Lundqvist and Marianne Wiktorin (eds.), Current Trends in British Housing - Proceedings from a British-Swedish Workshop on Current Housing Policy Research (The National Swedish Institute for Building Research, Gavle, Bulletin M 83:17, 1983).

Kemeny, Jim, The Myth of Home-ownership. Private

Versus Public Choices in Housing Tenure (Routledge & Kegan Paul, London, 1981).

Kilroy, Bernard, 'The Financial and Economic Implications of Council House Sales', pp. 52-96 in John English (ed.), The Future of Council Housing (Croom Helm, London, 1982).

Klingmüller, Ursula, et al., 'Gemeinwirtschaftliches Eigentum - Eine vorstaatliche Strategie gegen die Vernichtung preisgünstigen Wohnraums', Bauwelt, 73 (1982), pp. 1482-4.

Knight, Mike, 'When Owning Becomes a Nightmare', ROOF, 8 (November/December 1982), pp. 23-5.

Kornemann, Rolf, 'Umwandlung von Miet- in Eigentumswohnungen', Der Langfristige Kredit, Heft 15 (1983), pp. 480-6.

Kornemann, Rolf, 'Mehr Wohneigentum durch Umwandlungen?' Der Langfristige Kredit, Heft 20 (1983), pp. 625-30.

Kornemann, Rolf, 'Zur Umwandlung von Miet- in Eigentumswohnungen: Gunstige Konstellation für kaufwillige Mieter?, Der Langfristige Kredit, Heft 7 (1984), pp. 222-6.

Kröning, Wolfgang, 'Alternativen zum gewöhnlichen Wohnungsbau. Motive, Tendenzen, Beispiele fur veränderte Formen des Massenwohnungsbaus', pp. 74-97 in Institut Wohnen und Umwelt (Hrsg.), Wohnungspolitik am Ende? Analysen und Perspektiven (Westdeutscher Verlag GmbH, Opladen, 1981).

Labour Party, The Sale of Council Houses (Labour Party Research Department, London, Information Paper No. 16, 1979).

Labour Party, A Future for Public Housing - A Labour Party Discussion Document (The Labour Party, London, 1981).

Lansley, Stuart, Housing and Public Policy (Croom Helm, London, 1979).

Lauber, Daniel, 'Condominium Conversions - the Numbers Prompt Controls to Protect the Poor and the Elderly', Journal of Housing, 39 (1982), pp. 201-9.

Le Grand, Julian, The Strategy of Equality. Redistribution and the Social Services (George Allen & Unwin, London, 1982).

Lubbell, Harold A., 'Regulating Conversions in New York: A Model for the Nation', Real Estate Review, 11 (4/1981), pp. 42-5.

McCulloch, D., 'The New Housing Finance System', Local Government Studies, 8 (May/June 1982), pp. 97-103.

Malpass, Peter and Alan Murie, Housing Policy and Practice (MacMillan, London, 1982).

Merrett, Stephen (with Fred Gray), Owner-Occupation

in Britain (Routledge & Kegan Paul, London, 1982).
Meuter, Hartmut, 'Eigentumsbildung im Wohnungsb-
estand - Die Betroffenheit von Altbauquartieren
durch Umwandlung von Mietwohnungen', pp. 181-99 in
Adalbert Evers, Hans-Georg Lange and Hellmut Wollman
(Hrsg.), Kommunale Wohnungspolitik (Birkhäuser,
Basel/Boston/Stuttgart, Stadtforschungaktuell, Band
3, 1983).
Murie, Alan, The Sale of Council Houses - A Study in
Social Policy (University of Birmingham, Centre for
Urban and Regional Studies, Birmingham, CURS
Occasional Paper No. 35, 1975).
Murie, Alan, Housing Inequality and Deprivation
(Heineman, London, 1983).
National Decision Systems, 1980 U.S. Census -
Population & Housing Characteristics (NDS, San
Diego, 1982).
Norges Offentlige Utredninger, NOU 1980:6,
Eireleiligheter (Unversitetsforlaget, Oslo, 1980).
Peters, Heinz, Die Verwaltungsbeirate im Wohnungs-
eigentum. Praktische Tips für die Besitzer von
Eigentumswohnungen (Bauverlag GmbH, Wiesbaden und
Berlin, 1971).
Petzinger, Renate, and Marlo Riege, Die neue
Wohnungsnot. Wohnungswunder Bundesrepublik (VSA-
Verlag, Hamburg, 1981).
Przeworski, Adam, 'Methods of Cross-National
Research 1970-1983: An Overview', paper for the
Conference on Cross-National Policy Research,
organised by Science Center Berlin and Stanford
University, at Science Center Berlin, 18-21 December
1983.
Rae, Douglas, Equalities (Harvard University Press,
Cambridge, Mass., and London, 1981).
Robinson, Ray, and Tony O'Sullivan, 'Housing Tenure
Polarisation: Some Empirical Evidence', Housing
Review, 32 (July/August 1983), pp. 116-17.
Schifferes, Steve, 'Housing Bill 1980 - The Beginning
of the End for Council Housing', ROOF, 5 (January
1980), pp. 10-14.
Schmidt, Ernst-Günter, Die Eigentumswohnung hat
viele Vorteile, (Bauverlag GmbH, Wiesbaden und
Berlin, 1977).
Schneider, Oskar, 'Die Soziale Erneuerung der
Wohnungspolitik - politische Lösungsalternativen',
Politische Studien, 33 (1982), pp. 562-72.
Schröter, Albert, 'Ergebnisse der 1%-Stichprobe 1978
- Ein erster Überblick', Bundesbaublatt, XXIX (July
1980), pp. 431-8.
Schwartz, Nathan H., 'Reagan's Housing Policies',
pp. 149-64 in Anthony Champagne and Edward J.

Harpham (eds.), The Attack on the Welfare State (Waveland Press, Prospect Heights, Ill., 1984).

Sewel, J., F. Twine, and N. Williams, 'The Sale of Council Houses. Some Empirical Evidence', Urban Studies, 21 (1984), pp. 439-50.

Seyfried, Karl-Heinz, 'Zugzwang', Capital, 20 (Heft 9/1981), p. 128.

Shelter, Facts on Council House Sales (Shelter, National Campaign for the Homeless, London, 1979).

Short, John R., Housing in Britain - The Post-War Experience (Methuen, London and New York, 1982).

Siedt, Hans Gerd, 'Wohnverhältnisse und Mieten im April 1982. Ergebnisse der Mikrozensus-Ergänzungs-erhebung', Wirtschaft und Statistik (12/1983), pp. 961-7.

'Sozialer Wohnungsbau 1979', Wirtschaft und Statistik (9/1980), pp. 624-9.

'Sozialer Wohnungsbau 1981', Wirtschaft und Statistik (9/1982), pp. 675-80.

Sternlieb, George, and James W. Hughes, 'Condominium Conversion Profiles: Governmental Policy' pp. 289-312 in George Sternlieb and James W. Hughes (eds.), America's Housing. Prospects and Problems (Rutgers University Center for Urban Policy Research, New Brunswick, NJ, 1980).

Taschenbuch für den Wohnungswirt (Hammonia Verlag, Hamburg, 1981).

Tenschert, Erwin, 'Wohnungsumwandlung im Für und Wider. Eine Tagung mit wenig Neuem', Gemeinnutziges Wohnungswesen, 33 (1980), pp. 238-42.

The Report of the President's Commission on Housing (US Government Printing Office, Washington DC, 1982).

US Department of Commerce, Statistical Abstracts of the United States 1981 (US Department of Commerce/Bureau of Census, Washington, DC, 1981).

US Department of Commerce, Statistical Abstracts of the United States 1984 (US Department of Commerce/Bureau of Census, Washington, DC 1984).

US Department of Housing and Urban Development (HUD), Wise Home Buying (US Department of Housing and Urban Development, Washington, DC, 1980).

US Department of Housing and Urban Development (HUD), The Conversion of Rental Housing to Condominiums and Cooperatives. A National Study of Scope, Causes and Impacts (US Department of Housing and Urban Development, Washington, DC, 1980).

US Department of Housing and Urban Development (HUD), The Conversion of Rental Housing to Condominiums and Cooperatives, Volume of Conversion Activity in Selected Metropolitan Areas (US Department of

Housing Urban Development, Washington, DC, 1981).
US Department of Housing and Urban Development (HUD),
The Conversion of Rental Housing to Condominiums and
Cooperatives. Impact on Elderly and Low-Income
Households (US Department of Housing and Urban
Development, Washington, DC, 1981).
US Department of Housing and Urban Development (HUD),
The Conversion of Rental Housing to Condominiums and
Cooperatives. Impacts on Housing Costs (US
Department of Housing and Urban Development,
Washington, DC, 1981).
US Department of Housing and Urban Development (HUD),
1982 National Housing Production Report (US
Department of Housing and Urban Development,
Washington, DC, 1983).
US President's Commission on Housing, Interim
Report, October 30, 1981 (US Government Printing
Office, Washington, DC, 1981).
Veser, Jürgen, Umwandlung von Miet- in Eigentumswoh-
nungen. Die Folgen für den Betroffenen und die
Auswirkungen auf den Wohnungsmarkt (Institut für
Stadsforschung, Berlin, 1982).
Veser, Jürgen, Umfang und Struktur der Umwandlung von
Miet- in Eigentumswohnungen in Hannover (Institut
für Stadtforschung, Berlin, 1984).
Wappler, Alfred, 'Und sie ist doch eine gute Sache.
Die Umwandlung von Mietwohnungen', Gemeinnütziges
Wohnungswesen, 33 (1980), pp. 244-54.
Welham, P.J. 'The Tax Treatment of Owner-occupier
Housing in the U.K.', Scottish Journal of Political
Economy, 29 (1982), p. 139-55.
Whitehead, Christine M.E., 'Privatisation and
Housing', pp. 116-32 in Julian Le Grand and Ray
Robinson (eds.), Privatisation and the Welfare State
(George Allen & Unwin, London, 1984).
Wollman, Harold, L., Housing and Housing Policy in
the US and the U.K. (Lexington Books, Lexington,
Mass., 1975).
Wollman, Hellmut, 'Housing Policy in West Germany -
Between State Intervention and the Market', in Klaus
von Beyme and Manfred G. Schmidt (eds.), Policy-
Making in the Federal Republic of Germany (Gower,
Farnborough, 1984).
Wullkopf, Uwe, 'Wohnungsbau und Wohnungsbaupolitik
in der Bundesrepublik Deutschland', Politik und
Zeitgeschichte, Band 10 (1982), pp. 11-25.
Wullkopf, Uwe, 'Ist der Abbau sozialer Disparitäten
in der Wohnungsversorgung noch lohnendes Ziel der
Wohnungspolitik?' pp. 9-20 in Institut Wohnen und
Umwelt (Hrsg.), Wohnungspolitik am Ende? Analysen
und Perspektiven (Westdeutscher Verlag GmbH,

Opladen, 1981).

INDEX

232